Landscape of the Soul

Landscape of the Soul

Confronting the Ethos of Progress
and Restoring American Spirituality

W. VANCE GRACE

WIPF & STOCK · Eugene, Oregon

LANDSCAPE OF THE SOUL
Confronting the Ethos of Progress and Restoring American Spirituality

Wipf & Stock
An Imprint of Wipf and Stock Publishers
199 W. 8th Ave., Suite 3
Eugene, OR 97401

www.wipfandstock.com

PAPERBACK ISBN: 978-1-7252-6460-1
HARDCOVER ISBN: 978-1-7252-6461-8
EBOOK ISBN: 978-1-7252-6462-5

Manufactured in the U.S.A.   05/18/20

*For Doug, who reinforced a love of the wild
while teaching me it's never about
methodology*

Contents

Introduction

Growing Up Western

DAD WOULD HAVE ROUSED us out of bed while it was still dark. We had a long drive ahead of us: the fifteen miles along Interstate 80 to Rock Springs where we would turn south on Wyoming Highway 430, a narrow strip of asphalt that didn't warrant paving past the state line with Colorado where it would become another unexceptional gravel road. Apparently, what qualifies for paving and naming a state highway in Wyoming comes with different standards. Either way it was a lonely and seldom-traveled stretch of road. We would head another twenty-five miles south of Rock Springs to a turn-off somewhere around the Mud Springs Ranch onto Mud Springs Road. Dad was a land surveyor and had a full day of work ahead of him in the southern Red Desert, with two helpers in tow, likely somewhat unwillingly considering the time of morning.

I was probably ten or eleven years old at the time. My brother, two and a half years older, would undoubtedly have been the more difficult to stir. It was likely sometime around our spring break from school, otherwise Dad would have been venturing out with an actual adult assistant. Of course, "spring" in Wyoming is a bit of a misnomer. In the late 1970s and early 1980s, the high desert of southwest Wyoming experienced snow coming early and deep, and anything that wasn't blown to Nebraska could be piled up until a warm-up started—if it ever did—sometime in early June. Mom would have us a lunch packed for the day, hoping she had added enough for Dad to actually get something to eat late in the day. Frequently when going surveying with Dad, especially if it were a cold day, we would at some point find our way into the relative warmth of the work truck where we could

1

easily devour a lunch for six in a matter of minutes, including the thermos of strong, hot coffee Mom had inevitably added. I'm not sure why Dad continued to agree to this arrangement.

We were likely heading for another nondescript spot in the sagebrush sea of southwest Wyoming, nearly due north of the border which indicates the separation between Colorado and Utah. Dad would follow dirt road after dirt road, penetrating deep into the vast expanses of Bureau of Land Management land where eventually we would run out of even a fading two-track trail to utilize. He would have hundreds of pounds of survey equipment loaded in the vehicle: bundles of wood lathe, florescent flagging, steel T-posts and the requisite post driver. All this gear would have to be lugged to and fro across the desert in order to mark out the boundaries of an oil- or gas-drilling pad, or the route of the access road which would eventually be built to the pad. Obviously, ten- and twelve-year-old boys were of limited benefit for such work—unless there was some benefit in having the interior of your truck destroyed and an entire day's worth of food wolfed.

The landscape south of Rock Springs is a tangled maze of mostly dry creek beds, badlands, barren bluffs, and mesas rising upward from an elevation of 6,500 feet. In the spring the roads become a soupy mixture of bentonite clay which can coat even the most aggressive off-road tires with a two-inch-thick layer of mud, rendering the tires more appropriate as racing slicks on an asphalt oval track. Why Dad did not have an actual survey hand that day I will never know; I suppose children worked cheap back in those days. The three of us were soon encountering deep, drifted snow trapped in gullies and holding on to the northern exposure of hillsides our quickly diminishing road was supposed to be traversing. At some point, four-wheel drive would simply not be sufficient to see Dad's Bronco through increasingly large drifts. But Dad was a good and conscientious hand and had already ventured far from town in order to get this particular project in the books. We finally came to an expansive drift which was too deep and too long to try to dig and bully a path through. Dad shifted into four-low and headed for a sagebrush flat below the slope where he hoped to bypass this unusually large drift. In hindsight, there is probably good reason the road followed the contour of the hill instead of being routed through this lower ground. Equally clear, soon enough, was where all of that snow melt had been heading when it came off the hillside.

We bounced off the hillside toward the level, heedless of the myriad cacti and sagebrush, trying to weave a way between the downhill tail-end of the drift and a deep arroyo in the center of the flat. When the Bronco finally cratered to a halt we were buried up to the doors—four tires completely invisible. Dozens of miles from anywhere, a crisp, spring Wyoming morning, not a soul within a hundred square miles, a time before any mobile phone service, and a ten- and twelve-year-old for help. It was bound to be a long day. At times in mud up to his hips, Dad began shoveling what mud he could from the undercarriage of the vehicle. At first it likely wouldn't have seemed an entirely bad way to spend the day for my brother and I. We weren't in school and were actually being encouraged to dig in the mud and explore the region looking for rocks and any dry material we could find as we attempted to help Dad as best we could. We would typically spend hours on the edge of our small town wandering through the desert anyway, so this had become something of an adventure. It wouldn't seem so fun seven or eight hours later when, soaking wet and thoroughly chilled, we would be no closer to freeing the Bronco than when we had first plunged into the flat.

Through the entire day, Dad would dig and lift alternating corners of the Bronco with his high-lift jack. He would stack the rocks and brush my brother and I could gather underneath tires in an attempt to give the wheels some purchase. The truck might move a few feet before sinking in again, when the process would begin anew. My brother and I would alternate our time between exploring the arroyo, digging mud and gathering rocks, and eating Dad's lunch. By the time the sun went down we were nearly out of fuel, cold, wet, tired, and no closer to being unstuck. And certainly no closer to Rock Springs some thirty or forty miles away. Dad decided it was time to walk.

Dad was a great walker. He spent his days walking through the high desert, carrying loads of fenceposts and lathe, counting steps to determine distances. He might spend a great deal of time locating corner section markers from original surveys to work back to the location he was staking out—always walking, carrying and counting, hour after hour, day after day. While not a tall man, he had a tremendous working gait which allowed him to cover great distances in a short period. This was not the case for an average ten-year-old like myself; I had neither his endurance nor his fortitude and I would be embarrassed today to know how many miles I had to be carried on his shoulders that evening as we made our way for the highway with darkness falling. An unsuccessful attempt to start a bulldozer some halfway out put us back on the walk. Sometime in the night we finally reached the lonely highway where an unlikely passing motorist provided a ride back to town. Mom drove over to Rock Springs to pick us up. The truck was pulled out the next day with more competent help than a ten- and twelve-year-old could provide.

We are indelibly impacted by these experiences. Even while we were immersed in play and enjoying our environment, we were participating in changing its reality. I grew up in Wyoming's southwest corner on the edge of the Red Desert. At around ten million acres, the Red Desert rises upward from around 6,000 feet in elevation to the continental divide at over 7,000 feet above sea level. As a region it ranks among the lowest population densities in the country. Travelers speeding across Interstate 80 the 100 miles between Rock Springs and Rawlins typically look out their windows on their way to somewhere else and marvel at the apparent wasteland spreading to the horizon. But to only see a wasteland is to miss the reality of the Red Desert which is home to the Killpecker Sand Dunes: the second-largest active sand dune field in the world. From the speed of a passing vehicle one cannot appreciate the stunning landforms in Adobe Town, Devil's Playground, and the Organ or Honeycomb Buttes. Far from being empty, this region is home to the nation's last remaining desert elk herd; it contains wild horses and the country's longest mule deer migration route, while providing habitat for the quickly fading greater sage-grouse. The Red Desert contains the geologically unique Great Divide Basin which traps any water within its confines, never releasing it to either the Atlantic or Pacific watersheds. The lack of lights from any metropolitan areas, the high, dry air, and the clear atmosphere mean that night skies are darker here and stars noticably brighter.

For many it would be considered a source of privation to grow up in a small town in the sagebrush steppe, far from any metropolitan areas; immersed in subdued tones of grey and tan with little growth to the landscape; exposed to the incessant wind and cold for much of the year. I feel as if I have been uniquely privileged to have spent my formative years in southwest Wyoming. Because of the nature of Dad's work, I had an unusual opportunity to wander aimlessly in a great deal of vast, nondescript, roadless expanses one wouldn't otherwise have any reason to wander through. This has instilled in me an appreciation for desolate and commonly perceived waste areas, as well as the habits of walking, looking, and internalizing vastness. At the same time, however, we were also facilitating the land's change. My dad, with his rambunctious boys often in tow, provided the means for an industrial landscape to make an imprint on the Red Desert, the larger sagebrush steppe to the north and west, and the Colorado Plateau to the south. I walked through landscapes thirty and forty years ago that exist now only in memory.[1]

We are each inevitably shaped by—even as we in turn shape—our context, our environment, our landscape. In his book, *Winter in the Blood,*

---

1. While the Red Desert contains less than one person per square mile (the number which qualified for Frontier status in the 1890 US Census), estimates are that 84 percent of the landscape has nonetheless been industrialized, primarily by oil and gas infrastructure. Development in what has been called "The Big Empty" continues for the purposes of the extraction of oil, gas, coal, uranium, and trona.

Montana writer James Welch writes a story about a troubled Blackfoot teen struggling to make his way in a world of tension between the Montana cities—peopled primarily by whites—and the teen's own reservation culture. Early on, by way of introducing the conflict of the character's soul, Welch has his narrator proclaim his place in the world:

> I felt no hatred, no love, no guilt, no conscience, nothing but a distance that had grown through the years. It could have been the country, the burnt prairie beneath a blazing sun, the pale green of the Milk River Valley, the milky waters of the river, the sagebrush and cottonwoods, the dry, cracked, gumbo flats. The country had created a distance as deep as it was empty, and the people accepted and treated each other with distance.[2]

A year or two later I was again with my brother as we rode with our dad south across the unusual east-west ranges of Utah's Uinta Mountains. In crossing this range, we left the Red Desert and the larger sagebrush sea of the interior west to enter the environs of the Colorado Plateau. It was a long working trip for my dad—perhaps ten days—but the quintessential summer vacation for two young boys. It would be nearly two weeks in the sunshine and heat, living out of motel rooms and regularly eating at fast-food dives. We would make frequent stops at local grocery stores in northern Utah and Colorado to load up on junk food and lunch supplies for the days wandering in desert canyons and up steep pinyon- and juniper-covered hillsides. By day we could explore whatever patch of sand we happened to be on, hunting lizards and horned toads. By night we enjoyed the outdoor pools in Vernal and Moab and Grand Junction. It was a twelve-year-old's dream. In retrospect this was a particularly meaningful trip because it served as my introduction to the region we know as the Colorado Plateau.

Like the Red Desert surrounding the home of my youth, the Colorado Plateau is a massive and unique region making up an important chunk of the West. Encompassing 240,000 square miles in an oblong running north from the Four Corners region, the Plateau takes in western Colorado, eastern Utah, and portions of northern New Mexico and Arizona. Generally surrounding the Colorado River and its major tributaries where the rivers emerge from their alpine settings, this distinctive uplift varies from 2,000 feet of elevation at the bottom of the Grand Canyon to the islands of desert mountains that rise to nearly 13,000 feet. The plateau is bordered by the high peaks of the Rocky Mountains and the deserts of the Great Basin and Mojave Desert. While the Grand Canyon is the most notable feature of the region, the Colorado Plateau includes countless arches, deep slot canyons,

2. Welch, *Winter in the Blood*, 2.

immense mesas, and tablelands. Strange, sharp, knife-edge ridges seem to rise out of nowhere to thousands of feet, while seas of petrified sand dunes are littered with innumerable towers and domes. Lightly traveled before the uranium boom of the 1950s, the region continues to be sparsely populated though increasingly visited for its beauty and the presence of ancient artifacts and Native American dwellings. The land forms of the plateau continue to inspire the romantic ideals of the Old West.

Dad had a full slate of new roads and well pads to stake out for the oil and gas industry which was in a boom cycle in the early 1980s. We would get up in the dark each morning from a cheap motel and drive out to the end of some random desert road or up into an isolated canyon where Dad would identify the location of leases secured by production companies for future development. As usual, his work took him into areas not yet marked by travel or development, which was precisely why I thought he might have the best job in the world. My brother and I might help carry what supplies we could into remote locations and might hold the sighting rod occasionally, but when the work was undertaken in earnest, the intricacies of Dad's surveying work were soon lost on us. This was all new and untouched landscape to us so we would spend most of our days ranging as far as we could before being called back at dusk for the ride back into civilization and hopefully a swim in the pool.

Twenty-five years later, my wife and I, with our three children, moved back to call this region home. A great deal has changed in western Colorado since the early 1980s and in looking back I can't help but reflect on the role my dad, my brother, and I had on facilitating this change, if only in a small way. Western Colorado and eastern Utah have seen their share of industrial booms and economic busts along the way. Many of the wild canyons we visited and some of the vast open spaces would now be unrecognizable to my twelve-year-old self. Roads, old well pads, and the accompanying pipeline routes and additional oil and gas infrastructure have proliferated into the very areas we enjoyed as so wild and isolated—an occupation and development we were partially responsible for aiding. My own role in changing these landscapes increased into adulthood as I took work on a drilling rig for a number of years in western Colorado. I've learned to walk better now—like Dad—and my youthful enthusiasm for wandering these desert spaces has never waned; in fact it has increased through the years. And yet I have now a greater capacity to change these very places through my involvement in our built environment than I ever had before.

The relationship between the built and the natural, and my role in each, has come to be of vital importance to me in my later years. With decades of reflection I now recognize that the human built and the natural environment are, and perhaps always have been, messy and difficult to separate. Growing up on the outer edge of a small town in southwest Wyoming my playground was the desert surrounding us. My friends and I spent the bulk of our days off of school climbing the rocks and exploring the canyons on the outskirts of town. At the same time, we were utilizing the dirt bike and four-wheel-drive trails that made their way up every conceivable slope. We figured ourselves outdoorsmen and explorers even while we played in the already manipulated landscapes of abandoned mine shafts. Later in my teenage years we utilized the empty canyons for weekend parties and floated down the river through town that created a narrow and winding strip of green in the desert. It was never really empty and not very wild by the 1980s, and yet somehow this all felt very wild to us. In my innocence this was indeed an empty landscape. I now recognize this area was both/ and: vast regions of the untouched natural and the context of a growing industrialization.

Regardless of the reality of what this landscape is or historically has been, growing up and spending so much time in desert places made an enormous impact on who I am today and how I see the world in both its natural and built-upon state. I can resonate with what John Van Dyke wrote over a hundred year ago: ". . . the waste places of the earth, the barren deserts, the tracts forsaken of men and given over to loneliness, have a peculiar attraction of their own. The weird solitude, the great silence, the great desolation, are the very things with which every desert wanderer eventually falls in love."[3]

Growing up as I did and accompanying my dad as he performed his surveying work serves to illustrate the dual role of landscape I hope to pursue in the rest of this work. For years Dad's work was primarily in the service of the oil and gas and mining industries. This meant that his particular tasks frequently required him to be in previously untouched territory. New claims and leases would need roads built to them while the boundaries where the actual work would occur would have to be established. When we could, my brother and I would tag along in a wide area ranging from eastern Idaho and southern Wyoming to northern Colorado and Utah. More often than not we were in utterly wild environs which we walked into during the summer or reached by snow machine in the winter. I came to believe that virtually all of the West was like this: wild, open, isolated, and untracked. I grew up with a unique exposure to an empty quarter.

It was certainly a unique experience to be out in the open so often with Dad or with my friends as we traveled past the edge of town. We were rarely

3. Van Dyke, *Desert*, 19.

hemmed in by cities or people or even roads. Trees were sparse, and at 6,000 feet above sea level in the dry Wyoming air, the perspective of space and land was expansive. The very breadth of experience of the sky over the limitless sagebrush sea is a massive externality that works on a soul over time. This space was doing something in me I wouldn't recognize or appreciate until years later.

Wallace Stegner was in his day perhaps the most prolific writer about the West that I grew up in. It was his perspective, and one I have come to share, that more than the inhabitants of other regions, Westerners find their shaping identity in, and derive their meaning directly from, landscape.[4] This is what I was being exposed to on a regular basis. And while it may have been made up of more greys and tans than green and may have been little more than a sagebrush plain to those on their way to the Tetons or Yellowstone, it was my ground, my sand, my piece of exposure to the reality of the earth. "We can love a well-lived-in place even when it is essentially unlovable. . . . If a place is a real place, shaped by human living, and not a thing created on a speculator's drawing board and stamped on a landscape like a USDA stamp on a side of beef, it will interact with the people who live in it, and they with it."[5] And while my dad's work inevitably ended up on a drawing table to have a BLM lease number stamped on it, to us it was a real place we confronted in wind and cold and heat and occasionally rain. I learned to love the inimitable space of the desert because of it. At the time I wasn't conscious enough of the changes we wrought.

This is the other side of the coin: surveying work is, by its very nature, the source of change on that wild environment we were endeavoring to live in and learning to love. More than simply marking lines on paper, surveying is the engineered means of making both inhabitation on and extraction from land possible in this country. Surveys were designed to codify, name, and inventory land and resources for the purpose of controlling and developing those lands and the resources they contain. A culturally historic and therefore far-reaching decision was made in an 1853 congressional authorization for a publicly funded survey to determine the best route for a railroad crossing of the North American continent. The completion of the Transcontinental Railroad in 1869 likely had the greatest single impact on this country's westward expansion. "With the laying out of the Pacific railroad a new age had begun . . ."[6] In what historian William Goetzmann labels "The Great Western Reconnaissance," the Corps of Topographical Engineers

4. Stegner, *Sound of Mountain Water*, 11.

5. Stegner and Stegner, *American Places*, 207.

6. Goetzmann, *Exploration and Empire*, 301.

undertook a massive scientific inventory of the interior of the country in the 1850s. These surveyors were instructed to "make a general examination of the plants, animals, Indians, and geologic formations of the country." This data was "meant to comprise a total geographic inventory of the West which would have meaning and utility for westbound Americans."[7]

As the 1850s wore on and increasing numbers of people were responding to gold strikes in California and later in Colorado, Americans expressed a growing demand for explorations that would have local social and economic utility as opposed to earlier theoretical scientific inventories that tended to focus on never-seen-before plants and ancient bones.[8] The emerging surveys delineated routes, named prominent landscape features, identified water and timber resources, and recorded the presence of various mineral deposits and the potential of forage for livestock grazing. The corps inventoried and named as marks of value and possession and did so to facilitate growth and settlement in the interest of fulfilling the needs for progress. The act of surveying exposes one to the land even while it functions as its change-agent.

In his history of exploration, Goetzmann emphasizes that these early surveys would serve to first establish and then enhance competing visions of the West; visions which continue to persist today: "the Garden (meaning a belief in the economic potential of the West) and the Desert (meaning the belief that the West was a land of scarcity that would take centuries to develop)."[9] This both parallels my own experience surveying as well as anticipates the dual role of landscape which I hope to develop throughout this work. Is there a particular value in exposure to the desert as it is, precisely because of its scarcity and apparent emptiness? Or is our greatest value derived from the utilitarian uses and potentialities of what we can build and effect in the name of progress?

While a great deal has changed from the time I spent my youth in these areas to the more recent relocation to life on the edge of the Colorado Plateau, certain realities persist. I am still a wanderer at heart and have never been able to escape the need to experience the effect of sand and wind and vast expanses. I was an accidental—if somewhat reluctant—participant in those initial explorations of mostly empty spaces. Of late I have become a much more purposeful devotee. Today we live in close proximity to areas once thought to have little to no utility for human habitation—the very thing that draws me to a closer connection with such landscape. In an early

7. Goetzmann, *Exploration and Empire*, 303.
8. Goetzmann, *Exploration and Empire*, 305.
9. Goetzmann, *Exploration and Empire*, 305.

exploration to the heart of Canyon Country, Captain John N. Macomb wrote in 1859, "I cannot conceive of a more worthless and impractical region than the one we now find ourselves in. I doubt not that there are repetitions and varieties of it for hundreds of miles," and he further opined that "modern enterprise would do well to avoid the unredeemable canyon country."[10] The expedition's primary chronicler, Dr. John Strong Newberry, contrasted the party's time traveling through the Rocky Mountains, with its "picturesque scenery of the foothills, their flowery valleys, and sparkling streams, the grateful shade of their forests," to what lay before them as a "weary way across the arid expanse of the Great Western Plateau; a region whose dreary monotony is only broken by frightful chasms, where alone the weary traveler finds shelter from the burning heat of the cloudless sun, and where he seeks too often in vain a cooling draught that shall slake his thirst."[11] Things had not improved nearly a decade later when the Colorado Plateau was "A sprawling wasteland described in 1868 by William Tecumseh Sheridan, the general of Union Army fame, as 'utterly unfit for white civilization.'"[12]

For more than a decade I have been searching out the loneliest and least traveled spots throughout the Colorado Plateau precisely because of a love for what Van Dyke identified as the weird solitude, the great silence, and the grim desolation. This has undoubtedly colored my way of experiencing the world, as will become clearer as our purpose in this work unfolds. A recent three-day January trip took me alone into the northern San Rafael Swell where the temperature never reached twenty-five degrees and my time following any trail amounted to only a handful of hours. I frequently visit a nearby mesa precisely because it has never experienced livestock grazing or settlement, remains trailless, and only has one or two hard-to-locate access points which lead to nearly 20,000 acres of sloping tabletop cut by deep canyons. I have utilized long-abandoned Native American paths, miners' tracks, and historic livestock trails to access the benches and canyons of the seldom-traveled Dirty Devil region in Utah—always a place bathed in complete solitude. These forays confirm the realities Wallace Stegner affirmed: "The Utah deserts and plateaus and canyons are not a country of big returns, but a country of spiritual healing, uncomparable for contemplation, meditation, solitude, quiet and peace of mind and body. We were born of

---

10. Nelson, *Wrecks of Human Ambition,* 96–97.

11. Nelson, *Wrecks of Human Ambition,* 97–98.

12. Voyles, *Wastelanding,* viii. ". . . notions that the Colorado Plateau was uninhabited wasteland unfit for farming draw us quite a clear map of . . . the interplay between nature [and people]" (ix).

wilderness and we respond to it more increasingly for relief from the termite life we have created."[13]

One of the premises of this work is that we all live by a particular mythology. I have provided some intimations of our own American mythology already and hope to flesh this idea out more clearly in part 1. We are
inclined to approach a myth as something fundamentally untrue—a fairy
tale, something pretend or made-up with little basis in reality. But "myths
are better understood as attempts to answer the same types of questions
that philosophers and theologians do, questions concerning the nature of
reality and the meaning of human existence . . ."[14] Far from being a made-up
story for children, "Myth at its deepest level is that collectively created thing
which crystallizes the great, central values of a culture. It is, so to speak,
the intercommunications system of culture."[15] For any of us inhabiting a
specific culture, which would be all of us, our myths are caught and created
and confirmed by our exposure to our peculiar context in our small corner
of the world. My own desert experiences, then, have resulted in the challenge which this book represents to a specific form of a prevailing American
myth. This will hopefully become clear as my central point as we progress.
For now, suffice it to say that Terry Tempest Williams has dialed in on my
own myth creation:

> In the Colorado Plateau—roughly the four corners region of
> Utah, Colorado, New Mexico and Arizona—I believe we are in
> the process of creating our own mythology, a mythology born
> out of this spare, raw, broken country, so frightfully true, com-
> plex and elegant in its searing simplicity of form. You cannot
> help but be undone by its sensibility and light, nothing extra.
> Before the silence of sandstone cliffs, you stand still, equally
> bare.[16]

If our mythologies—our narratives, if you will—on both a culture-wide
as well as personal scale are created and confirmed by our experiences in a
specific context, then there is an additional aspect to my own story which
equally informs my purpose in writing *Landscape of the Soul*. As much as I
would like to perpetuate the image that I grew up under a lonely sagebrush
in the desert, my life is equally informed by my involvement in (and at times
a tenuous attachment to) American Christianity. A large portion of my life
has consisted of preparation for and participation in the vocational aspects

13. Stegner, *Wilderness at the Edge*, 8.
14. Jardine, *Making and Unmaking*, 139.
15. Roszak, *Making of a Counterculture*, 214.
16. Williams, *Red* 4.

of North American evangelical Christianity. While in my later years I have grown increasingly disillusioned by many aspects of this movement, I continue to believe that it contains vital resources to inform our place in this world. I find little biblical support for the movement's current marriage to conservative political power structures. In too many instances evangelicals have demonstrated a fixation on wealth and the defenses of a particular middle-class Americanism at the expense of the "other"—both in terms of the human and natural contexts—and in contradistinction to the central forming narrative of gospel.

My struggles with my involvement in this aspect of American culture partially hinge on the point Walter Brueggemann makes when he says, "The contemporary American church is so largely enculturated to the American ethos of consumerism that is has little power to believe or act."[17] While standards of living in America far surpass that of the majority now on earth or throughout history, America ranks second to last among developed countries in government foreign aid. America comes in nearly last among rich nations in categories such as childhood nutrition, infant mortality and access to preschool. The United States is the most violent rich nation on earth, with a murder rate four or five times that of European peers and a prison population five or six times greater than that of other wealthy nations.[18] I am not attempting to pin these conditions solely on the evangelical church in America, but just as Nero was accused of playing the fiddle while Rome burned, American Christianity seems to be further entrenching into middle-class comfort while so much goes awry around us. "The middle-class subculture has existed in such a close relationship with Christianity that it is sometimes difficult to distinguish what is American from what is Christian."[19]

This isn't a book about the failures and struggles of the evangelical church in America, but about one particular manifestation of a cultural value that has resulted in our inability to access the spiritual resources that would be transformative not only for the adherents of Christianity, but members of society at large. For while I remain at odds with many expressions of Christianity in America, this book is a decidedly Christian book because I maintain many affinities with other, healthier aspects of the faith. I understand that the spiritual life is critical to our true humanness and I believe there is a great deal in the biblical narrative which informs our way of being in the world. Over against a somewhat problematic and narrowly

17. Brueggemann, *Prophetic Imagination*, 1.

18. See McKibben, "Christian Paradox."

19. Dyrness, *How Does America Hear the Gospel?*, 12.

materialistic view of the universe, I am drawn to the externality of a Creator and creation which is capable of affecting us: a givenness by another, independent of our activity or striving.

While Western culture over the past 500 years has focused on and provided countless material and scientific resources, I recognize crucially needed spiritual and communal resources in the way of Jesus and the early church. Despite being widely criticized as primarily responsible for our ever-growing environmental crises,[20] there are other ways to understand this faith as actually informing and resourcing our care of creation.[21] I am drawn to the tensions and mystery inherent in the biblical witness—though too often unacknowledged by much of American evangelicalism—which are very resonant with the realities of most of our lives. Primarily I am compelled to stick with the biblical narrative because of the way it informs our way back to *shalom*: an expression of the way things ought to be.[22] Jesus and the community he envisioned informs our involvement in the process of the repair of the world which I believe gives existence meaning.

My past has at times been shaped by substantial involvement in the American Evangelical subculture. I have spent years listening to preachers and teachers who encourage us to pay close attention to the development of a vibrant spiritual life; as a pastor and church-planter I delivered those same messages countless times. I spent four years studying the Greek language of the New Testament and two years trying—mostly failing—to learn the intricacies of the Hebrew language of the Old Testament. My years in college and graduate school were spent poring over systematic theology tomes which organized and disseminated doctrines in an orderly and coherent manner. For decades I worked to develop and perfect spiritual exercises and disciplines in an attempt to produce a vigorous internal life—even while I encouraged the same in others. There have been innumerable books and messages and rallies and classes and endless personal study.

In later life, and after much exposure to the depths of my own soul and increasingly the depths and heights of creation, I have had to set aside some of the clarity and systematizing and easy answers. In my current post-evangelical[23] condition I recognize a great deal more of the liminal space present in the Bible and the movement it produced. I have endeavored to

20. See especially White, "Historical Roots of Our Ecological Crisis" and Turner, *Beyond Geography*.

21. See especially Hall, *Imaging God*; Bouma-Prediger, *For the Beauty of the Earth*; Santmire, *Nature Reborn*; Van Dyke, *Redeeming Creation*; Ellingson, *Care for Creation*; Stoll, *Inherit the Holy Mountain*.

22. See Plantinga, *Not the Way*.

23. See Tomlinson, *Post-Evangelical*.

embrace the tensions inherent in the way of Jesus. I believe that there are indeed many uncomfortable spaces present in the narratives that make up the biblical story; spaces too much of modern Christianity seems unwilling to recognize, let alone occupy. While we are creative beings with an incredible capacity for deep thought and a tremendous ability to form and build, the ambiguity remains that we were never meant to find that which we most deeply need in the context of our built environment. And that is no less true in terms of the building up of our own spiritual lives.

Like many other Christians of my own distinct perspective, I endeavored to improve the world—having myself been rescued from a life trending toward self-destruction. At some level I wanted to make things better, to see progress and improvement come. I remain captivated by the vision of the kingdom of God and our part in the repair of the world, even while I have become convinced that too many of our current expressions of Christianity are actually being counterproductive in this regard. Hence this current attempt at a corrective paradigm.

In contrast to its calling as "salt and light" in the world, The American Evangelical Church has too often modelled itself after the values of the culture surrounding it. I will present as a particular manifestation of that culture our present ecological crisis. I will also contend—and this is the larger purpose behind *Landscape of the Soul*—that our ecological crisis is not a peripheral occurrence but is indicative of the deeper crisis in our spirituality. I intend to demonstrate how our way in the world has created ongoing systemic environmental damage. But I will argue that this portends an equally critical crisis in our spiritual lives. The two issues—environment and spiritual life—act in parallel ways and the ways which we conceive of our relationship to the external world are fleshed out in the ways we conceive of the life of the soul. As the costs rise to deal with the impacts of an increasingly engineered world, so the debt is coming due in Western spirituality, which appears bereft of the resources necessary to inform the inner life and by extension participate in the repair of the world.

It is my contention in *Landscape of the Soul* that American Christianity has become so acculturated to a confidence in our capacity to engineer and construct everything necessary to secure our own progress that our spirituality has become little more than an extension of our own built environment. The result lies in the reality that the church has negated the resources that God would otherwise provide. As life itself is a gift, so our spiritual or interior life must be primarily affected and shaped by something external to ourselves, something we do not create. The natural world, the not-created-by-us, those places we have not yet engineered, can be a context to produce in us a vibrant life of the soul.

The point I am hoping to make is illustrated by a story Wendell Berry tells about building a pond on his farm in Kentucky. He hired a man with a bulldozer to clear trees from a steep wooded hillside and then cut into the hill on the upper side, piling the excavated earth on the downhill side. At first the pond appeared to be a success as it almost immediately began to fill with enough water to support a few head of stock. When an unusually wet fall and winter with the cycles of freezing and thawing took hold, the soil on the uphill-side grew soft and heavy with water and a large slice of land on the wooded hillside slipped down into the pond. Berry sees the pond and the subsequent mess as a scar on his land. He speaks seriously of his peace being damaged because of how closely his life is connected with his farm. Berry's conclusion is that, "a man with a machine and inadequate culture—such as I was when I made my pond—is a pestilence. He shakes more than he can hold."[24] The soul has a landscape created by another, external to us and our efforts, and we can build upon and push around that landscape as with a bulldozer, and in so doing effect irreparable damage. I hope to develop the idea that this damage stems precisely from the inadequate culture we adhere to. We must recover the sense that we cannot, most pointedly as Christians, derive what we most need from our built environment.

What follows is a criticism of a particular failure of Western culture, but it is offered with an eye toward a counternarrative which I hope will encourage some repair of the ability of our spiritual resources to affect the presence of *shalom*. Even as Christians we have largely shown ourselves as incapable of affecting any real degree of change in our North American culture despite the resources of the way of Jesus. I believe this is because we are as subject to some dark and damaging cultural realities as anyone else.

One approach is to take as a model the natural world—which Jesus often did in his teaching through parable—as a clue to being able to bless our world. Two centerpieces of Paul's theology are faith and grace: truths which he emphasizes work *on* us and which are indicative of things which bring about a response to what only a noncontingent Creator can accomplish. This work will be steeped not only in culture and theology but also in the natural world, particularly that of my own placedness as an inhabitant of and traveler in the Colorado Plateau. I hope to expose to the reader the rhythms of landscape in the anticipation that it will impact the landscape that is the soul. I concur with Theodore Roszak, who, in his work on the creation of a counterculture, concludes that,

> there must be a stance of life which seeks not to simply muster
> power against the misdeeds of society, but to transform the very

---

24. Berry, *What are People for?*, 8.

sense men have of reality. This may mean that, like George Fox, one must often be prepared not to act, but to 'stand still in the light,' confident that only such stillness possesses the eloquence to draw men away from lives we must believe they inwardly loathe, but which misplaced pride will goad them to defend under pressure to the very death—their death and ours."[25]

The road ahead in this work will have to figuratively follow Dr. Newberry in "a weary way across an arid expanse" to traverse some territory not often enough acknowledged by a faith seemingly focused on life in the hereafter. This includes a specific, inherited cultural paradigm, as well as the context in which this paradigm is most clearly manifesting. Christianity in the North American context has too often adhered to an idea of timelessness which results in a form of double-blindness. On the one hand, subscribers think they are acultural: somehow above the influence of the surrounding culture and outside of the vagaries of time in which we live. We are too frequently unaware of how profoundly our faith and culture mix. On the other hand, the timeless nature of this faith all too often produces a failure to take seriously the ways in which we as humans affect the physical world we inhabit and are responsible for. We will have to navigate cultural underpinnings as well as the ways in which that culture impacts the physical world in order to move toward what I feel is one aspect of a biblical vision for repair.

I have divided what follows into three parts. Part I addresses the two issues of our double-blindness: human culture and the physical environment. Chapter 1 examines one dominating aspect of our cultural ethos inherited from the period of the Enlightenment: expansion and the concomitant belief in progress. Christopher Dawson reminds us that,

> Every period of civilization possesses certain characteristic ideas that are peculiarly its own. They express the mind of the society that has given them birth, no less than does the artistic style of the social institutions of the age. . . . Now the idea of progress has occupied a position of this kind in modern civilization. . . . It has permeated the whole mind of society . . . It has been, in fact the working faith of our civilization.[26]

And while it seems more in vogue following a century of wars, threats of atomic annihilation, ecological crises, mass shootings, and the rise of global terrorism for more recent writers to question the ongoing reality of

---

25. Roszak, *Making of a Counterculture*, 267.

26. Dawson, *Progress and Religion*, 15.

a belief in progress, it nevertheless continues to be part and parcel of our approach to the world. Dawson points out that contrary to academic social critics, in the opinions of the general public and the "man in the street," progress continues to denote "little more than mental acceptance and a moral approval of that process of *material* and social change in the midst of which the modern man lives."[27] Progress was already being challenged at the end of the nineteenth century, as it continues to be challenged today. "Nevertheless, the absolute ideas that had governed social thought since the eighteenth century had entered too deeply into the mind of the average man to be easily shaken off."[28] We will explore in this opening chapter how this continues to be a formulative motif for Western culture.

Chapter 2 will dial in on this motif in its precise expression in the American West, my own context and one that has provided an especially clear expression of our cultural bias. As a region of expansive land (although by no means empty) and new opportunity for development, the American West provided a unique context for builders to practice their ethic. Just as there has been a wave of writers questioning the reality of our adherence to the idea of progress, much recent scholarship has challenged the role America's western frontier has actually played in the trending of our cultural life.[29] Regardless of the strength of the role of the frontier in American history, we can most certainly witness a peculiar expansion of the belief in our ability to make life better (progress) through the application of technology in the built environment in our western environs. And it is precisely in these settlers' approach to the West that we can clearly delineate middle-class American cultural values.

Not simply a relic of history, I will argue that the patterns of society that expanded into the interior west in the nineteenth century continue to characterize our way of interacting with our world into the twenty-first century, both externally and internally. Zeroing in on the American West not only serves as a particularly clear illustration of our confidence in what the built environment can provide, but the presence in this region of a great deal of what is yet undeveloped will also be crucial as we move into the section on how to address the crisis in which we now find ourselves. The American West was romanticized in the context of free land, individual liberty, and action and drama which led to its central role "as the final and culminating

27. Dawson, *Progress and Religion*, 17; emphasis added.

28. Dawson, *Progress and Religion*, 29.

29. See Limerick, *Legacy of Conquest*; White, *It's Your Misfortune*; Cronon, et al., *Under an Open Sky*.

home of the American Dream."[30] The American dream as a forming mythology continues to express itself in a commitment to economic progress
as indicated by the industrialization of the West and at the expense of not
only environmental resources but, as I contend here, spiritual resources too.
It is a caution given voice by Wallace Stegner when he writes, "It is perhaps
unkind to observe that the romanticizing of the West also led to acute political and economic and agricultural blunders, to the sour failure of projects
and lives, to the vast and avoidable waste of some resources and the mo-
nopolization of others, and to a long delay in the reconciling of institutions
to realities."[31]

This leads us directly to chapter 3 which will specifically address the
cost borne in the physical environment as a result of our adherence to
progress and its expression in the modern American West. The systems of
belief that define our culture are not benign theories that keep academics
employed. These ways of being in the world have profound significance in
emotional, spiritual, mental, and very physical ways. Our special belief in
progress is not centered on any specific moral or intellectual advance which
may be limited to a theoretical or ephemeral realm. Our beliefs and the
practices they give birth to have wide-ranging utilitarian, pragmatic, and
hence, for us, economic manifestations. Our cultural myth of progress is
clear in the marks we have made on the physical world, which come at tremendous social cost. This way-in-the-world becomes clear throughout the
West in the debates surrounding large-scale dams; the countless abandoned
uranium, copper, and gold mines which impact western communities daily;
and even the seemingly everyday and benign existence of a road.

The growth of the West's industrial landscape demonstrates a value
judgment relative to the built environment. While this chapter is heavy with
the economic cost involved in industrializing our world, the more important point regards how this context reveals something about our humanness. At the opening of the twentieth century, John Van Dyke wrote:

> To speak about sparing anything because it is beautiful is to
> waste one's breath and incur ridicule in the bargain. The aes-
> thetic sense—the power to enjoy through the eye, the ear, and
> the imagination—is just as important a factor in the service of
> human happiness as the corporal sense of eating and drinking;
> but there has never been a time when the world would admit
> it. . . . The main affair is to get the dollar, and if there is any
> money in cutting the throat of beauty, why, by all means, cut

---

30. Stegner, *Beyond the Hundredth Meridian*, 176.
31. Stegner, *Beyond the Hundredth Meridian*, 176.

her throat. That is what the 'practical men' have been doing ever since the world began.[32]

Part II—chapters 4 and 5—will explore more closely how the belief systems and resulting actions detailed in the previous section have become not merely an ecological crisis but a spiritual crisis for American Christians and the church in general. This serves as a pivot point for *Landscape of the Soul*. We have invariably become what our culture values, which results in prioritizing the built environment over all other considerations. The implications for American spirituality are profound. We have elevated productivity over *shalom*; often confusing the first as a necessary precondition for the second. I will contend that we cannot derive what is most crucial for us from the built environment, specifically the life of the spirit that we try so hard to develop. Because anything that we create is at best a contingent reality, including our own spirituality, it will inevitably fall short of the noncontingent reality of our Creator. It is my argument here that we must expose ourselves to the rhythms of the natural order, created not by us but by God as the only noncontingent being. We do not have the capacity to build our own world as it ought to be. This is why the obsession with the idea of progress as somehow inherent in the manifestation of the built environment has resulted in the current ecological crises. It is also why we are struggling with the parallel crisis in Western spirituality. I believe that our relationship to our environment has indeed become our spirituality. We will draw on the biblical concepts of righteousness, *shalom*, sabbath, and kingdom as an aid in establishing this reality.

As an attempt to navigate a way toward repair, Part III will draw on the rhythms and figures of the natural (the-not-built-by-us) as embodied by some of Jesus' parables of seed and soil from the gospel of Mark, chapter 4. Chapter 6 utilizes the idea of the soil as a framework to talk about the proper cultivation of our soul in order to be in a position to receive the seed, the focus of chapter 7. As a challenge to what would be the typical Western response to something needing cultivation, I will argue that our most pressing need in this regard is primarily to stop doing anything even to the point of what I will develop is a type of "nonthought."

Based on apophatic categories of theology—that which cannot be said about the perfection that is God—this is an acknowledgment and embrace of his fundamental mystery. Our spirituality cannot be primarily formed through our efforts, so a necessary first step for the church in our current climate is to free ourselves from the built environment of even Western efforts to secure our own proper state of being. Not a few of the defining

32. Van Dyke, *Desert*, 60.

figures of the biblical story—Moses, Elijah, Jesus, Paul—all found it criti-cal to disappear into the wild environs in what I understand as an act of negation *before* the next step of receptivity could take place. This is what I conceive of as the cultivation of the soil: the something affected on us by another. It is precisely the silence and solitude and simplicity of natural environments that cultivates us toward being receptive for a further work. This section will draw heavily from the wilderness perspectives of Beldon Lane, as well as my own forays into the deserts of the West.

Chapter 7 then focusses on the image of the seed, again from Mark 4, as a figure for our receptivity. This chapter also focusses on Paul's categories of faith and grace as something that God effects in us. If grace is God doing what doesn't get done any other way, then it is critical for us to approach the Creator as receivers rather than our penchant to be producers. We will hope to come to terms with an application of the idea of sacrament in this chapter as a category which can be directly applied to the natural order of creation. As physical and created beings it is vital that God provides physical representations of spiritual realities. If we conceive of sacrament as simply a setting which God provides to us as a means of rubbing up against grace, then we can approach the natural world on these terms and perhaps find it releasing something critical into our lives and to the world we walk in. This category is further opened for us by some of the thoughts of Karl Barth.

The final movement in this perspective on the repair of our spirituality comes in chapter 8, which takes its impetus from the parable of the growth of the seed in Mark 4:26–28. In following the images of emptying and re-ceiving, the emergence of the impact of our spiritual resources on the world have the mark of an automatic growth. The predominant category in this final movement is that of hospitality as conceived by the early church. This is inevitably the place to which any work that deals with the interface of Chris-tianity and culture leads—the "What do I do now?" stage. The point here, however, is not the creation of an agenda for the church but the creation of space. We will endeavor to build our argument throughout this work in an effort to combat our fondness for making things happen in light of the col-lateral damage this perspective often unwittingly produces. Hospitality in and of itself is not meant as a grand program for the renewal of the church; hospitality is instead the creation of space where people can experience the goodness that is God. As such, it is rooted in the idea of the Hebrew concept of *yasha* with its original connotation of "a wide-open space." Space and salvation are under the direct purveyance of the Creator. This is how we effect change in our own spiritual life toward the restoration of communal vibrancy. It follows the emptying and cessation and the giving-up of our fix-ation on the engineered so that anything we do is then done with care from a coherent center and not on the basis of the perpetuation of unexamined assumptions. We will conclude with a particular view of how this works out by looking at the scandalous parable of the good Samaritan from Luke 10.

Before I get started, one final disclaimer: contrary to appearances, I am not a Luddite.[33] I utilize my vehicle to access distant trailheads; I avail myself of outdoor gear dependent on various applications of technology; I take part in the market economy like most Christians in America. I am not above reproach. I have perhaps done more than my share of contributing to our built environment, most notably while working as a roughneck in western Colorado. The many advances our culture has made in terms of quantity and quality of life are not denied. My intent is to shed some light of perspective on what are all too often unacknowledged costs of our single-minded passion to build and change everything by our own efforts. There is always and inevitably a trade-off. I go to great lengths to note some of the enormous costs this way of being-in-the-world exacts from our environment. And yet, this is not the primary purpose of this work. The larger lessons to be learned have to do with how these costs are borne by our souls. The price is indeed high and we have been paying the price not only through physical and environmental degradation but equally through the deterioration of our personal spiritual conditions.

33. From nineteenth-century England, which referred to bands of workers who were destroying machinery in protest of the automation of certain trades. It generally refers to anyone who is opposed to new uses of technology.

Chapter 1

Our Inherited Cultural Mythology

IN THE INTRODUCTION I relied heavily on my formulative years being exposed to and shaped by the act of surveying as I followed my father around the deserts and hills of the interior West. It was my introduction to empty—soon-to-be-occupied—space but also a figure of what I will develop in this chapter as our particular cultural ethos. In the late nineteenth and early twentieth centuries, crews of government survey personnel traveled throughout the West placing small markers at critical locations. Those small brass and steel discs, about the diameter of a soda can, were positioned in widely spaced clusters, usually three or four at a time, allowing for distance and elevation measurements to be triangulated from a central known point. My dad often spent hours kicking through sagebrush and sand searching for these historic markers, over the top of which he would center his tripod and surveying instrument, thereby providing a definitive starting point for the mapping he was being paid to conduct. I was always astounded at his ability to locate these most often hidden markers. My own searches were rarely if ever much help. These seemed hidden in the midst of nothing but a barren sagebrush plain, stretching as far as the eye could see, all sand and undulating hills, a nondescript and, to me at least, random place of uniform emptiness.

I find it ironic to have so often encountered these markers in my more recent wanderings, and most often in the most random and supposedly untouched land I could be in: no roads or even trails for miles in any direction. I have a fondness for loading a backpack with a few days' worth of supplies and either ascending or descending isolated canyons on the Colorado Plateau. Poring over maps at home, I can identify countless canyons that have no kind of route marked into or through their inner environs. Obviously not all of these canyons prove to be untouched. Some have been historically inhabited by Native American peoples, utilized heavily for living, farming, and gathering, and hence littered with artifacts and ancient rock art. Some areas continue to bear the remnants of livestock trails constructed in the early years of the twentieth century—trails which provided access for sheep and cattle to utilize water and forage at the bottom of a canyon—even if these trails were rarely mapped. Even the typically heavier impact of Jeeps employed during the uranium boom in the Colorado Plateau during the fifties and sixties is not always indicated on a map. Often these areas can contain social trails established by canyoneers, backpackers, and other adventurers even if they are not acknowledged by USGS maps.

Though these features appear from time to time, I have been in many desert canyons which have none of the marks of human passage even when a canyon may possess a name on a map; and many such canyons still exist unnamed. In any unnamed and trailless canyon one must always acknowledge the possibility that there will be no viable entry or exit to such a remote location. This is a crucial consideration when one intends to exit a canyon and cross a ridge or plateau in order to enter a neighboring canyon. Depending on one's starting point, the intent is to either ascend or descend a canyon and—provided the upper reaches of a canyon are not blocked by an impassable dryfall—cross a high ridge in order to drop into and then reverse the process in a neighboring canyon. Utilizing parallel canyons to create a loop hike is an easy task when it occurs on paper, but an entirely different experience when it takes place on the ground.

So, I am always astounded when I encounter a survey marker in such out-of-the-way places. Something I could rarely find as a child now appears out of nowhere with no effort. This has happened frequently enough to almost become unnerving. It seems to make little difference where I travel of late as the markers are bound to show up, almost as if I somehow attract their presence. I recently came across these discs embedded in stone in the Sherman Mountains of southeast Wyoming and what I thought were anonymous locations in canyons of southwest Colorado. The markers inevitably have a date of placement stamped on them, frequently 1919 or 1933, often an elevation, and always a warning: "Penalty $250 for Removal." Some are marked by nearby rock cairns but just as many simply appear in a random patch of sand.

By far, most of my meetings with these markers have come in the untracked desert wilderness of eastern Utah's canyon country. Several years ago, I was walking into the Maze District of Canyonlands National Park on a four-day solo backpack. On a whim, I climbed to the high northeast ridge of Elaterite Butte above the deep twisting canyons of the inner maze. Elaterite is a high butte of broken maroon towers appearing like a ruined Medieval fortress 1,200 feet above the Elaterite Basin to the west and more than 1,600 feet above the deep canyon complex to the east. Having no trail and not leading to any other discernable points, this ridge seemed as wild and untraveled as any place could possibly be. And yet there on the narrow spine of the ridge, 1,000 feet above the basin floor, appeared a 1919 survey marker.

More recently I was in the Devil's Hole region of the San Rafael Swell, skirting cliff bands of sheer red rock nearly 2,000 feet above the San Rafael River. Again, an inhospitable and seeming empty tangle of detached towers standing at the head of narrow, steeply dropping canyons falling to both the east and west of the narrow mesa I was ascending. Another survey marker, this one placed in 1933. Likely the most surprising occurrence was in a large canyon complex on the Kaiparowits Plateau one November when I was ascending a steep and narrow, unnamed side canyon branching from another unnamed side canyon which itself drained into a larger but still trailless canyon draining the plateau to the south. This was one of the largest trailless areas I have identified and is part of the last region in the lower forty-eight to have been surveyed. I was deep in a region accessible only through days of walking. Climbing a steep slope to bypass another dryfall in the canyon I was surprised to stumble across another survey point in the most unlikely spot I could imagine. Obviously, this spot is no longer so improbable as it inevitably has a presence as a location on somebody's map.

These backcountry sightings are likely not as random as I once considered them to be and they clearly demonstrate one of the defining ethoses of our culture. These very physical markers, small steel discs hidden in the empty corners of the desert, illustrate what gives shape to our ways of being in the world. Their purpose is to give order and structure and thereby ascribe purpose to a vast expanse of rocks and cactus and sand. Even the most out-of-the-way, solitary, untouched place must be given a name and an identifier on a map because this is precisely who we are as a people and how we meet the world we live in. Survey markers, beyond their physical property as a piece of steel, demonstrate a form of religious belief in our culture which centers on the transformation of nature for the purpose of progress.

To associate a steel disc with a form of religious belief may seem like a stretch at this point, but it is this very relationship I hope to establish in this chapter. The great rule of our society is that nothing can be of value which is not first identified, mapped, named, and thereby put to productive use. The marks of this rule surround us every day in the physical environment we inhabit, apparently even in its hidden corners. Anticipating our larger point to be developed in later sections, it follows that this rule will dominate the deserts, the wilderness, the wastelands that make up even portions of our inner selves. These spaces cannot be of any value to us as they stand. Everything must be codified, fixed, made productive. The empty—the experience of space—is intolerable to us because it is out of our control and therefore either frightening or fruitless. Anything empty or wild would indicate something we have not yet brought into productive use.

In order to establish the reality of this point, we need to start by demonstrating how this rule developed as a way of thought and life thereby giving shape to our way of being in the world. The authors we will explore below speak of a particular motif, imperative, law, character, myth, and even faith. This rule is what I will call an *ethos* which stems from the Greek idea of custom or character. An ethos is, "The distinguishing character, sentiment, moral nature, or guiding belief of a person, group or institution"[1]; it is "the characteristic spirit of a culture, era, or community, as manifested in its beliefs and aspirations."[2] Our ethos is what makes us who we are through our morals and beliefs and the manifestation of those in our daily practice and the creation of our cultural institutions. The ethos of a culture is partially established by the founding myths of that specific culture, an idea I alluded to in the introduction. Theodore Roszak points out that the idea of myth has "been identified as a universal phenomenon of human society, a constitutive factor so critical in importance that it is difficult to imagine a culture having any coherence at all if it lacked the mythological bond."[3]

Even in our modern North American culture we are not exempt from identifying our ethos, stemming from the Enlightenment and scientific thought and the resulting Industrial and Technological Revolutions, as the product of a particular cultural mythology. This is simply a way of talking about how we developed the values we currently live by: "If the culture of science locates its highest values not in mystic symbol or ritual or epic tales of faraway lands and times, but in a mode of consciousness, why should we hesitate to call this a myth?"[4] It is further likely that even our highly advanced scientific culture itself cannot be construed as ever being truly free of mystery and magical ritual because, "These are the very bonds of social life, the inarticulate assumptions and motivations that weave together the collective fabric of society and which require periodic collective affirmation."[5] Our given society in a given historical situation has simply

1. https://www.merriam-webster.com/dictionary/ethos.

2. https://www.dictionary.com/browse/ethos?s=ts.

3. Roszak, *Making of a Counterculture*, 214.

4. Roszak, *Making of a Counterculture*, 214.

5. Roszak, *Making of a Counterculture*, 148.

invested the *idea* of the "objective consciousness" of science and technology with our sense of meaningfulness and value.[6]

The anthropologist Clyde Kluckhohn points out that, "The essential core of culture consists of traditional (i.e., historically derived and selected) ideas and especially their attached values; culture systems may, on the one hand, be considered as products of action, on the other hand as conditioning influences upon further action."[7] To identify that core—based on those historically selected ideas—will help us develop a perspective on not only why we do what we do, but will also in the end serve as an aid to facilitate the embrace of being a source of the repair of the world. I believe, with other social historians and critics, that the core resides in a unique adherence to the idea of progress stemming from an equally unique coalescing of historical occurrences.

According to the historian William Goetzmann, the newly encountered, previously unknown regions of the world in the nineteenth century Age of Exploration were a source of new and unique opportunity for the culture because vast regions were discovered which were perceived as not only holding untapped and nearly unlimited material wealth but also a wealth of new opportunity. These new regions were perceived as being uninhabited—or at the very least inhabited unproductively—which granted a form of sanction for those lands to be colonized. The newly mobile citizens of the Western world confronted the unknown "with Christianity, ideas of progress, new techniques in science, and dreams of romantic imperialism." This historically exceptional meeting of the physical environment with a newly developing Western worldview resulted in Western culture developing a new paradigm of expansion, development, and progress in economic growth, "which became a crucial factor in shaping the *long-standing* destiny of the newly discovered places and their peoples, and which *at the same time altered forever the established culture.*"[8]

The historical roots which form the core of Western civilization in its current manifestation are frequently traced back to Enlightenment thinkers, beginning toward the end of the seventeenth century, and the resulting full embrace of the Scientific Revolution. Isaac Newton (1642–1727) continues to be highlighted as especially influential for these movements. Newton's conception of the universe as adhering to rational and natural laws, fully discoverable by human reasoning, paved the way not only for the application of the growing scientific thought but also proved to reinforce the political thought of English philosopher John Locke (1632–1704) and

6. Roszak, *Making of a Counterculture*, 215.
7. Quoted in Dyrness, *How Does America Hear the Gospel?*, 7.
8. Goetzmann, *Exploration and Empire*, ix; emphasis added.

the economic categories of Adam Smith (1723–1790)—two figures who will prove influential in our brief survey momentarily. Newton's influence lies primarily in the establishment of our current thinking relative to both nature and humanity. The natural or physical universe, after Newton, is purely "mechanistic, mathematically ordered and concretely material," while modern men and women are those "whose rational intelligence [have] comprehended the world's natural order. . ."[9] Humankind derives nobility from the fact that "by [our] own reason [we] had grasped nature's underlying logic and thereby achieved dominion over its forces."[10]

Newton's understanding of reality as a fully rational system and the ability of humankind to discern that system flourished in the context of newly opened frontiers. As new ways of conceiving of our place in the natural world were unfolding in Europe, the New World provided a unique setting and unprecedented opportunity for the revelation of the purpose of human life and the development of human nobility. "The revelation began, Charles Taylor argues, with Francis Bacon who believed that the highest human dignity comes from a transformation of nature for the sake of human progress."[11] Richard Tarnas provides a succinct summary of the Enlightenment thinkers' impact on modern Western thought:

> Mankind's happy destiny at last seemed assured, and patently as a result of its own rational powers and concrete achievements. It was now evident that the quest for human fulfillment would be propelled by increasingly sophisticated analysis and manipulation of the natural world, and by systematic efforts to extend man's intellectual and existential independence in every realm—physical, social, political, religious, scientific, metaphysical.[12]

Our unique and newfound ability to understand and manipulate the natural world toward the ends of human dignity, fulfillment, and independence is what many historians, philosophers, and social scientists would now identify as a belief in progress. The idea of progress is specifically linked to our relationship with the natural world—how we understand, harness, and build upon it—and at the same time directed toward the ends which we identify as a more thoroughly fulfilling human existence. Our own conception of the good life is derived from the ways we work on our world to fit it to our own perceived needs and ends: "Progress, the work of our own minds and

9. Tarnas, *Passion of the Western Mind*, 280–81.
10. Tarnas, *Passion of the Western Mind*, 281.
11. Dyrness, *Earth is God's*, 59.
12. Tarnas, *Passion of the Western Mind*, 281.

hands, is not a neutral entity that stands outside of our life and thought; it is a force that has permeated profoundly into every fiber of our existence."[13]

Progress, in a sense, has become who we are as inheritors of Western culture, and in order to fulfill human purpose within this culture, humans must continually develop an ability to master their world through applications of technical means. This led the French philosopher Jacques Ellul to conclude that, "No human activity is possible except as it is mediated and censored by the technical medium. . . . Technique [we might say 'progress'] possesses monopoly of action."[14]

Authors speak of the overriding current or motif that gives structure to Western society as the idea of human progress. Who we are, how we conceive of and build our lives together, what we effect in terms of the "architecture" of society: all of these are distinctly shaped by an adherence to and pursuit of progress.[15] The idea of progress has distinct manifestations and value commitments which we will explore further below. Relative to the commitment of the *idea* of progress, Murray Jardine summarizes it in these terms:

> Modern Western culture, unlike any culture that has ever existed, has been characterized by the belief that humans can improve their earthly existence through the application of scientific and technological knowledge, which will lead to increased material well-being and individual freedom, possibly even to the point of total human liberation. . . . Belief in progress has been central to the self-understanding of modern Western societies.[16]

To speak of a "belief in progress" is to explicitly invoke a religious theme. Belief systems are internal (intellectual, emotional, spiritual) adherence systems which provide a coherence for external (social, physical, vocational) systems of action in the world. In the culture we inhabit the synonym for "belief" is often "faith." Faith is most often associated with specifically religious ideals which makes the association of the belief in progress a form of religious faith perhaps surprising. It is apparent in our culture, however, that the belief in progress "is essentially a philosophy of life; and like all philosophies of life, it does duty for a religion."[17] This is why authors can speak of adherence to progress in terms of an actual religious faith. The ethos of Western culture is that of specifically human progress which, "has often been described in terms of the inspiring dynamics of an authentic

13. Gouzwaard, *Capitalism and Progress*, 143.
14. Ellul, *Technological Society*, 418.
15. Gouzwaard, *Capitalism and Progress*, xxii–xxiii.
16. Jardine, *Making and Unmaking*, 15.
17. Baillie, *Belief in Progress*, 40.

faith" which consists of "the propelling, all-embracing visions which direct persons in everything they feel, think, and do."[18] Bob Gouzwaard, in his diagnosis of Western society, further emphasizes that,

> Consciousness of progress has nurtured into a faith, which, for the sake of the future of mankind, can summon man to deeds; and the breathtaking 'splendor' of those deeds parallels the moving of mountains, including the massive mountain of the Western social order. Faith in progress has become a faith capable of transforming its adherents into revolutionaries of the first order, for who would not follow the direction of an infallible guide which resolutely points the way to paradise regained?[19]

Faith in progress is a relatively recent development in terms of the whole history of humankind. This form of faith has at least two critical implications to consider for our purposes. First, the idea of progress as an arena for faith expression results in a uniquely Western expression of religious belief. This is most notably true in the United States where faith in progress has reached a fuller expression. Faith being what it is, it is difficult if not impossible to separate a "formal adherence to a distinct religio-ecclesiastical confession"[20] from forms of belief that we express in the culture at large. Christian faith and a general faith in progress appear in our culture as two sides of the same coin.

The second implication of this exercise of faith is the way it results in our granting sacred significance to the works of our minds and hands in our development of scientific theory and the application of that theory to specific technological applications. Faith in progress "is a faith in practicality, in the individual urge to act," and as such "faith in progress, much more than Calvinism, attributed a newly sacred significance to the technical and economic pioneering effects of the industrial revolutionaries."[21] So Jacques Ellul writes about the increased "sacralizing" of the world we ourselves build through technical processes. This is a form of being restored to a "supernatural world" because human beings project a "sacred delirium" into the belief in progress "through which he can control, explain, direct, and justify his actions" as a divine being.[22] Hence anything we take hold of gains an eternal significance. This applies equally to our methodologies directed toward specifically spiritual goals.

18. Gouzwaard, *Capitalism and Progress*, xxiii.

19. Gouzwaard, *Capitalism and Progress*, 41–42.

20. Gouzwaard, *Capitalism and Progress*, xxii.

21. Gouzwaard, *Capitalism and Progress*, 57.

22. Ellul, *Technological Society*, 192.

The faith in progress, like any cultural belief system, has very concrete expressions in terms of its effect on people's activities. The manifestations of this belief system have as their focal point a profound ability to reshape both nature and human society. Central or core beliefs of an individual and a society at large will find expression in the values, expenses, efforts, and pursuits of that individual or society. To this end, Ellul emphasizes that our adherence to the idea of progress harnesses all the variety of our technical abilities in order to master both the physical and social worlds. Applied reason is an attempt to take hold of chaos and put order to it.[23] This worldview entails a spiritual choice as to our actions, "namely that man's destiny is realized primarily in his relation to the natural things of the world. . . . We distinguish ourselves as human beings primarily by the shape we give to the world through thought and creative activity."[24]

It has been specifically since the middle of the eighteenth century that Western societies have taken on an increasing impetus to reshape the physical and social experience of humanity. We have not only increased our understanding of the physical environment as well as the means of exercising control over it, but likewise have embarked on experiments in advanced social techniques to shape our lives together.[25] The specific application of the faith in progress occurs on both places simultaneously in an effort to achieve greater human happiness and utility from nature.

> To make the notion of progress more concrete, we can begin by observing that the most obvious feature of modern Western civilization is that over the past five centuries, and especially in the last two hundred years, people in the Western world have discovered that they have a much greater capacity to understand, control, and even change their environments—and by this term I mean both natural and social environments—than they or any other people had previously realized was possible.[26]

According to the Western way of thought, then, in order for progress to occur in formulating a more conducive natural and social world, special attention needs to be applied to both of these realms: the transformation of the natural world and the human systems that make up our life together. The belief in progress and its necessary application on the natural world requires, first of all, close attention to the central role of labor, specifically in its relation to productivity and the economy. Adam Smith, the Scottish

23. Ellul, *Technological Society*, 43.
24. Gouzwaard, *Capitalism and Progress*, 24.
25. See Baillie, *Belief in Progress*, 37.
26. Jardine, *Making and Unmaking*, 15–16.

economist and author of the profoundly influential *Wealth of Nations*, specifically applied Enlightenment categories of progress to the Western economic order. Smith had particularly important formulative thoughts relative to humanity's relationship to nature. This worldview understands nature as the domain of humankind's self-realization and subsequently "economic value can only be achieved by way of man's active struggle with nature—in other words, by means of labor. Hence, there is no value other than labor value, elicited from nature by man. . . . Production is the result of labor; it is the most important expression of human dignity."[27]

The culture we inhabit has had nearly five centuries to internalize the priority and sense of value granted to the advance of technology and industrial production for the sake of economic progress. Like Adam Smith, John Locke was deeply influenced by Enlightenment thought. While his primary contribution to Western culture continues in our forms of political life, he developed an approach similar to Adam Smith in that he emphasized productive labor in the realm of nature as central to progress of modern men and women. The primary human goal for Locke is production toward the accumulation of wealth which is almost exclusively derived from one's confrontation with the resources of the natural world. "Locke tends to think of value as being material or economic. Nowhere in his theory does he consider the possibility that something might be of aesthetic or spiritual value. . . . [So] Locke states that the Europeans have the right to take possession of the land in North America because the Native Indians are not using it to create any value."[28]

In recounting the history of white settlement in the Uncompaghre Valley of western Colorado, Peter Decker points out an editorial published in the *Ouray Times* in the summer of 1877 which called for the valley's indigenous tribes to pack up and leave. "It was the industrious whites who could cultivate, improve and make valuable the land, thus adding to the prosperity of the whole country, not a few Indians who were of no benefit to themselves or anyone else except maybe the Indian agents and government contractors. The land is of no earthly use to the Indians and it is necessary to the prosperity of our section."[29] Regardless of our own "enlightened" response to such obviously racist categories, it remains true that the ongoing faith in progress is manifested primarily through an increasingly intense application of productive labor on the physical world in order to make it more conducive to economic prosperity. One who does not labor to this end is somehow morally deficient.

27. Gouzwaard, *Capitalism and Progress*, 24.

28. Jardine, *Making and Unmaking*, 49.

29. Decker, *Old Fences, New Neighbors*, 15. See a similar editorial submitted to the *Cheyenne Daily Leader* in 1870 by the Big Horn Association; quoted by Johns, "With Friends Like These," 22.

The second realm of emphasis, the structure of our social life together, flows from the focus on the natural world and serves to highlight the ways in which a focus on labor and production toward the aim of progress is not just affected in the physical environment. Centuries of attention to increasing the efficiency of labor in order to facilitate greater production has resulted in a particular kind of society in which our social life together is increasingly shaped to advance the primary goal of economic productivity. Social critics label this type of society as a "technocracy," which Theodore Roszak defines as, "that society in which those who govern justify themselves by appeal to technical experts who, in turn, justify themselves by appeal to scientific forms of knowledge. And beyond the authority of science, there is no appeal."[30] If human dignity depends on productive labor, then it naturally follows for our society that the more productive we can be the more fully human and advanced we can demonstrate we have become. This requires the application of increasing scientific knowledge to advancing technology which, in the end, acquires an unquestionable authority over the social structure. We find ourselves living in the technocracy.

Technocracy is the mature product of the scientific ethos and technological progress and as such holds a prominent and unchallenged position in Western culture. Technocracy's "assumptions about reality and its values become as unobtrusively pervasive as the air we breathe. . . . [Daily] the technocracy increases and consolidates its power as a transpolitical phenomenon following the dictates of industrial efficiency, rationality, and necessity." Herein lies the defining ethos of our culture which prioritizes what can be engineered and made productive through technology which holds the place "of a grand cultural imperative which is beyond question, beyond discussion."[31] The story of the development of the cultural myth we adhere to from Newton to Locke to Smith is the story of progress through labor and therefore the absolute necessity of the built environment: "Despite exaggerations, the text is clear: no other solution is possible, no other hope, than that represented by the improvement of human techniques. Every other solution is inefficient or mischievous."[32]

Much of the foregoing discussion of our Western cultural ethos has been drawn from writers who are critical of where our myths have landed us. Certainly, there is a great deal to be critical of as the triumph of technocracy locks us into a narrowly materialistic worldview which can be experienced

30. Roszak, *Making of a Counterculture*, 8.

31. Roszak, *Making of a Counterculture*, 9.

32. Ellul, *Technological Society*, 415.

as tyrannical as our lives are increasingly dependent on the rule of experts [33] Even by the middle of the last century

> modern science's brave new world had started to become subject to wide and vigorous criticism: Technology was taking over and dehumanizing man, placing him in a context of artificial substances and gadgets rather than live nature, in an unaesthetically standardized environment where means had subsumed ends, where industrial labor requirements entailed the mechanization of human beings, where all problems were perceived as soluble by technical research at the expense of genuine existential responses.[34]

We might ask in our twenty-first-century context whether we are still subject to a faith in progress.

Despite the criticisms being levelled, Western culture continues to exercise a profound faith in the grand narrative of progress through scientific and technological advance. The idea has become such a central core of life that the actual practices of our society appear to embody the belief in progress regardless of its critics This is the ruling paradigm that continues to shape our way in the world. In the introduction to a recent work addressing our "deep root metaphors"—those individual and collective views of the world—Tom Butler reminds us that these are the very things that often become invisible to people within a specific culture because people tend to internalize cultural practices without actually noticing their presence.[35] The ongoing view of the world that Butler argues is more prominent than ever is centered in a belief that the earth is merely a storehouse of natural resources subject to appropriation. There appears to be an increase in recent movements calling for humanity to rise to its global-managing responsibilities, which in turn is a justification for the further domestication of the planet. We are living in the age of human domination over virtually all natural processes.[36] In the words of Stewart Brand, "We are as gods and might as well get good at it."[37] To raise a challenge to this civil religion of progress is to place one on the margins of polite society; there is little choice in our current climate other than to embrace the realities of the modern, technoindustrial society which will naturally bring about the continued commodification of nature to serve economic growth.[38]

33. See Jardine, *Making and Unmaking*, 83.
34. Tarnas, *Passion of the Western Mind*, 362.
35. Butler, "Lives Not Our Own," ix.
36. Butler, "Lives Not Our Own," ix.
37. As quoted by Butler, "Lives Not Our Own," xi.
38. Butler, "Lives Not Our Own," xii.

A helpful summary of our condition is provided by David Ehrenfeld in his work *The Arrogance of Humanism*. Ehrenfeld is addressing the dominant theme in our culture which he identifies as "humanism," but his definition of this reality accords closely with what I have called the belief in progress. It consists of, "A supreme faith in human reason—its ability to confront and solve the many problems that humans face, its ability to rearrange both the world of nature and the affairs of men and women so that human life will prosper."[39] Ehrenfeld further invokes our faith in the expressions of pure reason: science and technology. He identifies the confusion of late relative to our use of reason, but is still able to affirm that this faith continues to permeate our existence and behavior and in fact remains well ingrained in Western culture. We have opted for the assumptions of human power not only due to their effectiveness but also because they tend to be good for our egos.[40] Especially informative in Ehrenfeld's discussion of the idea of progress (his "humanism") as it connects with what has been said so far in this chapter is his assertion that, "Humanism is one of the vital religions. . . . It is the dominating religion of our time, a part of the lives of nearly everyone in the 'developed' world and of all others who want to participate in a similar development."[41]

We can begin to weave these strands about progress together to form a tapestry which will show us something about ourselves and our ways of interacting with the world. Part of my forming assumption is that Christians in America for the most part possess the best intentions for formulating a healthy spirituality which would then make a positive impact on the world at large. The leading issue for me, however, is the category under which those two things take place. By now it should be fairly well established that we believe (in an explicitly religious sense) that our labor—generally our efforts to secure a better life—contain a sacred significance. The upshot is that we end up being dominated by human techniques and the role of experts in order to affect any measurable progress in our own lives and the larger context of the society we inhabit. It is specifically the paradigm of labor as directed by an expert which has such profound implications for the American church, both in terms of our own spirituality as well as in how we then participate in reflecting how things ought to be in the world at large.

Because the great rule of our society is centered on making everything worthwhile through production, it follows that we bring to our own faith exercises an unguarded priority for that which is human-engineered. The landscape of the soul bears these marks. Our own spirituality has become an

---

39. Ehrenfeld, *Arrogance of Humanism*, 5.

40. Ehrenfeld, *Arrogance of Humanism*, 6, 21.

41. Ehrenfeld, *Arrogance of Humanism*, 3.

extension of our built environment and therein lies the roots of its apparent anemic condition for far too much of the American church. What is built by our own efforts is at best a contingent creation which can only ever be a poor substitute for what would be produced by a noncontingent Creator.

There is a point at which our best efforts to construct a healthy physical and spiritual existence (the two are intimately intertwined) turns out to be actually quite counterproductive. The point is illustrated by Montana writer William Kittredge. Raised on an enormous farm and ranching empire in southeast Oregon, Kittredge grew up in the shadow of a father and grandfather bent on accumulating and putting under hoof and plow as much land as would be humanly possible. It was later in life when Kittredge recognized what their grand program had done to the land and, equally important, what it had done to their lives:

> And then it all went dead, over years, but swiftly. You can imagine our surprise and despair, our sense of having been profoundly cheated. It took us a long while to realize some unnamable thing was wrong, and then we blamed it on ourselves, our inability to manage enough. But the fault wasn't ours, beyond the fact that we had all been educated to believe in a grand bad land-factory notion as our prime model of excellence. We felt enormously betrayed. For so many years, through endless efforts, we had proceeded in good faith, and it turned out we had wrecked all we had not left untouched. . . . In Warner Valley we thought we were living the right lives, creating a great precise perfection of fields, and we found the mythology had been telling us an enormous lie. The world had proven too complex, or the myth too simpleminded. And we were mortally angered.[42]

Kittredge here does us the service of demonstrating the relationship between our efforts on our world and its effects on the inner life.

The mythology we live under is indeed problematic: It is the sense of confidence that our actions are the primary sources of progress for our own spiritual life and that of the culture surrounding us. This has become an unquestionable and unchallengeable formulative myth for our way of life in the world. At this point I want to introduce just two of the myriad criticisms levelled at the belief in progress, criticisms that will have specific bearing on our argument as we progress toward parts II and III. These criticisms center on the ways in which, first, our faith in progress becomes a dominating aspect of culture, and second, how this results in moral senselessness.

42. Kittredge, *Owning it All*, 61, 64.

Our sense of progress depends on the application of scientific techniques to produce anything of value. While the application of technical knowledge has indeed produced many positive advances for human existence worldwide, it has a dark side as well. The assumption of our kind of society is that technique inevitably leads to better things for everyone under its application. This kind of assumption, often unchallengeable in our cultural climate, grants a certain self-perpetuating autonomy to technical knowledge. So, for Ellul, "technique has taken substance, has become a reality in itself. It is no longer merely a means and an intermediary. It is an object in itself, an independent reality with which we must reckon."[43] The suggestion being that even "spiritual movements are totally confined within a technical world. Here is yet another example of the phenomenon . . . that technique encompasses the totality of present-day society. Man is caught like a fly in a bottle. His attempts at culture, freedom, and creative endeavor have become mere entries in technique's filing cabinet."[44]

In the current climate of progress based on human productivity, nothing is ultimately beyond the domination of the technical knowledge of experts. This sense led Vaclav Havel to assert that, "Technology—the child of modern science, which in turn is child of modern metaphysics—is out of humanity's control, has ceased to serve us, has enslaved us and compelled us to participate in the preparation of our own destruction."[45] Indeed, it would seem that nothing stands apart from the domination of a thoroughly engineered society:

> Charles A. Reich observed that 'Technology and production . . . pulverize everything in their path: the landscape, the natural environment, history and tradition, the amenities and civilities, the privacy and spaciousness of life, beauty, and the fragile, slow-growing social structures which bind us together. . . . Thus, a true definition of the American crisis would say this: We no longer understand the system under which we live . . . in turn, the system has been permitted to assume unchallenged power to dominate our lives, and now rumbles along, unguided and therefore indifferent to human ends.[46]

The domination of life under the rubric of production as empowered by the technology we create curtails any possibility of discovering value by another means. The possibility that we could be profoundly shaped by something other than our own efforts cannot occur under the dominating

43. Ellul, *Technological Society*, 63.
44. Ellul, *Technological Society*, 417–18.
45. Havel, *Open Letters*, 206.
46. Gouzwaard, *Capitalism and Progress*, 152–53.

paradigm of our faith in progress. Edward Abbey was particularly critical of this society we have inherited which began with a promise of a new age of freedom drawn from the supposed wealth produced by the Enlightenment, science, technology, and political emancipation. He likens our current condition to being engulfed by a nightmare:

> The technological superstate, densely populated, centrally controlled, nuclear-powered, computer-directed, firmly and thoroughly policed. . . . A technocratic despotism—perhaps benevolent, perhaps not, but in either case the enemy of personal liberty, family independence, and community sovereignty, shutting off for a long time to come the freedom to choose among alternative ways of living.[47]

It is just this alternativeness I am pursuing here which is precisely what seems so unlikely in light of the dominating structure of our attachment to the unquestioned value of the built environment.

Abbey's rant about the loss of freedom, community, and family due to the domination of life by technique leads to our second critique: the inability to make moral sense of the world which has followed the pursuit of progress. We may finally be in a position to acknowledge that the priorities of productive labor in order to manipulate the natural world for the sake of pursuing market categories of progress is a grossly inefficient way of developing a healthy—and therefore socially helpful—spirituality. The cultural paradigm that we have been developing in this chapter is dependent on the exchange of productive labor for progress to occur: We have to build something out of nothing (or at the very least exert our efforts) in order for the transformation from nonvalue to value to take place. These are explicitly market categories. Orientation to these categories produces a certain kind of society because the only progress ethically justified is that which maximizes benefits relative to costs.[48] When all human social relationships and all of human life generally is reduced to the model of the market, "the situation ultimately will be thoroughly destructive *morally*, socially, politically, and even economically."[49]

In the past 500 years, our Western culture has undeniably discovered new creative approaches and has developed the corresponding new technological powers necessary for an exchange to occur, allowing progress to happen. At the same time, we have been "unable to make moral sense of those capacities, resulting in psychological disorientation, cultural decay,

---

47. Abbey, *Down the River*, 117.
48. See Gouzwaard, *Capitalism and Progress*, 140.
49. Jardine, *Making and Unmaking*, 112; emphasis added.

and institutional breakdown."[50] Furthermore, according to John Baillie, our culture's moral sense has not been able to match the pace of technological progress: "the merely technical progress of civilization may to a large extent be assured by the advance of knowledge, something quite different is required to ensure moral and social progress. The hindrance now is not that we do not know enough, but that we are not good enough to use what knowledge we have in the service of the best ends."[51] This conclusion calls into question the actual *progress* our society has achieved because at its root this very paradigm is beset by a moral senselessness which cannot adequately resource our lives together. We cannot but come to a similar conclusion as that drawn by David Ehrenfeld regarding our ethos: "There is no morality or final purpose or even character inherent in our mechanisms of control—they can turn unpredictably on any teleology in whose name they are invoked."[52]

The time is overdue for drawing some conclusions about who we are and what it means for cultivating a healthy life of the soul with an ultimate eye toward what part we might play in developing a healthy society. We have developed the idea of our cultural ethos—our distinguishing character and guiding belief system—as being centered in the belief of progress. This ethos is identified through the categories we observed as crucial to the Western cultural mind: production and development, specifically to the point of societal transformation, and especially as these categories impinge on the physical environment. Production and transformation occur directly as the fruit of human rationality as exemplified in science and applied through human labor. The ultimate aim of this development of the world through the instrumentality of human labor is the creation of wealth specifically, and an increased sense of value more generally.

The creation of value carries with it a sacralizing effect regarding the tasks we put ourselves to. We are drawn to the conclusion that our adherence to the belief in progress is an exercise in value or worth creation. In the end, this tenor of our society is about our deep-set need for meaning and significance. Our efforts in the natural and social realms are, at their most profound level, efforts to create and bestow value—something of profound worth—into our very existence as human beings on earth.

An equally crucial thread running through this presentation of our way of being in the world is the reality that we are not actually the autonomous creators we give ourselves credit for being; we are actually under some kind of compulsion in whatever actions we undertake. Our attempts at

50. Jardine, *Making and Unmaking*, 130.
51. Baillie, *Belief in Progress*, 178.
52. Ehrenfeld, *Arrogance of Humanism*, 103.

value creation, and therefore meaning bestowal, have never taken place in a vacuum of human autonomy. The very categories of production and wealth and significance have always been mediated by the cultural myths we live by. The idea of progress has not relinquished meaning or value creation to the human agent but instead has retained monopoly of action and its own position of centrality to define our culture.

The directives under which we think we create are actually maintained by the technocracy under which we labor and the dominating categories of progress which remain unchallenged and indifferent. Our narrative is neither as empowering nor as freeing as we would like to think. We can reference Bob Gouzwaard and his diagnosis again at length:

> Western man is certainly not that 'unmoved mover' as at times he is depicted. He is no longer the autonomous subject who can sovereignly set processes into motion and who can also sovereignly, at a moment of his own choice, stop these processes again. To the contrary, Western man, as a result of the process of progress which he has initiated, is now caught in the predicaments of being managed rather that of being the manager. Progress the work of our own minds and hands, is not a neutral entity that stands outside of our life and thought; it is a force that has penetrated profoundly into every fiber of our existence.[53]

Standing at the center of the idea of progress is a belief—a distinct form of faith, if you will. We see that this manifestation of our cultural ideas and values is itself a form of religious belief, often replacing more formal expressions of a particular religious institution, but at the very least standing alongside and lending its aid to those institutions as the two have come to share identical goals. The idea of progress not only contains the "inspiring dynamics of an actual faith" but allows us to ascribe a sacred significance to our efforts. We aspire to be the creators of value and meaning, but have never actually been the autonomous creators that bestowal would require. We are thus thrust into the centrality and necessity of an act of faith.

Faith, at its root, is a form of exchange. Faith is to place trust or confidence in something or someone, most often demonstrated through necessary corresponding actions in behavior which embody that trust, in anticipation of a return of value, usually in the form of meaning. The exchange is always prompted by a perceived value, be it coherent answers, meaning, or the general categories of worth and significance. Western culture has therefore effected a faith exchange with this particular idea of progress. This is inevitably accompanied by a frenzied activity of mind and

53. Gouzwaard, *Capitalism and Progress*, 143.

body in anticipation of the return of desired value. This is not a neutral or unproblematic exchange.

I could place my confidence in a diet of Twinkies and expect to receive back eighty years' worth of perfect health. This would obviously be a bad exchange due to a misplaced confidence in what my diet of processed sugar was capable of providing. The problem lies in the lack of substance in the object of my faith to deliver the end for which I purchase and consume in the first place. In this ridiculous example, a Twinkie does not have the capacity to reciprocate my belief in its healthful properties precisely because it lacks the necessary substance. The faith exchange that has occurred in Western culture, regardless of our own religious affiliations, is that our efforts can produce the requisite meaning and value as long as we follow the cultural dictates within this ethos of progress. The issue with our misplaced faith is that the object of that faith is basically morally senseless and the only value it can subscribe to is the value of market categories, which cannot ultimately return that which our exercise of faith seeks.

We have centered on the idea of progress according to Enlightenment-era categories as a cultural ethos—as formulative myth. This is what Daniel Bell calls an ideology: a value system organized into a specific code and formulated as a set of religious dogmas which serve as a means of mobilizing a community. Furthermore,

> It is in the character of ideologies not only to reflect or justify an underlying reality but, once launched, to take on a life of their own. A truly powerful ideology opens up a new vision of life in the imagination; once formulated, it remains part of the moral repertoire to be drawn upon by intellectuals, theologians, or moralists as part of the range of possibilities open to mankind.[54]

These are the basic resources of our culture which do not disappear, but are renewable, "called upon and re-formulated throughout the history of a civilization."[55]

At issue in the current form of the Western ideology is the absence of a "moral or transcendental ethic" and the corresponding "extraordinary contradiction within the social structure."[56] In subscribing as we do to the ideology of progress, we have effected an exchange of our faith—our deepest hope and most profound trust—in something lacking the requisite moral substance to return true value. Undoubtedly many, if not most, American

---

54. Bell, *Cultural Contradictions of Capitalism*, 60.
55. Bell, *Cultural Contradictions of Capitalism*, 61.
56. Bell, *Cultural Contradictions of Capitalism*, 71.

Christians would maintain that their faith is placed elsewhere. If this were actually the case, however, then I maintain that our society would look very different. Genuine faith is accompanied by corresponding actions which demonstrate the confidence level in the object of that faith to return the sought-after value. "Can a person unknowingly belong to one religion while under the impression that he or she is part of another? If that person believes in the dogma of the former and only celebrates the latter, why not?"[57]

What I am driving at here is what defines us, what constitutes our ethos and its produced actions which make our world—internally and externally—look as it does. The perspectives on cultural maladies as well as potential correctives are, at their core, religious issues. At the center of what holds our culture together is some moral purpose, "a *telos*, which provides the moral justification for the society."[58] Our current ends and moral justifications for pursuing those ends are centered around the environment we build through scientific knowledge. In his *Cultural Contradictions of Capitalism*, Daniel Bell pursues the necessary religious categories of cultural formation at length: "Changes in culture and moral temper—the fusion of imagination and life-styles—are not amendable to 'social engineering' or political control. They derive from the value and moral traditions of the society, and these cannot be 'designed' by precept. The ultimate sources are the religious conceptions which undergird a society."[59] Our current condition is to have substituted the *idea* of religious faith with the idea of utopia because the latter allows us to realize our ends through history with the prowess of our technology; and yet it remains a matter of belief at its core: "The real problem of modernity is the problem of belief. To use an unfashionable term, it is a spiritual crisis, since the new anchorages have proved illusory and the old ones have become submerged."[60] In light of the condition of our physical landscape, to be explored at length in chapter 3, at issue is what will be the shape of the landscape of the soul. To quote Bell at length:

> Religions grow out of the deepest needs of individuals sharing a common awakening, and are not created by 'engineers of the soul.' My concern with religion goes back to what I assume is the constitutive character of culture: the wheel of questions that brings one back to the existential predicaments, the awareness in men of their finiteness and the inexorable limits to their power (the transgression of which is *hamartia*), and the consequent

57. Ehrenfeld, *Arrogance of Humanism*, 3.

58. Bell, *Cultural Contradictions of Capitalism*, 83.

59. Bell, *Cultural Contradictions of Capitalism*, 83.

60. Bell, *Cultural Contradictions of Capitalism*, 28.

effort to find a coherent answer to reconcile them to this human condition. Since that awareness touches the deepest springs of consciousness, I believe that a culture which has become aware of the limits in exploring the mundane will turn, at some point, to the effort to recover the sacred.[61]

As I indicated earlier, the great rule of our society is the production of value and we now understand that this stems from our own labor to bestow meaning. The problem is that we are not actually creators in this capacity. We are not autonomous but are in reality always acted upon by our myths and the independent reality of the technical culture they give birth to. The next two chapters further explore how our attachment to the built environment as a physical, and hence spiritual, reality has placed us in the position of a bad faith exchange. The prophet Isaiah ridicules our contingent creations as unable to make adequate sense of either our past or our future and challenges those creations to, "Do good, or do harm, that we may be dismayed and terrified." Despite the apparent value or harm affected by our actions, they are ultimately powerless toward ultimate ends: "Behold, you are nothing, and your work is less than nothing" (Isa 41:23–24). It is the nature of our own creations, being themselves derived from contingent beings, to lack the capacity to bestow value.[62]

Our primary aim is to pursue how to repair this situation through cultivation, receptivity, and space—categories very different from those explored in this opening chapter. In the end, our attachment to the built environment—the pursuit of meaning through labor—compromises our ability to understand the ideas of the constituted reality of mystery, grace, and the kingdom of God. These are the ideas which provide the categories for *shalom*: the way things ought to be. Before getting there, we will turn first to our cultural ethos as exemplified in American culture, especially the full and clear expression of that character in the American interior west. The American conception of value played out on the physical environment of the West and its as-of-yet, though shrinking, empty spaces will lead us to an examination of the cost of the myth here developed. This is all a question of the faith exchange we enact daily, and hence a question of value. The landscape we inhabit both reflects and forms the landscape of the soul.

---

61. Bell, *Cultural Contradictions of Capitalism*, xxix.
62. See Ps 115:4–8.

Chapter 2

Unleashed on the American West

I CAME TO MOUNTAINEERING relatively late in life. I climbed my first 13,000-foot peak standing above the small town in southern Colorado I lived in the year I turned thirty. Living where I did with my wife and three children through my twenties and early thirties, my domineering passions up until that first summit were hunting and fishing in the mountains of Colorado and Wyoming. At the time, I could not conceive of spending long hours on a trail or many days in the hills apart from the purpose of pursuing game or finding a high mountain lake or isolated stream. Though I spent countless days and nights in many of the most isolated environs of Colorado and Wyoming, I inevitably had a rifle on my back or a pole in my pack—oftentimes both. I have always loved isolated backcountry regions, but I had combined that passion with my western American sense that there should ultimately be a goal or purpose behind one's labor. Otherwise, treks to the backcountry would feel like aimless wandering which would somehow be at odds with a proper reason for undertaking anything.

Somewhat surprisingly to me, then, I took to the sport of mountaineering relatively quickly and with some gusto following that initial summit. With many isolated peaks in Wyoming and Colorado, a number still surmounted by glaciers and not a few requiring multi-day approaches, I was in the midst of a wealth of opportunity that continues to include high, unclimbed-by-me peaks even twenty years later. Colorado alone contains fifty-eight peaks above 14,000 feet in elevation, the most of any state, though officially only fifty-four "14ers" meet qualification as an individual peak.[1]

1. To qualify as an independent peak a mountain must have at least three hundred

If one adds the more than 600 peaks ranging from 13,000 to 13,999 feet, it becomes apparent that Colorado is a mecca for nearly endless mountain climbing. I was soon exploring all around the area I lived in for additional peaks to climb, and before long I was summiting at least one mountain every month straight through the year and sometimes topped out on multiple peaks at any given outing. In retrospect I realize that to some degree I had simply transferred my original form of approaching my time in the outdoors to a new endeavor. With a peak to summit—a definite point to reach—it no longer appeared to be just aimless wandering if I was not pursuing some kind of wildlife. The peaks inevitably grew more difficult as I sought less-traveled areas and routes, often waiting until the depths of winter to attempt a summit or climbing solo.

Being able to claim that one has stood atop every 14er in Colorado has become a badge of honor for many. The "peak bagging" culture is an enormous part of living in or visiting the state of Colorado. It is uniquely reflective of a part of our American character to make a day spent in the natural world into a mark of one's ability to conquer. Many mountaineers keep detailed lists of climbs completed and those peaks left to check off. Recently the *Colorado Springs Gazette* reported on a Colorado Fourteeners Initiative analysis that pointed out that Colorado Fourteeners saw 353,000 climbers in 2018, including between 35–40,000 on Quandry Peak alone. Mount Bierdstadt saw 1,023 climbers just on the single day of July 20.[2] When I set aside the rod and rifle for mountain climbing, I somehow thought I was suspending more purposeful pursuits in nature with a long walk above timberline. I had little idea that I was wading into a unique and overwhelming expression of the ubiquitous cultural pursuit of personal progress.

It could be understood if one would typically consider a mountain climbing expedition to serve as an opportunity to detach from the rat race of progress if for only a few hours, or perhaps, if lucky, a few days. Such a detachment from cultural realities is easier said than done. Mountain climbing in Colorado—and likely worldwide—has become simply another arena in which to demonstrate personal control and prowess, which are the hallmarks of our society. In the summer of 2000, Teddy Keizer set a speed record for climbing all of Colorado's highest peaks by completing fifty-five summits in ten days, twenty hours, and twenty-six minutes. That particular record stood for fifteen years until Andrew Hamilton set a new record of nine days,

---

feet of topographical prominence, which means that any connecting saddle to a neighboring peak must drop at least three hundred feet from either high point.

2. Boster, "Colorado 14ers," paras. 3, 10.

twenty-one hours, and fifty-one minutes.[3] Three years later, Hamilton became the first person to summit all of the peaks in a single winter season.[4] It is part of the mystique of our culture to make our interactions with even the natural world into a context to conquer, count, and quantify. We are enamored by first ascents and increasingly daring exhibitions of human feats in the wild which many never thought possible.[5]

In part because I wonder what this mentality does to us as humans, I have endeavored to travel in a different way of late. I have never compiled a list of all of my summits and many years ago I stopped signing summit registers. I do not think that my primary purpose in climbing a peak is to leave my mark. This entails a different mentality for doing anything in the culture we inhabit. We are acculturated to find or provide a definable purpose in every activity. This is part of the exchange we have intuited: if I do such-and-such then I expect the return of meaning or the sense of value an accomplishment provides. It is not enough to go for a walk in an environment we have not yet developed with our industry; we must know how many miles we have walked, how fast we have traveled and how many calories expended. We have to reach this summit or this pass or that lake in order to have the sense that we are traveling with purpose and therefore making some kind of progress. By way of contrast, I recently spent three days in a local canyon simply walking. There was no trail and no specific destination. I did not track my mileage and I was not in any recognizable location that I could later tell anyone, "I've been there." It is a far cry from my twenties when a specific purpose accompanied any such effort.

We move from an exploration of the religious belief in progress as a dominant cultural force to exploring the ways that faith is lived out. This is a view of the actions which our faith produces. Viewing our ethos as it both reflected and further shaped American culture in the specific context of the Interior West is a stark perspective on how the idea of progress works itself out in priorities and actions on the ground. When the myth contacts the open land and rich resources of the inner continent of North America, that myth is given legs—and an axe, a pic, a shovel, and a hammer. What was formulated as an ideal in the settings of northern and western Europe comes into full flourish as Americans expand westward. The continent west of the Appalachian Mountains and particularly west of the Mississippi River was a

---

3. Achs, "Andrew Hamilton Shatters Colorado 14ers Speed Record," paras. 1, 3.

4. Murray, "Andrew Hamilton Becomes First."

5. the recent success of the climbing films *The Dawn Wall* and *Free Solo,* which chronicle rock climbs in California's Yosemite Valley, are a case in point.

unique context for solidifying our faith in progress as it comes to maturity before the eyes of Americans in the nineteenth and early twentieth centuries.

I focus on the West not only because this is my personal context but also due to the reality that historically the American West was a stark setting for labor to be exercised, for scientific discovery to be utilized, and for new technologies of steam and plow and machinery to be applied. The unique historical situation occurring as Americans pressed westward into what they erroneously called "virgin land"[6] allows the roots of Enlightenment thought to sink deep into our national psyche and mature into a vast canopy covering our entire society. Even noting the supposed closing of the frontier in 1890, the rise of the forest conservation movement under President Roosevelt and Gifford Pinchot, and the ceasing of the widespread dispersal of the public domain early in the twentieth century, the early 1900s continued the development of our national ethos as science assumed increasing responsibility for engineering and managing western resources.

We will explore the solidifying of our national proclivity for growth and progress as settlers applied their thoughts and labors to the grand experiment as we see the ideal exemplified in successive stages of western settlement. The belief in progress in America can be most clearly viewed by a brief examination of the Mormon faith's settlement of Deseret. As I will argue, the Mormon faith can be viewed as the most American of American religions and has been especially explicit in articulating the ethos we live under today.

The character of the western mind comes to be fully embedded in American middle-class culture, which serves as a sort of baseline for identifying cultural aspirations. Because the wealthy constitute a minority group in any given society, a growing and somewhat anomalous middle-class becomes the standard for Americanness: a degree of comfortableness and respectability for all inhabitants of the culture to aspire to. The middle-class mentality captures the heart of actually being an American, and therefore flavors all of our endeavors—for our purposes especially our understanding of and approach to the spiritual life.

Our chapter on the American form of the ethos will draw to a close by noting some Indigenous American alternative views on life in this world as a way of anticipating the thoughts to be developed in parts II and III. And just as chapter 1 concluded by exploring a consequence of the faith exchange we enact in our cultural climate, so this chapter will point out that there are clearly identifiable outcomes accompanying our chosen way of being in the world. A confidence in the ability to establish value through

6. See Smith, *Virgin Land.*

efforts to build and make everything productive is never a neutral choice. Our societal and spiritual restlessness and the corresponding—seemingly contradictory—lack of confidence haunts the choice we have made to tie existence most closely to the progress we can affect through our own labor.

The ongoing, ever-present American fixation on growth and progress is the result of the coalescing of unique historical conditions which met on the North American continent in a sort of perfect storm. Since the sixteenth century, Reformation theologians had been emphasizing the focal point of human attention as residing in the concern for the future state of the individual soul. The earth was merely the platform on which the more crucial concerns of individual salvation were to be worked out, and was, in fact, a platform beset by tests and temptations and at times even demonic influence as figured in wild and unkempt peoples and places. At the same time, Enlightenment thinkers like Bacon and Newton were positing a world essentially devoid of either positive or negative spiritual significance. "Instead, nature was likened to monumental and intricate machinery. The challenge to the human mind was to learn first how all its parts worked and then how to better operate them to human advantage."[7] It was in the setting of the vast expanse of the newly settled (by Western Europeans) North American continent where these two streams converged in American Puritans and explorers.

Reformation and Enlightenment thought were surprisingly quite compatible when combined with the new soil of the United States. The natural world held its only significance as a stage on which to develop the fullness of what it meant to be truly human. University of Colorado professor Lloyd Burton points out that, from the perspective of Europeans now firmly ensconced on the eastern third of the United States, a convenient alliance with religious and scientific thought could occur:

> Just as the devil was the enemy of God and of godly humans, so was scientific ignorance of nature the foe of the rational mind. And just as it was the duty of the faithful to convert heathen wildness (both the wilderness and its indigenous human inhabitants) into tamed and obedient servants of Christian society, so, too, was it the duty of scientists and engineers to convert natural forces into expressions of human mastery over nature.[8]

The presence of a wide expanse of previously untapped natural resource wealth served as a unique platform on which to shape an American culture. Despite the perception of a long-standing war between religion and science,

7. Burton, *Worship and Wilderness*, 57.
8. Burton, *Worship and Wilderness*, 57.

in this new setting the two could, and often would, comfortably coexist and even reinforce one another's aims. From both the religious and scientific perspective, the natural world was only important as it served its role in developing human aspirations. In these terms, nature becomes peripheral and humanity increasingly inhabits a self-made environment which God has stocked with natural resources intended to serve the perceived ends of the scientific mind and the religious heart. There was an interesting melding of Enlightenment and Reformation thought in the American colonies as "nature became primarily a resource to be exploited in the human quest for *progress* and the regaining of *Adam's dominion* over the nonhuman world." Because nature was passive, dumb, and wild,

> it begged for development, exploitation and manipulation by human beings to eradicate a range of evils. . . . To rest content with the current state of economic, scientific, and technological progress would be irresponsible and an unheroic abdication of human destiny as set forth by God, which was to acquire complete dominion over the earth."[9]

This is the mindset which fueled the American advance into the western environs of the continent throughout the nineteenth century. In so doing, these categories of thought both reflected and further developed our mythology. Value does not inhere in things but has to be established, built, or even extracted by human effort. It is critical that we keep in mind our purpose in exploring these themes. This is not an exercise in history or philosophy, but an effort to come to terms with the ways in which we have learned to experience the life of the soul. The coalescing of science, technology, and religion in this country forms us into people who are restless to develop a life of significance and meaning. This emerged at the edge of the American frontier where, "the pristine wilderness beyond the settlements had captured the imagination of America. It had become the Garden of the world where the New Adam could realize his inherent dignity."[10] We continue the efforts to realize this dignity over 200 years later.

From the perspective of the early American reconciliation of scientific and Puritan religious thought, the western frontier practically begged to be confronted and developed. There was at once a religious obligation to serve as the Creator's representatives in cleaning up the unruly wild as well as the human imperative to progress through development in order to prove our worth. Movement toward the "empty" west of America "has offered a theater

9. Burton, *Worship and Wilderness*, 57–58; emphasis added.

10. Dyrness, *How Does America Hear the Gospel?*, 35.

in which American patterns of culture could be endlessly mirrored."[11] This is why a consideration of the frontier in American history can offer such clarity on our way in the world in the twenty-first century. Western settlers were emulating European thought categories and establishing the patterns of our culture that adhere today.

We can consider two such patterns of culture which are illustrative of how we continue to conceive of our place in the world and inform the larger purpose of this book. The expanse of frontier in American history exemplifies, first, our ongoing character as a restless society in which consumption is endlessly pursued. This is a very natural consequence of the American mythology blending both scientific and religious thought, which an open western frontier could merely reinforce and strengthen. Even as early as 1830, Alexis de Tocqueville could identify the American spirit:

> 'These Americans who go out far away from the Atlantic Ocean, plunging into the West, are adventurers impatient of any sort of yoke, greedy for wealth . . .' He was describing a transient, restless, rootless population who saw in their surroundings only a commodity, something not to be cherished, but simply consumed before moving westward to repeat the 'resettlement' process once again.[12]

A second pattern, still "endlessly mirrored" in American culture, is our penchant to place our highest value on the engineered or built environment as the source of the satisfaction of our needs—even our emotional and spiritual needs. I do not think that Wallace Stegner was being unduly harsh when he observed that,

> Europeans and their American descendants did not set out to live with this continent, learn its rules and its moods, love, honor and obey it. They set out to 'tame' or 'conquer' or 'break' the wilderness. They imposed their old habits on the new land, they 'improved,' as in homesteads, they 'developed,' as in towns. They replaced, destroyed, and polluted, they bent the earth and all its native forms of life to the satisfaction of their own needs.[13]

Of particular interest to our argument regarding the current merging of Christian spirituality and western culture is the way in which Christianity in America specifically empowered the advancing western frontier. In his history of the confrontation of white European settlement with one of

---

11. Goetzmann, *Exploration and Empire*, xiii.

12. Burton, *Worship and Wilderness*, 24–25.

13. Stegner and Stegner, *American Places*, 207.

the most foreboding and difficult landscapes of the western frontier—the Canyon Country of the Colorado Plateau—Paul Nelson affirms that, "The yearning for an ordered, efficient, and utilitarian landscape is one of the most basic themes of European Christianity's spread across the globe in the last five hundred years, if not the past fifteen hundred."[14] A utilitarian landscape would be specifically formed by human ingenuity and the restless creativity of almost limitless freedom because the world was created by God as a field of human activity. The natural world, as Max Weber posited for the Christian mind, was itself neutral and empty of all spirit life. "Such a non-sacramental world, bereft of spirit, its gods and groves and sacred megaliths reduced to euhemeristic ciphers, or else banished to devilish realms, could pose no resistance to those intensive investigations of nature that ultimately resulted in the West's celebrated ability to expand."[15] The American frontier, then, is part and parcel of the American religious experience.

The application of the Enlightenment's belief in progress which fa-cilitated the advancing American frontier and was equally empowered by American Christianity is exemplified in each successive stage of settlement across the western plains, into the inner-mountain west, and eventually a confrontation with western deserts. Major John Wesley Powell was the first to identify the Hundredth Meridian in the American plains as a rough line which marked a dramatic change in climactic conditions such that west of this meridian eastern forms of agriculture would not be sustainable due to a lack of adequate rainfall.[16] From a progress mindset, however, such a line was inconceivable. The Creator had established the world for human use and improvement and could not possibly have failed to create the Great Plains in such a way as to render human wealth development impractical on a landscape of such scale.

Elliot West has written one of the most complete histories of the American plains and he points out that early settlers were operating under expansive progressive visions in which any natural environmental limita-tions would be inevitably transcended through human ingenuity. "Most im-portant, settlers lived by a capitalist, market-oriented dream. Their goal was not that of every earlier inhabitant—to produce enough for themselves, plus some to trade for what they could not provide—but to convert everything they could into something to export and sell for a profit." The categories by

---

14. Nelson, *Wrecks of Human Ambition*, 3.

15. Turner, *Beyond Geography*, 175.

16. See Wallace Stegner, *Beyond the Hundredth Meridian*.

which they made sense of the world dictated that, "This would be one of the planet's Great Gardens . . . home to millions of cattle fed on God's hay."[17]

West's history contends that the natural limits of the Great Plains were never transcended, only tested. The "law of the minimum" was violated by a belief in progress and this, "pursued with the help of money and technology, led to violations far greater than any in the previous millennia."[18] The American Plains witnessed one of its most devastating summer droughts in 1886 which was followed immediately by a ferocious winter. Tens of thousands of cattle perished and scores of ranchers were driven into bankruptcy. The pattern continued in the region through droughts during the 1890s and the Dust Bowl of the 1930s.[19]

The high-mountain environs of the Interior West were confronted in similar fashion. When gold was discovered in Cherry Creek near present-day Denver in 1859, thousands of settlers flooded the Rocky Mountains to apply their technology to the harvesting of the wealth God had implanted here. According to Lloyd Burton,

> Anglo-American trappers, miners, loggers, and railroad construction workers intruded into these high-country places at will, taking whatever they wanted with relative impunity. . . . The connection that this new wave of immigrants had with the lands around them—like that of the conquistadors before them—was explicitly material in nature. When they looked into the high-country, they saw not deities but dollars waiting to be made—from the wildlife, timber, minerals, and pasturage that might be found there.[20]

As to be expected, the arid deserts and deep canyons of the American West were the last regions to be engaged with Enlightenment ideals and Christian categories of the purpose of creation. When the confrontation inevitably occurred, however, it revealed well-worn categories of progress through labor in especially clear terms. This is the setting of the uniquely American experiment we know as the Mormon settlement and expanse from the Salt Lake Valley, which will be explored more in depth below. For the time being we can recognize that, "The story of Euro-American Christianity's encounters and compromises with [Canyon Country] shows the profundity of ideas concerning the transformation of useless desert—Bad

17. West, *Contested Plains*, 329.

18. West, *Contested Plains*, 329.

19. West, *Contested Plains*, 329–30.

20. Burton, *Wilderness and Worship*, 152.

Land—into a fertile, ordered, Christian Garden—Good Land."[21] Deserts, arid with a crooked topography, were precisely the place where Western cultural ideals and the aims of Christianity would be most transformative: to make the land into "Good Land" by endeavoring to straighten the topography and provide for a well-watered garden. The Canyon Country "has rarely accommodated its visitors. They in turn have rarely accepted it on its own complex terms as they established their straight lines across the crooked landscape."[22]

The settlement and intended reshaping of the Canyon Country and the larger geographic region of which it is a part provides the setting for one of the clearest depictions of the ways our national myth plays out. The American mythos of progress through transformative labor lies at the heart of the Latter-day Saints' occupation of and subsequent spread from its center in Utah. The Mormon experience in the Colorado Plateau and the western sagebrush sea is instructive because not only were Mormon leaders specifically purposeful in their verbal and written advocacy of the ideal as they shaped their followers' views of the world, but additionally due to the way this movement and its effects are based on explicitly religious themes. The ways in which the LDS faith conceived of and interacted with their surroundings is worth exploring in depth because this faith can be viewed as the most American of American religions.

Due partly to the settlement of the "waste" regions of the West, but primarily due to perceived aberrant political devotion to church authority figures and early adherence to the practice of plural marriage, the Mormon faith has long been seen as an outlier in American society.[23] A different view, however, recognizes that this religious movement possesses many of the qualities of a distinctly and thoroughly American movement. There are solid reasons for understanding Mormon views of their interaction with the physical world as most clearly representative of the American ethos, and hence for my characterization that his subculture inhabits a peculiar place in the middle of what is often characterized as middle-class Americanness.

The Latter-day Saints provide a rare glimpse into a religious movement which was not only birthed in American soil, but which has matured into a successful and wealthy institution and continues to maintain a central role in the character of the Intermountain West. American children are raised to

21. Nelson, *Wrecks of Human Ambition*, 3.

22. Nelson, *Wrecks of Human Ambition*, 18.

23. Some of this perception appears to be changing. Robert Jones indicates a change has occurred over the past fifteen years as exemplified by the fact that avowed Mormon and 2012 presidential candidate Mitt Romney carried 79 percent of the White Evangelical vote. See Jones, *End of White Christian America*, 70.

view this nation as founded by a people migrating westward over an open sea, fleeing religious persecution, to establish a free and upright society in a new land. This is embodied in the Mormon understanding of their own roots; it is the grand narrative of the larger LDS experience. Following his visions in western New York state in the 1820s, Joseph Smith led thousands of followers westward to attempted agricultural settlements in the heartland of America in Ohio, Missouri, and Illinois. Smith's successor, Brigham Young, led followers further westward to settle in the Salt Lake Valley in 1847. Westward immigration trails are iconic for Americans, and occupying a central vision of Americanness is the picture of thousands of Mormon immigrants pulling handcarts across the Great Plains as they walked from Iowa City to Salt Lake City in 1856.

To maintain that Mormonism is the most American of American religions is to invoke a sense that this faith embodies many of the ideals of what we would call Americanness, while it also specifically perpetuates the myth of progress we are here pursuing. Mormonism is in all reality reflective of mainstream American culture in its mythology, much of its theology, and its democratic and thoroughly capitalistic outlooks. It was specifically in the frontier of what is now the state of Utah—what Mormons call Deseret— that this faith finally came to maturity and it is the frontier condition which developed many of the characteristics we now associate with American culture. Walter Prescott Webb articulated the impact of the frontier condition on the ongoing idea of Americanness is his work *The Great Frontier*. While still controversial in many regards, Webb is able to clearly associate many of our shared cultural values with the idea of the frontier explicitly present in American westward expansion. Despite the Native inhabitants of western lands, white Europeans viewed the land as "frontier" which referred to "a vast body of wealth without proprietors" which then provided a "sudden, continuing, and ever-increasing flood of wealth" to a growing and expanding population.[24] This condition was instrumental, in Webb's view, in establishing American characteristics of democratic government, boisterous politics, exploitative agriculture, mobility, and optimism. The frontier experience further solidified ideals of freedom, independence, aggressiveness, and industry which were expansive ideas giving impetus to a people moving against the passive force of nature.[25]

These ongoing American values were perhaps most clearly embodied by the Mormon experience in Utah. Wallace Stegner could opine that,

24. Webb, *Great Frontier*, 13.
25. Webb, *Great Frontier*, 5, 49.

> Brigham Young was a colonizer without equal in the history of
> America. In a desert that nobody wanted and that was univer-
> sally considered a fit home only for coyotes and rattlesnakes,
> he planted in thirty years over three-hundred and fifty towns
> and created the technique and made the surveys for others. One
> hundred of these towns were colonized in the first ten years,
> when transportation was fearfully difficult and expensive, when
> the nearest source of many essential supplies was over a thou-
> sand miles away.[26]

These early colonizing successes were "transformed into a series of
myths that transformed their settlement history into a sociopolitical ico-
nography still used to demonstrate that they were indeed a chosen, heroic
people." The myths centered on the ideas that Brigham Young was led by
divine providence—an explicit invocation of Manifest Destiny—to the
Salt Lake Valley where the raging desert was cultivated in such a manner
that climate was "ameliorated" and stream flows increased by God to meet
settlement needs.[27]

While typically criticized for holding aberrant theological ideas, Mormonism has always maintained just enough biblicism to make it recognizable as an American religion and their belief system continues to cultivate
a people who exhibit a high degree of middle-class respectability. There
remains additionally the Mormon understanding of a popular ideal that
America serves a central role in God's plan for the world and future. The
tenth of Joseph Smith's thirteen Articles of Faith composed in 1842 invoke
the belief that God's future rule will occur on the American continent and
that a future paradisiacal glory will be the result of the Mormon-American
experience, placing America firmly at the center of world history.[28]

The Mormon experience, then, is in many ways iconic as an expression
of American cultural character. Theirs is a story of a displaced people walking into the Frontier West, establishing an agricultural society which would
soon emerge into a regional trading center and would eventually grow to
control vast wealth and multiple business interests. The Mormon faith is
both thoroughly capitalistic[29] and, in many ways, deeply democratic.[30]

26. Stegner, *Mormon Country*, 65.

27. Jackson, "Mormon Wests," 146–47.

28. Nelson, *Wrecks of Human Ambition*, 136.

29. See Quinn, *Mormon Hierarchy*. Quinn extensively chronicles the history of the
LDS faith in the movement's growing attention to wealth accumulation and business
practices, which have resulted in billions of dollars in income.

30. Although the highest levels of church leadership continue to be limited primarily to white males, the saints have no paid clergy leading local congregations and rely on

The self-understanding of these Latter-day Saints provides clear insight into the larger American ethos of progress through industry as it is given full expression in the intermountain west. Part of the uniqueness of this faith and the reason it serves as such a clear personification of the larger cultural myth is because Mormon thought has been explicit in giving voice to what often appear as otherwise merely internalized values. As an example, Donald Worster points out that according to John Widstoe, a member of the LDS Quorum of the Twelve Apostles,

> The destiny of man is to possess the whole earth; and the destiny of the earth is to be subject to man. There can be no full conquest of the earth, and no real satisfaction to humanity, if large portions of the earth remain beyond its highest control. Only as parts of the earth are developed according to the best existing knowledge, and brought under human control, can man be said to possess the earth.[31]

John Widstoe simply gives voice to what is generally intuited by much of our Western—especially American—culture. As in Enlightenment and scientific thought, the natural world itself does not possess any particular rights. The natural world is a world of utility which should be controlled and changed in order to make it productive for human occupation and accumulation.[32] If adherence to the belief in progress maintains a sort of vague religious or faith component for the bulk of our society, it is simply brought into the open as an explicitly religious and even redemptive category for Mormons. This empowers an affirmation of technology as a divinely ordained instrument of domination over the natural world. "Technology, especially irrigation technology, has become invested with an intensely religious purpose," so, one might say with Worster, that in the Mormon view, God dwells in all of the machinery which serves as instrumental in their work of desert reclamation.[33]

The natural world being a context of human utility and the technology we apply to that setting being infused with divine power, it naturally follows that the earth and humanity's transformation of it actually becomes the setting of human redemption. A central theme in the Mormon

---

their membership to provide leadership at the local level. The growth of the LDS church is likewise an indication of democratic ideals as it historically relied on typical family groups to serve as colonizers from the Salt Lake Valley and continue to send out pairs of young men and women in two-year missions to serve as "volunteer" missionaries

31. Worster, *Wealth of Nature,* 119.

32. Flores, *Natural West,* 133, 141.

33. Worster, *Wealth of Nature,* 121.

self-understanding "is that the work of redeeming the desert from its steril-
ity is simultaneously a work of self-redemption for humanity."[34] The view is
simply the articulation of Francis Bacon's ideal regarding the achievement
of the highest human dignity produced in concert with the transformation
of nature for the sake of progress. The building of our physical environment
is the arena in which our meaning and highest value will be achieved and
this accords most definitively in the Mormon "narrative of environmental transformation in which the Mormons took a fallen desert wilderness
and restored it to the Garden [of Eden] from which humanity had been
expelled."[35] The American myth of progress as a form of faith is therefore
granted unusually clear articulation in this uniquely and thoroughly American religion which centers human salvation and paradise in the progress of
transformative labor.

What we now know as the United States has become the embodiment
of a belief in progress which serves as the source of our greatest sense of
personal value. The history of American settlement, exemplified in the Mormon experience, has created a kind of culture in which our engagement
with technology continues to fuel our conception of meaning and fulfillment. Even in the middle of the last century, on the heels of two world wars
and a prolonged worldwide economic depression intensified in the environmental devastation of the 1930s Dust Bowl, cultural theorists could still
speak of the optimism inherent in American culture as a result of the ways
in which the culture was formed:

> The evidence would suggest that if widespread doubts were
> entertained throughout Western Civilization, most Americans
> were still inclined to act upon the faith that the future held forth
> the promise of even better things to come. America, at mid-
> century, was not yet prepared to reject as no longer relevant
> or viable the belief in progress, rooted as that faith was in the
> experience of generations. Continuity of thought and hope sur-
> vived the discontinuities posed in an age of anxiety. "Progress"
> was still the "business of America." The nation, "forever on the
> march," was certain that it was advancing into a better land.[36]

34. Worster, *Wealth of Nature*, 117.

35. Flores, *Natural West*, 129.

36. Chambers, "Belief in Progress," 224. Clarke Chambers provides here an exhaustive survey of literature on American views of progress, including its presence, waning,
and revival. While the literature by now is somewhat dated, Chambers's affirmation that
the optimistic belief holds sway in America continues to reverberate today.

Such faith continues to be rooted not only in experience of the past but in the aspirations of the American middle class.

The breadth of the middle class in the United States as a unique historical occurrence grants this reality an unusual authority to reinforce and perpetuate cultural values. It becomes significant, then, when Robert Bellah in his *Habits of the Heart* characterizes middle-class America as "a group that seeks to embody in its own continuous progress and advancement the very meaning of the American project."[37] This leads American theologian William Dyrness to the conclusion that "American middle-class culture has been almost entirely preoccupied with technical means divorced from questions of a final purpose and goal."[38] It breeds a "strong, every-man hero" who recklessly, and at times naively, attacks problems and is accompanied by a final optimism in the value of any project.[39] Humankind's advancing technical abilities, honed and perfected over 500 years of confrontation with a natural and social world that at times seems unable or unwilling to acquiesce to the human project, are ends in themselves as they empower a people to throw labor and resources at everything that confronts them.

It is this very empowerment and the actions it engenders which seems to serve as the root of our sense of value. If something can be accomplished by technical means then it follows that it should be pursued because it is precisely in the change we effect on the natural environment that we have been socialized to believe carries its own sense of worth. This middle-class Americanism fuels the twin focal points of labor and production which were introduced in the previous chapter as embodying the Enlightenment project. William Whyte identified the core of the American belief system as, "The pursuit of individual salvation through hard work, thrift and competitive struggle."[40] So Dyrness claims that "Americans learned to define themselves by their relation to their work" which, while creating a people of incredible vitality and creativity, has also made it difficult for those same people to define themselves in genuinely human terms.[41] The relative prosperity of middle-class Americans demonstrates a people who are, as a whole, creative and capable and who largely believe they have the capacity to wrest personal significance from their environment—social, economic, natural—through effort and struggle. We tend to apply labor categories, then, to virtually everything in life, including physical health, leisure pursuits, and even the

37. Quoted in Dyrness, *How Does America Hear the Gospel?*, 14.

38. Dyrness, *How Does America Hear the Gospel?*, 55.

39. Dyrness, *How Does America Hear the Gospel?*, 12.

40. Whyte, as quoted in Samuelson, *Good Life*, 5.

41. Dyrness, *How Does America Hear the Gospel?*, 42.

development of spiritual vitality. Anything of value requires the application of our effort.

A fixation on production naturally follows this focus on labor. In the arenas of life in which labor categories are applied—which appears to encompass all of life as even leisure pursuits require intentional preparation and effort on our part to be meaningful—there must be an identifiable "something" that is generated. This focal point of production is delineated through exhaustive lists and strategies and quantifiable results. Beyond keeping track of personal income and wealth, Americans count even personal development in terms of pages read, miles biked, or the number of parks and peaks visited. Production as the necessary result of the labor we feel compelled to engage in contains the corresponding sense of growth. Growth is how we identify improvement. In a chapter entitled "The Paramount Position of Production," John Kenneth Galbraith accords the idea of production the zenith of our society and self-identity: "The importance of production transcends our boundaries. We are regularly told—in the conventional wisdom it is the most frequent justification of our civilization, even our existence—that the American standard of living is 'the marvel of the world.'"[42] The centrality of production as a sense of value transcends politics, race, religion, and ideology. We don't measure success of one year against the next in reference to health, education, violence, or the number of people attaining spiritual enlightenment, but merely in terms of the increase in production. Elsewhere Galbraith observes that "The belief that increased production is a worthy social goal is very nearly absolute. . . . That social progress is identical with a rising standard of living has the aspect of a faith."[43]

It becomes easy to see why the value of the measure of increased production can transcend political and religious belief and acquire the dynamics of a faith when even our American religious and spiritual life is measured in these terms. A prime example is the Crystal Cathedral opened by Robert Schuller in Orange County, California in 1980. Despite selling the property and declaring bankruptcy in 2010, Schuller's message and movement spurred an entirely new movement in the American religious experience which today continues to illustrate American Christianity's thorough-going adherence to the belief in progress and how one goes about participating in that dream. "The appeal of megachurches like Schuller's was simple—they validated and encouraged a powerful trifecta of material success, personal

42. Galbraith, *Affluent Society*, 97.

43. Quoted in Dyrness, *How Does America Hear the Gospel?*, 54.

growth and fulfillment, and political conservatism."[44] While Schuller may have been on the cusp of a new movement of "megachurches"—defined as a congregation of at least 2,000 members—this reality soon came to embody American Evangelicalism. In 1970, there were only ten megachurches nationwide, but twenty years later there were 500, and by 2005 there were 1,500 such congregations. Despite a slowing rate of growth in recent years, these churches still maintain an average annual budget of nearly 6 million dollars.[45] The core beliefs of progress through one's ability toward the goal of greater production embrace the whole of American culture and undoubtedly colors our understanding of and approach to the life of the soul.

Before progressing to a critique of this social reality, I think it would be instructive to point out that there have been some annunciations of alternative ways of being in this world. Most pointedly and eloquently—certainly most ironically—these voices have emerged from the very continent and from the very same western American context as that which seems to have fueled our cultural values over the past 200-plus years. The indigenous populations which predate western European settlement by hundreds, if not thousands, of years, had developed a starkly different understanding of life while inhabiting the very regions that became "frontier" for American society. In *Death Comes for the Archbishop* Willa Cather has her protagonist, Father Latour, reflect that,

> Just as it was the white man's way to assert himself in any land-scape, to change it, make it over a little (at least to leave some mark of memorial of his sojourn), it was the Indian's way to pass through a country without disturbing anything; to pass and leave no trace, like fish through the water, or birds through the air. It was the Indian manner to vanish into the landscape, not to stand out against it.[46]

It is a similar sentiment indicated in an essay by Julene Bair who says,

> Despite cold and a host of other hardships, the Indians, whether they wove wool in southwestern hogans and adobes or tanned buffalo hides in plains tepees, developed a different set of values. The Hopi are actually grateful they live in a desert. In too easy a climate, they were told by their maker, Spider Woman, they

44. Jones, *End of White Christian America*, 26.

45. Jones, *End of White Christian America*, 26–27.

46. Cather, *Death Comes for the Archbishop*, 233.

would fall into ignorance and irreverence. . . . The unreliability
of the rain keeps them diligent in their rituals.[47]

This view of purpose in existence which contrasts so clearly with our
modern Western view is perhaps most clearly illustrated by a statement
made by the Puebloan Chief Ochwiay Biano to Carl Jung in 1925:

See how cruel the whites look. Their lips are thin, their noses
sharp, their faces furrowed and distorted by folds. Their eyes
have a staring expression; they are always seeking something.
What are they seeking? The whites always want something; they
are always uneasy and restless. We do not know what they want.
We do not understand them. We think that they are mad.[48]

The American application of Enlightenment and Reformation thought
has settled a continent (which was actually not unsettled), elevated its inhabitants to levels of wealth never before known, resulted in an insulation
for most Americans against the vagaries of weather and hunger and disease,
and increased personal health, resulting in increasingly long life-spans. We
seem to have done well for ourselves. The relative safety and security we
enjoy is the fruit of enormous and in many cases irreversible changes on
the physical world we inhabit. The relentless pursuit of knowledge feeds the
growth of technology and industry which is generally celebrated in our society as an indication of our dignity and god-like stature. The effects of our
labor and productivity on the natural setting surrounding us are accepted as
necessary and even valuable indications of our ability to progress. What we
as a culture have been slower to recognize, however, is that any change on
the external environment causes a corresponding change on our personal
interior environment. Such change inevitably shapes what we value and
desire and therefore what we give our attention and efforts to. We do not
simply create a culture and change the physical environment; that culture
and environment work in profound ways *on* us as well.

Because we are social creatures and are subject to the socializing influence of the people around us, themselves subject to a particular history
and place, we are all inhabitants and inheritors of culture. It cannot be any
other way. We have simply grown to intuit the values related to the world
we build. At the same time there is nothing to inherently render those cultural conditions we live under a freedom from criticism or exposure. The
double-blindedness of much of North American Christianity mentioned
in the introduction—its tendency to believe itself to be acultural and the

47. Bair, "She Poured Out Her Own," 90.

48. Jung, *Earth Has a Soul*, 42.

failure to value the physical world—has a corollary in our culturally historic myopia. We have been conditioned by growth and progress to believe that value is exclusively future dependent. The tendency is to denigrate ancient wisdom and practice because to be human is to move continually forward toward new and therefore better levels of knowledge and enlightenment. The cultural climate that forms us provides for its own perpetuation so that it becomes increasingly difficult to appreciate that there are indeed other ways to define life in this world.

In some ways the Enlightenment and Reformation severed important connections with resources of the ancient world. Human destiny and dignity lie in the future—in the ways we work out our individual redemption. It matters little if that redemption is understood in religious or scientific categories because in the end both regard the world simply as a platform on which to enact human ends; the physical context counts for little. Ancient wisdom and practices have been superseded by humanity's ability to shape his or her own reality. In the end, even an interpretation of cultural influence such as this one is irrelevant because the only thing that counts is what comes next as we apply the new piece of knowledge to the new and inevitably better form of technology. This is what we understand to give life meaning.

These are precisely the kinds of belief systems that shape a particular kind of people. The devotion to growth and progress as exemplified in American history and the modern middle class has specifically formed our restlessness as well as—nearly inexplicably and seemingly contradictorily— our lack of confidence. We have already encountered the societal sense of restlessness—the inability to settle, to rest, or to be comfortable—in the very nature of the frontier as a beckoning reality drawing a nation ever westward. Restlessness is inherent in the adherence to a belief that growth and progress are never-ending realities dependent only on our ability to be industrious and to keep the momentum moving forward by pursuing new boundaries. Restlessness breeds a need for continuous movement and innovation which characterize American society and significantly increase our discontent and anxiety.[49] This inability to slow down and experience a satisfied state has reached down to infect the very soul and spiritual life of Americans and is antithetical to the themes centered around a healthy landscape.

Our inheritance of the cultural climate we have examined in this chapter has indelibly shaped us as a people who cannot but inhabit an increasingly demanding society, which psychiatrist Peter Whybrow has indicated creates "an accelerated, competitive lifestyle that steals away sleep

49. See Samuelson, *Good Life*; Whybrow, *American Mania*.

and kindles anxiety, threatening the intimate social webs that sustain family and community. For many Americans the hallowed search for happiness has been hijacked by a discomforting and frenzied activity." For Whybrow this is indicative of *mania*, "a dysfunctional state of mind that begins with a joyous sense of excitement and high productivity but escalates into reckless pursuit, irritability, and confusion, before cycling down into depression."[50] It is precisely such mania that we are endeavoring to provide an alternative to as we develop here an honest appraisal of cultural forces, followed by the categories of the cultivation of our own soil and the reception of the seed of grace and embrace of space.

The contention that our cultural inheritance is equally exemplified by a lack of confidence is not nearly so evident as, though no less prevalent than, our restlessness. We are conditioned to believe that our scientific prowess applied through industry and technology has resulted in the greatest period for human thriving in all of history. Any unsolved problems we encounter will inevitably fall to an ever-advancing human knowledge. But a belief in progress and commitment to ever-greater productivity at the same time cultivates its own deep dissatisfaction with any current state of affairs because we live under the constant fear that somehow this is not enough. We can never be allowed the thought that either ancient wisdom or modern intellectual abilities are somehow adequate. We live under nagging doubts about the current condition of our political, economic, and religious life, to say nothing of our relationships and virtually any social or technical field, because progress informs us that greater advances are always possible.

Sociologist Zygmunt Bauman indicates ours as a culture which believes it has progressed beyond categories of existential guilt as the essential criterion for evaluating life's choices to our current condition of "the depressions arising from the terror of *inadequacy* . . . as the most characteristic and widespread psychic afflictions among the denizens of the consumer society."[51] Our lack of confidence drives us ever forward to discover the next best thing. In turn, this perpetuates a perennial spiritual dissatisfaction which maintains a dependency on our never-ending constructive efforts. "Humans are insecure in their ambiguous situation of finitude and freedom. So, they seek security against the vicissitudes of nature by pretending to unlimited technological capacities and by exceeding the limits providentially established."[52]

---

50. Whybrow, *American Mania*, 3–4.

51. Bauman, *Does Ethics Have a Chance*, 51; emphasis original.

52. Nash, *Loving Nature*, 121.

These opening two chapters have demonstrated a society which is thoroughly religious: subsumed under certain myths and beliefs. If our cultural faith adherence is not an explicit invocation of a specifically defined religious ideal—in terms of adherence to a particular religious institution—it is nonetheless held together under a veneer of faith. Whether institutionalized or not, the religious categories those of us inhabiting North America find ourselves in constitutes a strong system of belief. And belief prompts action. We will inevitably act on those things we believe to be most crucial for and valuable in existence. This is our way of showing up in and acting on and in the world.

This is precisely why I have gone to the length I have in this chapter to demonstrate that the American Frontier experience is part and parcel of the American religious experience. Western settlement constitutes the platform on which to work out what was conceived as the greatest human flourishing ever known. For Euro-American Christians it was their very salvation; for Enlightenment thinkers it was ultimate human dignity and meaning. In either case, the Western Frontier amounted to the same thing: the place to establish value which must always be built or extracted by our effort. In this sense the idea of Manifest Destiny could thrive and impel a people into the unknown to engage in whatever wealth creation they were healthy, industriousness, or lucky enough to perform. It was the most natural thing in the world and apparently the very reason the frontier existed: to serve as the setting on which salvation—however conceived—would be fleshed out. On this undeveloped front technology shows itself to be redemptive. It matters little whether that technology was derived from human ingenuity or divine revelation, it was and is understood as the means of delivering our greatest victories and thereby our deepest meaning.

This serves to demonstrate that we inhabit a thoroughly religious culture. American Christianity has rarely engaged in the kind of thinking and acting that would distinguish one form of religious belief from another. Despite loud protestations to the contrary, Christianity in this country merely accepts the belief in progress as an adequate expression of its own identity. The Christian empowerment of frontier expansion, as well as the confidence in the built environment which we will examine in the next chapter, are clear indications of this reality.

Faith and belief will at some point emerge in sacrament. A sacrament is a physical figure of a deeper spiritual reality. Due to our embeddedness in the physical condition of the world we inhabit, our beliefs will inevitably take on a physical expression. Because sacraments entail the physical elements of bread, wine, water, oil, and voice, they are artifacts of our culture, specifically as inhabitants of a physical universe. For Catholic and much

Orthodox thought, sacraments are a means of divine grace while for most Protestants they are a sign or symbol of spiritual reality. Regardless of one's own confession, sacraments are a physical manifestation of ideals. If faith will inevitably issue in sacrament, then the modern American access to grace is primarily through labor and production. These are the sacramental—physical—acts that transcend an individual's religious camp. Our faith is manifest in an adherence to work to bring about growth. It breeds an unqualified attachment to the built-by-us environment.

Before moving to the next chapter, which will explore the ways our cultural ethos has worked out in some of our physical environments, I want to end this current chapter by anticipating the themes to be developed in parts II and III. There are alternative ways to conceive of our life in this world. Hebrews 4:1–13 provides just such an alternative vision centered around the idea of rest—an idea that stands in direct opposition to our ways of finding meaning in the world. The writer highlights "rest" as an idea frequently developed in the biblical canon. It is specifically "God's rest," and is therefore associated with the very purposeful cessation of design and work which culminates the act of a Creator as the crowning act of creation. This seventh act is passed on to the people of God in the form of sabbath and indicates completion, an idea of enough, and, as we will explore later, the sense that at some point there is no need to keep adding. Sabbath, God's rest, prefigured the idea that human production will never be sufficient in and of itself and is not really the point of life anyway. Life is not to be lived merely on the basis of what our efforts accomplish, build, or accumulate. We inevitably ruin what we touch without a sense of limit—a sense of enough.

For the author of Hebrews this is not a mere aside. I have gone to the lengths I have in these opening chapters to demonstrate our singlemindedness for labor, production, and progress because this serves internally as our form of spirituality, and externally as our religious practice in American culture, regardless of our ecclesiastical confession. It is at the center of existence. The failure to have a capacity for a form of sabbath rest elicits from the writer of Hebrews the strongest form of warning. To fail to enter rest—the whole category of reasons for initiating Sabbath—is disobedience, a lack of faith. It is actually to be feared due to what such failure does to the soul. The failure to understand God's rest and the intent behind the idea is to be misaligned with the Creator, our central purpose, and creation itself.

Our inherited form of cultural belief naturally becomes our actions. Our redemption—our sacrament, if you will—has become our labor and productivity. This unleashes the condition of our world we turn to now and the deeper crisis we will look to in part II.

Chapter 3

The Cost

SEVERAL YEARS AGO, I made the drive south on US Highway 550 over the imposing and narrow Red Mountain Pass in order to make my way into the South Fork of Mineral Creek in Colorado's San Juan Mountains. My goal was Vermillion Peak, the 13,894-foot highpoint along a long and broken, north-south-running ridge that separates Ice Lakes Basin from Poverty Gulch. Approaching Vermillion from the east entails a start at around 10,400 feet and an ascent on a quickly steepening trail along and over cascading streams which lead into the lower basin lakes emerging just above treeline. My visit that year occurred in late June and just happened to correspond with an early peak of wildflower blooms in the open meadows of Ice Lakes Basin. Despite the relatively quick gain in elevation, the trail into the basin is relatively short and accessible to many people and hence it serves as a popular access point for viewing wildflowers in an alpine setting in western Colorado. Photographers and wildflower enthusiasts were streaming down the trail following their day-hike into wide views of clear waterfalls and exploding color carpeting the alpine tundra. Tents dotted the hillsides around Upper Ice Lake and despite the warning implied in the name, adventurous souls were attempting swims in the stunningly deep aquamarine of the lake.

I climbed the ancient glacial moraine above the upper lake to establish my solitary camp in the shadow of the Golden Horn, lying just to the north of the highpoint of Vermillion. The following day I summitted both Vermillion and Fuller Peaks while resident marmots rifled through the overnight gear I had stashed in order to lighten my load for climbing. The lack of wildfires that summer combined with a bright, clear, dry day meant I was treated to long views all across the western San Juan Range. Dark forest green, fields of bursting color, and blue-green lakes punctuated the red and grey rocks of the upper mountain. It was as classic a mountain scene as one could find anywhere in the Rocky Mountains, and an obvious attraction for many lovers of scenic beauty.

The wide appeal of Ice Lakes Basin was not always centered on its stunning views, mix of colors, and variety of wildflower species. Early in the twentieth century this basin was part of the wide mining district that established the remote western Colorado communities of Silverton, Ouray, and Telluride. Most of these high-mountain basins throughout this large region contain extensive marks of mining operations that propelled hundreds of miners into some of the most remote and harsh environs in Colorado. It's not always clear what these initial explorers thought of the scenic beauty surrounding them. What is clear is that the miners were primarily concerned not with isolated, beautiful wildflowers but with the monetary wealth the mountains could provide. In the highest basin above Ice Lakes, directly below the slopes that make up Vermillion proper—at about 12,800 feet—remnants of mining operations a century old continue to litter the otherwise pristine alpine tundra far above timberline.

It can actually be somewhat disorienting to spend miles climbing through a wilderness setting rife with the sound of falling water, surrounded by the bluest water imaginable, bathed in yellow, white, purple, red fields of flowers and towered over by the red-orange walls of the ridge of Vermillion Peak, only to surmount a hill of moraine to find oneself in the middle of the leftovers of an expansive industrial setting. Though the buildings themselves have long succumbed to the deep winters and harsh, high-altitude sun above 12,000 feet, enormous cables, bedframes, and wood stoves still occupy their space in what must have been at one time a bustling center of noise and activity. Outside of what was undoubtedly a miner's cabin are strewn literally hundreds, if not thousands, of rusting metal cans. The contents of these conveniences of civilization had been consumed through many summers of mining and the empty cans apparently simply pitched outside to rust in the elements; marks that will likely never leave the site.

This short trip into a region heralded today for its stark beauty was an epiphany of sorts for me. I was surrounded by a vast display of bright color, walking under a sky of deep blue during the seventy-degree calm day, and sleeping under a canopy of endless stars during the night. In the midst of stunning and arresting splendor, another era of human visitors had sought a very different source of value from these mountains. It has become my image of our fundamental attachment to the built environment. The presence of so many piles of rusted metal strewn about in an otherwise pristine and idyllic setting betrays a mentality that this land of little more than rock and ice was understood as valuable only insofar as it gave up its monetary wealth: gold and silver ore from the depths of the mountain. And even if Ice Lakes Basin is today a destination for wildflower photographers rather than hard rock miners, the basic belief in the value of the human-built still holds. The marks are everywhere around us. The situation is as the German philosopher Arthur Schopenhauer opines: "In the mind of a man who is filled with his own aims, the world appears as a beautiful landscape appears on the plan of a battlefield."[1]

The spring of the following year found me in the Animas River drainage a few miles east of Ice Lakes for a snow climb up the northeast face of 13,807-foot Niagara Peak. Though most of the high country was still under many feet of snow, the Alpine Loop Road had been cleared as far as Animas Forks which meant that I could access the mountain by way of Burns Gulch. The early morning cold allowed me to forgo donning my snowshoes for the approach and find solid purchase for my crampons on a quickly steepening northeast face Niagara Peak is not an often-sought-after summit, lying far from Colorado's more populous centers and furthermore lacking the allure of rising to the requisite threshold of 14,000 feet. Niagara stands in a vast region of rugged and seldom-visited peaks. The view from the summit reveals little more than miles of rock and snow and ice. Upon reaching the summit ridge, my climb thrust me into the teeth of a strong, biting wind, pushing spindrift directly into my face from off of the summit. I had to navigate a steep incline of corniced snow on the ridgeline with enormous vertical drops on either side. My crampons were becoming liabilities rather than aids as they began to ball-up from the sun-softened snow. It felt as if I could be at the end of the earth itself.

But this was anything but the end of the earth. Despite the appearance of unbroken and absolute wild, especially under its winter sleep, Niagara actually exists on the edge of one of the most industrialized landscapes of the West. Niagara Peak is part of the high, long ridge that makes up the eastern wall of the Animas River drainage. The Animas River flows from north to south out of the San Juan high country through the communities of Silverton and Durango, one of the hardest-to-access rivers of the American West. Even considering the advances of modern highway travel, Silverton is accessible only by crossing two narrow, twisting mountain passes from Durango in the south or the treacherous and high Red Mountain Pass from Ouray in the north. The modern road over Red Mountain Pass has repeatedly swept state highway snow plows off its flanks in devastating avalanches.

---

1. Quoted in Turner, *Abstract Wild*, 7.

The upper Animas is a hard place not only to access but in which to live. San Juan County, Colorado has the distinction of being the only county in the entire country that has not a single acre of arable land. The time period from last frost to first frost most years consists of a paltry thirty days.

Its relative isolation, however, is in contrast to the amount of change enacted on this region by human activity, specifically over the past 100 years. If one views the Animas country on a detailed enough map, the symbols designating mining activity occur in every apparent nook and cranny. It was in the Upper Animas River Canyon in 2015 that a dam was breached at the mouth of the Gold King Mine, releasing a toxic orange sludge into the river that would eventually make its way downstream to the San Juan and Colorado Rivers.

Our opening chapters established an American ethos as a worldview centered on the overarching value of change through labor to facilitate production for the sake of progress. Our roots in Western cultural categories of thought establish that ultimate value, dignity—human redemption, if you will—stems from the changes we effect on the inert, natural environment in order to make it serve human needs, understood in terms of our own comfort and consumption. This view of reality prioritizes the human, the built environment, as the locus of our most profound meaning. This cultural climate has critical personal, as well as far-reaching societal and environmental, consequences.

The current chapter will explore just a few of the costs we have incurred as a result of this overriding confidence in the built-by-us environment. At the same time, it is critical to keep the larger purpose of this book in mind as we examine what our penchant for the priority of the built has bought us. Our inner being—the landscape of the soul—has become an extension of our attachment to progress through the application of our building and changing prowess. The uncritical changes we have too often affected on the physical world serve the more important purpose of revealing the damage we have unwittingly wrought on our souls. Indeed, the external and internal worlds we inhabit shape and reinforce one another. These environmental prices we pay for our hubris are borne equally by a certain spiritual degradation.

This is important to keep in mind as we look at the environmental costs of our faith in progress. Despite its isolation and harsh living and working conditions, the mountain region surrounding Colorado's Animas River was a center of growing population and building activity during the 1870s, empowered by the 1872 General Mining Act. A natural outgrowth of the Western cultural paradigm of the necessity of human intervention to enact (or *extract*) value, the General Mining Act was intended to encourage the settlement of and national profit from the mountain region of the interior west Unchanged nearly 150 years later, this law gave away land to whoever staked a mining claim and allowed for unlimited, royalty-free extraction from those claims. In the isolated and harsh mountains of western Colorado, the intentions of this act were fully realized:

> Hordes of people would pour into the mountains from Kansas, Missouri, Sweden, Italy, China. Within a couple decades, every mountainside near every mining camp—Gladstone, Howardsville, Silverton, Eureka—would be shorn of all of its trees. Massive mills and boardinghouses would perch where sheep once roamed, and hundreds of miles of tram lines would be strung across hillsides. Tunnels would be blasted and drilled into mountains until those innards resembled Swiss cheese, the streams would run grey, yellow, or orange on a daily basis.[2]

In relatively short order, this hard-to-access high country, which is even today nearly 400 road miles from Denver, was transformed into a bustling industrial and profitable center. "In 1881, approximately six hundred tons of ore were pulled out of Silverton area mines. A couple of years later, it had jumped to fourteen thousand tons and climbing. The population of Silverton and surrounding towns ballooned into the thousands." By the early 1890s San Juan County was a mining powerhouse with more than 1,200 miners working in 176 mines, thirteen mills, and two electric plants.[3] A few short decades before this boom, surveyors had questioned whether the region would ever amount to much because the isolated valleys were too hard to get to, the climate was too severe for year-round habitation, there was no nearby coal for fuel, and nothing would grow here. But by 1901, another USGS surveyor, Frederick Ransome, would reflect that "no natural obstacles have ever long withstood the restlessness and indomitable perseverance of the seekers after precious metals."[4]

One of the Silverton area's most profitable mines was the Gold King. By the time it officially closed in 1924, the mine had produced more than 700,000 tons of gold, silver, lead, and copper ore, valued at $8.4 million ($120 million in 2017 dollars).[5] But the legacy of the Gold King lies not merely in the wealth it provided for a group of eastern and international investors, but in the hundreds of miles of mine shafts that were bored underneath Bonita Peak. The most infamous of these tunnels was the American Tunnel, bored to a depth of 6,233 feet in the early 1900s. The tunnel was dug at an elevation

2. Thompson, *River of Lost Souls*, 35–36.
3. Thompson, *River of Lost Souls*, 56–58.
4. Thompson, *River of Lost Souls*, 35.
5. Thompson, *River of Lost Souls*, 95.

below the bulk of the Gold King's most productive diggings to provide a safer and cheaper extraction point for ore from the upper mine. In 1960, the American Tunnel was extended to a depth of 9,000 feet in order to accomplish the same goals for the still-operating Sunnyside Mine working on the other side of Bonita Peak.[6]

While providing access to precious metals buried in the depths of mountains, mine tunnels also make an important chemical process possible which affects these regions long after the profits have gone. The tunnels dug for the extraction of ore, which then must be processed at mills, opens a hole which allows oxygen and water to meet minerals which were previously safely buried by earth. The combination of the rock with air and water results in a chemical change that becomes dangerously poisonous to plants, animals, and humans. Mine shafts inevitably intersect groundwater and fractures which carry snowmelt percolating through the rock from above. Underground mines either have to be continually pumped free of water in order to be accessible to miners or they have to be somehow drained, as the American Tunnel was naturally doing for the miles of mine tunnels above it on Bonita Peak. In fact, the American Tunnel was unusually good at its drainage capabilities. In June of 1978 the entirety of the pristine high alpine waters of Lake Emma, sitting at 12,600 feet—anywhere from 5 to 25 million gallons—was sent into the American Tunnel as the lake was breached by the tunnel below.[7]

Every year of a mine's operation more miles of minerals are exposed to open air. And every winter in the San Juan Mountains snow continues to fall, adding more water to the mix. Hydrogen, oxygen, and sulfide-bearing rocks combine to form sulfuric acid, making the water in mines far more acidic than otherwise healthy river and stream water. "As the nonacidic groundwater moves through the mine, it dissolves and picks up naturally occurring metals in the rocks over which it flows, a process known as metal-loading. Mine drainage is typically loaded with iron, zinc, cadmium, lead, copper, aluminum, arsenic, and silver. Mercury can get mixed in, too, sometimes even uranium."[8] This is the toxic soup that was accumulating in the 150 miles of Sunnyside Mine's tunnels after a concrete plug (bulkhead) was placed a mile deep in the American Tunnel in 1996.

We don't always recognize these kinds of long-term consequences when we prioritize the perceived value of making a landscape productive. Hard rock mines such as the Gold King and Sunnyside create an ongoing poisonous mixture of ever-accumulating water which will need to be treated

6. Thompson, *River of Lost Souls*, 94, 194–95.

7. Thompson, *River of Lost Souls*, 217–18.

8. Thompson, *River of Lost Souls*, 61–62.

in perpetuity. This was the kind of remediation work being performed by an EPA contractor at the mouth of the American Tunnel in August of 2015 when a dam was breached, allowing 3 million gallons of water to blast out of the mine in a matter of minutes. The water, carrying 880,000 pounds of zinc, cadmium, aluminum, arsenic, and iron hydroxides, careened into Cement Creek and into the Animas River.[9] Thirty-six hours later, an electric-orange mixture of sludge would flow through the expensive outdoor mecca of Durango on its way downstream to the San Juan and Colorado Rivers. Similar water continues to daily build up in the bowels of hundreds of abandoned mines throughout the West.

The view of the world as a platform on which to exercise our highest value of change through labor and production has resulted in a landscape marred by countless abandoned attempts at enacting our sense of human meaning. And it is likewise the American perception of the inherent value of the industrial landscape that frequently results in a lack of recognition of and accountability for the ongoing conditions of a poisoned landscape. A recent *High Country News* article points out that outdated mining laws passed in an era bent on development allow many industries to simply place operations on standby while waiting for commodity prices to rebound. This is especially characterized by the uranium industry in the Four Corners region of the West, and Appalachian coal mining in the eastern United States. Idling a mine rather than definitively closing it allows operators to forego expensive reclamation work. Despite unlikely future profitability, these mines are allowed to continue on paper in a sort of functional limbo which earns them the designation "zombie mines."[10]

Like the trapped water filling the Silverton, Colorado mines, the toxic legacy of these industrial operations can exist for decades as sources of significant health issues. Mining, in whatever form, creates toxic waste piles of either solid rock or liquid waste which is often held in collecting ponds behind earthen dams. The longer those waste materials are allowed to linger, the greater the risk for catastrophic failure. Already one in three miles of southern West Virginia rivers is impaired due to Appalachian coal mining and tens of thousands of acres, mostly former forests, lie barren at idled coal operations.[11] The Mount Taylor uranium mine in northwest New Mexico was idled in 1990 and allowed to flood, and yet continues to remain on standby thirty years later. To resume operation would require eight to ten years of

9. Thompson, *River of Lost Souls*, 5.
10. Olalde, "Forever Mines," 25.
11. Olalde, "Forever Mines," 31.

expensive pumping and water treatment.[12] Active mining operations have been linked with cancer and birth defects, both of which continue as inoperable mines still release their poison laced with arsenic, lead, and uranium into groundwater. Arid, western winds daily lift airborne toxins from piles of waste rock, affecting wide regions beyond the mines themselves.

Despite attempts in 1991 and again in 2011 to address outdated laws and close loopholes for no-longer-operating mining efforts, the American tendency to value a profit-driven industrial landscape meant that the changes were never brought to fruition. As a result,

> Several dozen uranium mines and more than 150 coal mines sit idle and have not produced for years. . . . Mine operators have exploited regulatory loopholes to warehouse their operations, changing the status of their permits on paper while little to no activity happens on the ground. . . . Many of the mines identified in this investigation have remained 'temporarily' paused for decades at a time . . . and most will likely never produce again.[13]

The rusting piles of cans in an otherwise pristine setting, the accumulation of toxic water beneath mountain peaks, the ongoing problems of industrial mining waste: they all reflect the culture's adherence to values of those like John Locke, who prioritize confrontation with the natural world's resources.

It is not merely monetary value, however, that drives the effects on the world we inhabit and which serves to illustrate our ethos. Our way of thinking is as often driven by a mostly uncritical prioritizing of the value of scientific thought and the products of that paradigm. Evidence lies in the legacy of uranium extraction in the Four Corners, primarily undertaken to feed the proliferation of atomic weapons in the middle of the twentieth century. The Animas River we just examined meets the San Juan River in Farmington, New Mexico, which then flows westward for nearly 200 more miles before it empties into the Colorado River. The San Juan River forms the northern boundary of the Navajo Nation, the single largest American Indian reservation in the country and home to one of the clearest demonstrations of the cost borne by our giving preference to and belief in the goodness of scientific and technological ability.

A significant historical threshold was crossed when American scientists detonated the first atomic bomb in the desert of New Mexico on July 16, 1945. The Atomic Age, which would require the United States to acquire and stockpile the mineral uranium necessary for nuclear fusion, was

12. Olalde, "Forever Mines," 26.
13. Olalde, "Forever Mines," 26.

ushered in. While ethical questions were faced during the development of the weaponry in the early 1940s, and such questions continued to be raised during the nuclear proliferation of the Cold War, it is entirely conceivable that the development of this technology was inevitable in a culture that has always placed such an unquestioned value on scientific thought and development. We might consider ourselves fortunate that these weapons have only been deployed in a single war since their inception. The cost of this progress, however, continues to be inordinately borne in the industrialized environment of a single people: the Navajo.

The Navajo Nation comprises over 17 million acres, encompassing northeast Arizona and portions of southeast Utah and western New Mexico. This also happens to be the location of some of the most accessible uranium deposits in the United States. Uranium mining on the Navajo Nation is a picture of scientific knowledge driving an industrial landscape that continues to dramatically affect a people. Even as late as 1950, more than 80 percent of the uranium stores were being imported from overseas. The establishment of the Atomic Energy Commission (AEC) was designed to change this reality, and in 1956 the head of procurement for the AEC "announced with pride that yearly domestic uranium ore production had risen from 70,000 tons in 1948 to three million tons . . ." America was the leading provider of uranium for the free world.[14] A great deal of this ore was being extracted from the Four Corners Region, and a disproportionate amount from the Navajo Nation, where regulators were far laxer on health and safety requirements and mining leases could be had for a fraction of market value.[15]

For centuries the Navajo had been a pastoral population, primarily raising sheep on the desert of their expansive reservation. Seemingly overnight they found themselves in the midst of an industrial, built environment. In her history of uranium mining's legacy on the Navajo Reservation, Judy Pasternak writes,

> Uranium was their Holy Grail. Their country desperately needed it to make atomic bombs. . . . Through the most anxious Cold War years of the 1940s, 50s and 60s, mining companies swarmed Dine Bikeyah. . . . All that time, the Navajos dug up uranium happy for the blessing of steady jobs and all that their new wages could buy. . . . They had little concept of its capacity

14. Pasternak, *Yellow Dirt*, 75, 104.

15. Monument 1 Uranium Mine was secured in 1942 for $739.83 and a 10 percent royalty. Monument 2, which contributed 820 pounds of yellow cake to the Manhattan Project, was secured by a payment of $3,000 and a 10 percent royalty. This would net the tribe $200,000 per year while the lease was actually worth millions and the standard royalty rate at the time was 40 percent (Pasternak, *Yellow Dirt*, 44, 90).

to wreck their health until too late, when 'Yellow Dirt' had crept into every aspect of their daily lives: their homes, their drinking water, their playgrounds, even their garbage dumps.[16]

The price for progress was tremendous. Prior to this period of mining proliferation, cancer was virtually unknown among the Navajo and scientists were amazed at their seeming natural immunity from a basic American disease. Never being educated on the dangers of the radioactive material they were now working so hard to extract, this previously "immune" people started dying of cancer at rates many times higher than the general population. Safety regulations required among other mining populations were rarely enforced in the Navajo Nation and many residents utilized the tainted mine tailings in the foundations of their homes and even blocks and stucco for the exterior and interior of the houses. Water runoff from mining waste polluted surface stock ponds as well as groundwater wells, sickening people and killing livestock. "The Navajo uranium miners *averaged* cumulative exposures that were about forty-four times higher than the levels at Hiroshima and Nagasaki."[17]

The cost of the industrialized landscape continues to be experienced by the Navajo long after the uranium boom subsided, leaving a new dependence on a wage economy and ruined health alongside a land still pocked with mine shafts and tailings piles. On July 16, 1975, Navajos at Church Rock were awakened at 5:30 AM by the sound of rushing water. A twenty-foot breach had opened overnight in a United Nuclear Mill waste pond dam, releasing 93 million gallons of radioactive liquid into the Rio Puerco. It was the largest accidental release of radioactive material in US history—larger than the more well-publicized Three Mile Island meltdown in Pennsylvania three months later.[18]

Due to the historical categories of Manifest Destiny, progress, and the ways in which American Indians have fit—or failed to fit—into those conceptions, the legacy of uranium mining on Navajo lands remain mostly out of our line of sight and concern. The marks of the built and changed landscape in another mining community, Butte, Montana, are impossible to ignore. The Anaconda Copper Mining Company had nearly 5,200 employees working in the Butte area extracting copper from thousands of miles of underground tunnels in 1955. A decline in copper prices in the mid-1950s, however, necessitated a change from the expensive and inefficient underground mines to the much more efficient open-pit style of mining coming in vogue worldwide.[19] Production of copper ore steadily rose as enormous

16. Pasternak, *Yellow Dirt*, 6–7.

17. Pasternak, *Yellow Dirt*, 154; emphasis added.

18. Pasternak, *Yellow Dirt*, 149–50.

19. Leech, *City That Ate Itself*, 112–13.

trucks hauled away massive amounts of earth near the core of the city of Butte. In 1962, 215,000 tons of ore were processed at the Anaconda smelter, twenty-six miles away. Ten years later that production would rise to 250,000 tons of material *every day*.[20] The massive removal of so many tons of earth opened the Berkeley Pit to such a degree that in 1972 "Anaconda finally stated a preference for a long-range, orderly relocation of Butte's central business district to a new area."[21] The city was slowly devouring itself for the sake of the copper mine's expansion.

Falling copper prices in the early 1980s saved the historic downtown of Butte. When mining finally ceased in early 1984, the Berkeley Pit was a mile wide, a mile and a half long, and 1,700 feet deep. It contained more than twenty-five miles of haul roads *within* the pit and its depth had surpassed the height of the Empire State Building as early as 1975.[22] It was a massive hole in the earth that was about to become an enormous poisoned lake. Pumps had been running continuously for nearly 100 years to keep groundwater from flooding the copper diggings. When the pumps were turned off, engineers estimated it would take anywhere from twenty to 120 years for water to refill the thousands of miles of tunnels beneath the pit and become visible at the pit's bottom. It took little more than a year.[23] Today the Berkeley Pit adds 2 to 3 million gallons of acidic, metal-laden water every day to the 400 *billion* gallons of contaminated water already in the pit. There is no cost-effective means of treating such a large body of pollution, so only 3 million gallons are withdrawn for treatment each day in order to maintain the pit's equilibrium. This process will go on indefinitely.[24]

The Berkeley Pit brought into the open the effects of progress through industrialization that until 1955 would often be hidden in the bowels of the earth. In his history of Butte and the Berkeley Pit, Brian James Leech writes that open-pit mining

> was such a dramatically different way to work that it quickly became a symbol of mechanization's social consequences. The wide-open spaces of the pit made possible the use of bigger and bigger machines . . . . The pit's success also created industrial hazards that angered many of Butte's residents and the expansion threatened the very existence of closely bonded neighborhoods.[25]

20. Leech, *City That Ate Itself*, 146, 148.
21. Leech, *City That Ate Itself*, 279.
22. Leech, *City That Ate Itself*, 309, 149.
23. Leech, *City That Ate Itself*, 335.
24. Leech, *City That Ate Itself*, 337–38.
25. Leech, *City That Ate Itself*, 102.

In addition to the industrial and social costs of expansion, the environmental cost became apparent when the Berkeley Pit and the Clark Fork, into which much of its water drained, became the EPA's largest Superfund cleanup site, by area, in the nation.[26]

What is particularly notable about the Berkeley Pit as a monument to human categories of progress is how its increasing depth and width were specifically justified in the community it was devouring by the company conducting this massive removal of earth. While other impacts of technology were hidden beneath mountains, obscured by bureaucratic legalese, or veiled behind a curtain of cultural marginality, the Berkeley Pit dominates the landscape as one drops off the Continental Divide into the Clark Fork drainage. The value of this project, both the result of and a glaring monument to progress through the human-engineered, was actually to be celebrated. "Brochures at the Berkeley Pit viewing stand also pushed the view that anyone who enjoyed mass consumption must also support the pit. They often explicitly linked tourists' and customers' lives with Anaconda's copper products."[27] The Anaconda Company began airing television commercials in the 1960s and 70s to promote (if not justify) its operations and published frequent employee newsletters in an attempt to garner support in a community previously dependent on the hidden nature of underground mining. "All the media made it evident that open-pit mining was a *sublime* technological marvel. Increasingly larger machinery helped to extract material, and more efficient systems began to process it."[28]

Today the Berkeley Pit is a tourist attraction, sporting a gift shop and a three-dollar fee to walk out on the viewing platform. The community of Anaconda, where Butte's ore was processed (smelted) lies twenty-six miles northwest of Butte and contains the Anaconda Smoke Stack State Park. The smoke stack is the tallest masonry structure in the world at 585 feet, and was built in 1918 in an attempt to lift the poisonous emissions from the smelter high enough into the atmosphere that harmful particles could dissipate without harming the area's residents.

In his collection of essays about the loss of connection with natural environments, author and mountain guide Jack Turner invokes this connection between the engineered world and the museum when he writes, "Created environments also reek of the 'museal' quality made famous by Theodor Adorno's essay 'Valery Proust Museum.'" Turner quotes Adorno: "The German word 'museal' [museumlike] has unpleasant overtones. It describes objects to which

26. Leech, *City That Ate Itself*, 332.
27. Leech, *City That Ate Itself*, 115.
28. Leech, *City That Ate Itself*, 141; emphasis added.

the observer no longer has a vital relationship and which are in the process of dying." To further make his point, in this same essay Turner invokes Anthony Giddens's work, *The Consequences of Modernity*, where Giddens writes that, "The 'End of Nature' means that the natural world has become in large part a 'created environment' consisting of humanly structured systems whose motive power and dynamics derive from socially organized knowledge claims rather than from influences exogenous to human activity."[29]

We tether our existence to our world through particular lines of connection. The ideas about value and meaning serve to secure our physical presence on earth; to fasten us to the world in which we live. The anchors were set in the Enlightenment ideals of human ability from which we extend the lines of connection which consist of our roads, cities, tunnels, rail lines for hauling ore, and the pathways of nuclear fusion. The anchor points and the tethers that extend from them create us as a certain kind of people. Our Western ideals are a fairly recent development in terms of the whole history of humankind and some of the deterioration of life is already becoming apparent. The lines of connection for thousands of years ran through families, tribes, spiritualities, and a dependence on an environment that could not be thoroughly engineered. The natural world, the not-built-by-us, no longer serves to fasten us to existence and herein lies part of the poverty in our current spirituality. Julene Bair writes,

> Without a spiritual tradition that recognizes the balance of nature and holds it sacred, our relationship to the land and its bounty is like a child's in a candy store with no adult present to restrain it from gorging. . . . We conduct ourselves within an economy that depends on the depletion and degradation of the real things—plants, animals, soils, air, water—that sustain us.[30]

When what connects us to or grounds us in existence—our tethers—depend on our own intelligence, ingenuity, or technical ability, then our lives become meaningful or successful only in these terms. The restlessness and lack of confidence that characterize our culture demonstrate our inability to measure up to the necessary significance in those terms. Our connective pathways consisting of roads, rail lines, tunnels, and engineered waterways lead to a particular destination. And it is not yet a destination that has demonstrated its adeptness at resourcing the vision of a better existence for all people—not just those who are the smartest, richest, or most capable.

Historic and modern mining projects aimed at the extraction of wealth from the earth are prime indicators of our cultural ethos in action. Another

29. Turner, *Abstract Wild*, 109.
30. Bair, "She Poured Out Her Own," 90.

primary value of the paradigm we live by is the ability to engineer and thereby control naturally occurring processes for our own perceived benefit. This value is clearly exemplified in the proliferation of dams, specifically those west of Powell's Hundredth Meridian where water is as valuable as any mineral and often more volatile than nuclear fusion. Jonathon Thompson, who wrote the history of the Gold King Mine spill we looked at earlier, points out that

> The history of white settlement of the West is one of trying to wrest control over the natural world, particularly water, and redirecting it to fit our needs. After World War II, this effort climaxed with a paroxysm of dam- and tunnel- and canal-building on the Colorado River and its tributaries: the San Juan, the Gunnison, the Dolores, and the Green. It was the largest plumbing project the world had ever seen, and its centerpiece was certainly Glen Canyon Dam, behind which the waters of the Colorado started backing up in 1963.[31]

The dams one can see when driving all across the West are monuments to our cultural belief in progress.

Glen Canyon Dam was built by the Bureau of Reclamation on the Colorado River in the heart of the arid plateau country. Construction occurred between 1956 and 1966 at a cost of $1.9 billion. The dam sits in Arizona, just south of the Utah state line, but the 20 million acre-feet of water storage in the 180-miles-long reservoir lies predominantly in southern Utah. The Bureau of Reclamation was responsible for constructing impoundment dams throughout the western states to facilitate water storage, and that water was then intended for the irrigation of the arid lands west of the Hundredth Meridian. Glen Canyon Dam was part of the Colorado River Storage Project, which additionally funded the towering Flaming Gorge Dam on the Green River in northern Utah. These dams, along with countless others that were built and some that never made it past the planning stage, seek to capture the heavy flows of spring snowmelt from the high peaks that would historically have been lost downstream. The water, it was contended, could be more appropriately utilized to water crops through the heat of the dry summers.

The dreams of an engineered environment and the dams those dreams engendered are problematic at best. As the Colorado River and its tributaries drain the sandy regions of Colorado, Utah, and Wyoming, these rivers accumulate an enormous amount of silt and debris. This silt was for centuries spread throughout the flood plains of the lower Colorado River as spring flows spread the river wide and allowed the silt to settle on and replenish topsoil on the Colorado River Delta and in what is now Imperial

31. Thompson, *River of Lost Souls*, 204.

Valley. Since the 1960s, this silt has been impounded behind the dam in Glen Canyon, slowly filling Lake Powell with soil intended to reinvigorate regions beyond. Along with valuable topsoil, the dam traps millions of gallons of poisoned water as fertilizers, fuels, and the runoff of metal-laden mine waste are washed into this enormous impoundment pond. As a stagnant body of water in a hot desert, Lake Powell increases evaporation—up to 9 percent per year—as well as the water's salinity which can render the water useless for irrigating crops further downstream.

In his history of the Colorado River Storage Project, Marc Reisner reflects,

> Never in US history had so little economic development been proposed at such an exorbitant public cost, for all the billions were buying, besides extremely expensive public power, were a few patches of new irrigated lands whose composite size was smaller than Rhode Island. The subsidies, it turned out later, would be worth as much as $2 million per farm, perhaps five times as much as the farms themselves were worth.[32]

The vision to force an unwieldly and unproductive landscape to fit human definitions of value has always unleashed such unintended consequences and has created a mythology that too rarely accords with reality. As Western writer Bernard DeVoto once wrote,

> The jubilant Mormons told the world as early as 1849 that they had made the desert blossom as the rose. . . . They gave the biblical phrase to the West at large; it has long been a stereotype. The West, understand, has made the desert blossom as the rose. The stereotype happens not to be true. The West has not made the desert blossom. By means of the most formidable engineering works man has ever constructed, it has transferred portions of the mountain snowpack to minute areas that lie along the edge of the desert.[33]

The Army Corps of Engineers was the counterpart of the Bureau of Reclamation during the dam-building era of the mid-twentieth century. The corps, however, endeavored to build dams as primarily flood control devices on otherwise flood-prone rivers. It was again an act steeped in a belief in the human ability to engineer an environment to make it more conducive to our perceived ends. The broad and shallow Missouri River was transformed into a deeper and narrower channel in order to both facilitate a

---

32. Reisner, *Cadillac Desert*, 144.
33. DeVoto, *Western Paradox*, 272.

better river shipping business and to more easily control the river's floods. A series of dams on both the mainstream Missouri and most of its tributaries were approved by Congress in 1944 in an effort to fully control a massive water system draining parts of ten states and two Canadian provinces. But a recent *New York Times* article points out that the vast machinery encompassing the river "was designed for a different era, a time before climate change and the extreme weather it can bring."[34]

In March of 2019 engineer John Remus found himself in charge of six dams on the swelling Missouri River with a difficult choice to make. A bomb cyclone hit the upper Midwest with massive amounts of rain falling on frozen soil. The unusual amount of water was then directly routed into a swelling river rather than being absorbed into the ground. Remus's choice: "Try to hold back the surging Missouri River but risk destroying a major dam, potentially releasing a 45-foot wall of water? Or should he relieve the pressure by opening the spillway purposely, add to the flooding of towns, homes and farmland for hundreds of miles?"[35] The dams were not designed to handle the influx they were confronted with and spillways were opened. Afterward, Remus was reflective: "It's human nature to think we are masters of our environment, the lords of creation. But there are limits."[36] Such limits extend to our capacity to form an adequate interior life as well. Writer Thomas Berry notes,

> What is happening was unthinkable in ages gone by. We now control forces that once controlled us, or, more precisely, the earth process that formerly administered the earth directly is now accomplishing this task in and through the human as its conscious agent. Once a creature of earthly providence, we are now extensively in control of this providence. We now have extensive power over the ultimate destinies of the planet, the power of life and death over many of its life systems.[37]

It is the idea of having such power that drives our way of being in the world and more often than not provides us with a sense of our own unlimited ability to extract value and meaning. In so doing we can unleash unanticipated and uncontrollable interactions and, I would contend, open an enormous pit in our soul.

The evidence that we believe we can improve the world and our own existence simply by building more and building better are all around us everyday in hundreds of small things. Seventeen-hundred-foot-deep pits,

34. Kelly, "Fight to Tame a Swelling River," para. 3.
35. Kelly, "Fight to Tame a Swelling River," para. 2.
36. Kelly, "Fight to Tame a Swelling River," para. 4.
37. Berry, *Dream of the Earth*, 42.

seven-hundred-foot-high dams, 3 million gallons of orange water, and thousands of cancer victims are all glaring and obvious indicators of the costs involved in our pursuit of progress. But each of us lives the bulk of our lives in a built environment and we scarcely consider the degree to which this condition establishes our sense of highest value and meaning. Bob Gouzwaard, in his critique of Western society, observes that in dealing with progress Christians have generally failed to extensively question the *direction* of progress: "Synthesis with the entire development of society is the mark of modern Christendom" so that we share responsibility not only for the presence of good in our social order but evil as well.[38] We all inhabit a landscape—internally as well as externally—of our own making. This inevitably forms us as a certain kind of people.

Consider something as commonplace as roads as a source of formulative meaning. We all utilize roads daily to walk, ride, or drive on. They serve not only to facilitate a smooth functioning in daily life, but equally as sources of meaning for a technically oriented society. The presence of a road—paved or not—can evoke pride in an advocate of human capacity and at the same time provoke derision from a proponent of a return to a pre-industrial condition.

In contrast to the focus on rivers as primary travel corridors of an earlier era, "Roads are static, inorganic, and unnatural; while they can be moved and create change when built and rebuilt, they indicate permanence and sheer resistance to change."[39] Modern roads, specifically some of the iconic highways in the rugged mountainous West, demonstrate a high degree of technological prowess and are traveled by millions every year: Red Mountain Pass, Going to the Sun Road, Trail Ridge Road, the final piece of the Interstate highway system completed through Glenwood Canyon in 1992—the very names invoke engineering marvels. "It may be that this overt intention toward the landscape—the impulse to improve upon nature and subdue it for human purpose—has largely contributed to the image of roads as a dominant force."[40]

Roads were critical to enacting the Enlightenment vision of transformation to productive use. A line in an early mining law granted "the right-of-way for the construction of highways across public lands not otherwise reserved for public purposes," and by the twentieth century roads had "come to signify [the] industrialization of the modern age."[41] Roads also

38. Gouzwaard, *Capitalism and Progress*, 117.

39. Rogers, *Roads in the Wilderness*, 167.

40. Rogers, *Roads in the Wilderness*, 168.

41. Rogers, *Roads in the Wilderness*, 4.

serve as a flashpoint for controversy, especially for regions like Utah where so much rugged and unsettled country is met by a people uniquely bent toward the value of the human-built. Utah roads such as Hole in the Rock Road are historical identity formers while many other "roads"—those into Arch Canyon, Negro Bill Canyon, Recapture Canyon, the Burr Trail—embody contrasting visions of human presence in and use of the landscape. Differing visions of establishing value form the heart of this book and are specifically enacted by diverging views of something as everyday as a road. In his history of Utah roads controversies, Jedediah Rogers frames the issue:

> Many southern Utah residents are ideological if not blood descendants of the original pioneers who settled here. They cling firmly to a conquest narrative that the land is theirs by birthright and divine decree; theirs is a quest to domesticate the wilderness. Others, both locals and "outsiders," hold a diametric view: that the land demands distance from the human touch and ought to be protected. These dueling visions are consequential; it matters how one thinks about and perceives the land, and the dialectic has contributed to persistent tensions here.[42]

This consideration of roads further frames important issues as we progress toward the transition of our involvement in personal and social repair. The categories we use to find meaning in work and production will be the same categories we bring to establishing a productive and meaningful spiritual existence. And as I have been contending throughout, our society presents many clear illustrations of where we stand. "Development in Colorado and across the United States is transforming natural landscapes at the rate of two football fields per minute. . . The amount of land converted by human activities in Colorado increased by 676,827 acres between 2001 and 2017. . . The human footprint nationwide expanded by 24 million acres over those sixteen years."[43] This rate of land conversion actually surpasses the much-more-talked-about rate of deforestation in the Amazon region of Brazil. The president of Conservation Science Partners, Brett Dickson, remarks that, "In losing our natural landscape, we're losing a part of the American soul—especially in the West."[44]

This shouldn't be a surprising reality when we consider the entire tenor of Western society. Jacques Ellul takes aim at our technologically dependent culture and its inherent consequences on the earth we inhabit: "Every technique tends, more or less, to constrain nature; accordingly, the artificial is

---

42. Rogers, *Roads in the Wilderness*, 3.

43. Finley, "Development Devours U.S. Natural Landscapes," paras. 1–2.

44. Finley, "Development Devours U.S. Natural Landscapes," para. 4.

opposed to the natural." The necessity and only logical conclusion of this way in the world "is a mastery that *excludes, eliminates,* and *replaces* the natural." Because the world that is being created by our ever-growing technical ability is an artificial world it is radically different from the natural world and "destroys, eliminates, or subordinates the natural world and does not allow this world to restore itself or even to enter into a symbiotic relationship with it."[45] Regardless of any token efforts we might advocate for in salvaging some of our natural landscape, the core of our sense of highest and best use continues to reside in a confidence in our ability to build and engineer a better world. Because this has become our innate understanding of a meaningful existence, it colors the entirety of our thinking and acting.

The prioritizing of the built environment, whether external or internal, is accompanied by enormous—if at times hidden—costs. The examples we have looked at in this chapter provide a glimpse into expansive regions that bear the consequences of our passion for industrialization, often in perpetuity. These consequences and the affected landscapes inevitably devour resources that could otherwise be utilized to alleviate other kinds of suffering in our communities and world. In western Canada, the province of Alberta has long been a center of industrial development in the proliferation of oil and gas infrastructure. Regulators estimate that cleanup of the impact of industry could take *2,800* years and cost more than $260 billion. That means that the task will fall to the efforts and expenses of the next *ninety-three* generations.[46] In West Virginia, restoration and remediation of more than 3,300 sites abandoned by coal companies *before* 1977 will cost $4.5 billion and could take centuries. It will cost a billion dollars just to extinguish all of West Virginia's forty-three fires currently burning in abandoned mines. There is more poisoned water within mine pools in the state than there is in the state's lakes.[47] The numbers are beyond comprehension.

In 1980, Congress passed the Comprehensive Environmental Response, Compensation, and Liability Act (CERCLA), more commonly referred to as Superfund. The law was designed to provide funding and regulation for cleanup of the nation's worst hazardous waste sites, and was created as a legacy of our single-minded attention to development and industrialization in a wide variety of natural and urban settings. The EPA website currently lists 1,335 sites on the National Priorities List (NPL) while 424 sites have been considered "remediated" and removed from the list.[48] Over the span of

45. Ellul, *Technological Society*, 216, 79; emphasis added.

46. McIntosh and De Souza, "Alberta Warned."

47. Virtanen, "WV Officials," paras. 3, 11, and 14.

48. https://www.epa.gov/superfund.

forty years, less than one-third of the nation's *most* polluted sites have been restored to a safe condition, to say nothing of the hazardous waste locations that were never identified under Superfund designation and yet continue to compromise vast regions. Just in the past twenty years, half of the Superfund's lifespan, American taxpayers have spent more than $21 billion in cleanup costs "while hundreds of companies responsible for contaminating water paid little to nothing, an analysis of congressional budget data shows."[49]

The examples could (and have) fill an entire book. My intent has been to provide a few glaring examples, primarily from my own regional context, to provide a sense of the cost to be borne in our prioritizing of the built environment. Beyond the unreasonable material and environmental costs involved in this worldview, however, my larger point is the cost paid in our stilted spiritual selves, which is the spring from which life and culture emanates. Our inner landscape—the landscape of the soul—too often reflects these ruined environs. This examination of some of the costs involved, perhaps more clearly than the history and sociology of the previous chapters, show us who we are and what we value. Because value issues in action, our belief in progress issues in our built environment. That environment brings with it its own justification: profits, wages, scientific interest, control, etc. As such, the condition becomes self-referent and self-perpetuating.

As Wallace Stegner so eloquently points out, "The problem is that places work on people very slowly, but people work on places with the singlemindedness of a beaver at a cottonwood tree. Occasionally they make the desert blossom as the rose, as the Mormons are fond of saying. As often, they simply make deserts."[50] Uncritically engaged, as it too often appears to be, our attachment to our work on our world destroys community dynamics, environments, individuals, and any sense that meaning might lie outside of our efforts in a creation external to our own striving. The dark side of this attachment is the toxic brew that percolates beneath the surface of our being and can take years to surface. We should be aware of the whole host of problems the release of these underlying convictions can produce and question whether it will be too late to salvage our soul's landscape when they do. When we near the end of our sojourn on earth, will we be content with the meaning we have procured by our own efforts? It is doubtful as it is not within our capacity to create anything meaningful enough. That is the argument we will pursue in part II.

By way of application, I want to conclude this examination of the cost of our cultural ethos by opening the door to a consideration that our way

49. Anderson, "Taxpayer Dollars," para. 1.
50. Stegner and Stegner, *American Places*, 207.

in the world has profound implications which go beyond environmental and monetary costs, as high and worthy of consideration as these costs inevitably are. As I have been saying throughout, our embrace as a society of Enlightenment categories of progress and labor and the conception of value makes us into a particular kind of people. What kind of people, essentially, are we, then? Sociologist Zygmunt Bauman provides a chilling perspective. To quote Bauman at length:

> I suggest . . . that the bureaucratic culture which prompts us to view society as an object of administration, as a collection of so many 'problems' to be solved, as 'nature' to be 'controlled,' 'mastered,' and 'improved' or 'remade,' as a legitimate target for 'social engineering,' and in general a garden to be designed and kept in the planned shape by force (the gardening posture divides vegetation into 'cultured plants' to be taken care of, and weeds to be exterminated), was the very atmosphere in which the idea of the Holocaust could be conceived, slowly yet consistently developed, and brought to its conclusion. I also suggest that it was the spirit of instrumental rationality, and its modern, bureaucratic form of institutionalization, which has made the Holocaust-style solutions not only possible, but eminently 'reasonable'—and increased the probability of their choice.[51]

We're getting to the point of recognizing how our cultural values have a profound impact on our spiritual life and therefore shape the context in which each of us live and act. Bauman's observations are a sobering and frightening view into what can become the condition of the soul of any one of us captivated by our Western, and specifically American, cultural ethos. Apart from a position that understands our own limitations, exercises humility, and seeks the source wherein true humanness is received, not built, we will inevitably become a people who can only conceive of anything worthwhile as that which we manufacture, even to the point of our own spirituality. And "for these men [and women], technique is in every way sacred: it is the common expression of human power without which they would find themselves poor, alone, naked, and stripped of all pretensions. They would no longer be the heroes, geniuses, or archangels which a motor permits them to be at little expense."[52] To be truly human, not subject to the limiting and violating force of technological determinism, is where we begin to turn next.

51. Quoted in Volf, *Exclusion and Embrace*, 281.

52. Ellul, *Technological Society*, 145.

Chapter 4

The Landscape of the Soul

THE PREVIOUS THREE CHAPTERS invoke the themes of an overarching cultural mythology clearly dependent on religious categories. The architects and builders of the cultural artifacts we most often utilize—our streets, vehicles, homes, powerplants, technology, and information infrastructure—design as they do based on deep senses of meaning and value which are modern confessions of faith. Even the seemingly mundane tasks of life are infused with a significance that transcends the everyday acts themselves. The philosophers of our culture inform the builders of the physical infrastructure which cooperate to enact a vision of the right kind of society. The rightness of this world is conceived in terms of highest and best use of resources in order to propel our world toward what is understood as most worthwhile. Actions, and the artifacts those actions produce, emanate from beliefs regarding what is worth applying out efforts to in the limited years we have to act.

These are undeniably religious ideals and we adhere to them as fanatically as any fundamentalist has ever adhered to their faith. The ideas of progress that create our dependence on the engineered-by-us world utilize specifically religiously hued images which serve to tether our faith to a specific way of being in the world. What we build and accomplish is about purpose, about value, about dignity, and even about humanity's salvation and redemption. This is our way to (or perhaps *back* to) paradise. Frequently in American history the image of the garden is invoked. Progress is our way back to Eden.

It makes little difference how one understands the story of the garden of Eden in Genesis chapters 2–3; as a figurative or literal story of our origins as a part of the physical creation. The image and idea of the garden, of an Edenic state, is one of the most forceful cultural images adhered to by the Western mind. At one and the same time Eden indicates an idyllic and innocent first condition of humanity and it also points to a kind of paradisiacal sense of the place to which our intelligence and ingenuity can lead us in the future. Western settlers understood Eden as well-watered and well-stocked, a natural state of perfection where humanity is in charge at the apex of creation. The Old Testament vision of Eden—whether as a place of emergence or as a model of destination—is reflected in one way or another in virtually every human society throughout history. It is the paradigm for all that's right with the world.

The paradigm of the garden inspired a whole nation of explorers, settlers, boomers, investors, and builders. The nation was uniquely set up for the realization of full humanness. Any region that didn't at first appear garden-like would soon be changed through the abilities of the scientific mind to introduce water, crops, livestock, and power. The earth, specifically North America, was—or soon would be—the new Eden. It is questionable whether the shapers of thought in the earliest settlement of this new Eden realized the irony of their new faith: this Eden would be entered and subdued precisely through the application of human knowledge, the very grasping after which got the first couple expelled from Eden in the first place.

This chapter marks a shift to an alternative cultural narrative, one provided by the ancient biblical text which has demonstrated remarkable staying power over many millennia as a vision for how the world ought to look. Part II will generally follow the pattern of part I, developing culture as a way of being, which then produces ways of acting, all with a view toward the resulting meaning to be derived from this faith exchange. As we undertake this transition to the biblical view of the world and meaning, it is critical that we do so in a way that guards against reading these texts from within our own narrowly conceived cultural paradigm, which was fully developed in the previous chapters. While we can never fully separate ourselves from the culture which shapes our being, we can at the very least be aware of imposing our own sense of meaning on the text which was not formulated from within a Western context.

This is especially important as we look at some of the elements of Genesis: the book of beginnings. Genesis, in fact the whole of the biblical canon, was not formulated from a Western cultural perspective as a scientific treatise intended to satisfy our thirst for precision and completeness. These narratives consist of the necessary elements for cultural formation and meaning. That meaning and the type of people it created can be gleaned from any number of different levels of literalness ascribed to the various accounts that make up the biblical literature. My own understanding of and adherence to the biblical narrative does not hinge, for example, on whether creation occurred in seven days or seven eons, but on the compelling nature of the vision exuded and its ability to accurately portray life and meaning.

The Bible was compiled with the specific purpose of forming a particular people with a particular way of being in the world. It is therefore primarily about cultural formation. Chapter 1 established the view that our own scientific view of reality is a specific cultural narrative which in turn supplies our sense of meaning and produces certain actions in and on this world. In light of the ways in which our own approach to reality and meaning have produced a restless and fragmented society and has resulted in enormous costs to the environment, I am convinced that a search for an alternative way of being is in order. I am drawn to the biblical alternative because of the way it supplies uniquely compelling views of our place in the world ordered around what I understand as three overarching themes holding this form of cultural formation together.

The first of these themes has to do with the nature of creation. The biblical narrative gives us a convincing sense of why there is something rather than nothing and further provides a persuasive sense of how humankind fits into the world as both a part of and somehow unique in creation. Secondly, the Bible provides an honest sense that things are not as they should be due to the dissolution[1] of that creation. Every society throughout history has attempted to address the disconnect between what it knows life should look like and the reality which is too often manifest in individual and social suffering. Finally, there is built into the narrative the sense of how things could be different; how we might participate in the restoration of a condition of *shalom*. The movement of the earth and its inhabitants toward some kind of heaven, utopia, or basic harmony is embedded in every culture we have ever known. This last piece will specifically be the theme of the following chapter.

The opening chapters of Genesis provide the source of these resounding confessions. Specifically, we are provided the sense that this world was formed by a creator who transcends while he also inhabits the creation, that the creation was "very good"—it was a place of *shalom*—and the world doesn't look as it ought because of humanity's desire to be its own source of

---

1. Rather than invoking the term *sin*, which is too often individualized and therefore minimized in Western culture, I use the word *dissolution* throughout this work as it provides a stark image in pointing to a condition of "death or decay" which stands in particular contrast to the image of creation existing in a state of *shalom* with its connotations of life and flourishing.

meaning. The details of the how and when and where of these realities were far less important to the authors of these accounts than they are to us. The point of Genesis is to establish that our world is founded and superintended by God through his creative and sustaining act. And in contrast to our efforts to level mountains, redirect rivers, and straighten crooked paths so we might have a conformity of landscape and experience, God formed the world of diversity, beauty, mystery, desolation, turbulent activity, and even silence. It is a rich, if at times uncontrollable, landscape of unfathomable diversity in which everything adheres in interdependent relation. The creator also fills this landscape with movement and interaction. Additionally, the opening two chapters of Genesis, in an otherwise very brief account of an expansive and diverse world, doubly highlights humanity's place in the middle of the creative act. We not only share the sixth day of creation with other living creatures, but humans are specifically formed from the very dust of the ground.

Genesis 2:7, which mentions the dust from the ground, also mentions the unique additional *something* that characterizes humanity: the breathing into our nostrils of the breath of life. We are fully a part and fully embedded in the creation, and yet our humanness entails something additional, something uniquely added. Humanity contains a special breath of consciousness—our soul, our capacity for spirituality—which uniquely shapes our position as created beings. What we identify as our spirituality is our ability to internalize the external. We are inherently self-reflective about and uniquely conscious of the environment we inhabit, which means that we do not simply react to our world on the basis of unreflective instinct. Our conscious response to the elements external to us, both our environment and other conscious beings, becomes what we call culture. We accumulate history and have the capacity to choose (internalize) certain elements of those external happenings in order to provide the meaning for which self-reflective thought (spirituality) strives.

This ability to take the biological and physical world and formulate it into a source of conscious identity which can inform a cooperative culture means that as humans we are incredibly creative and capable. At the same time, we cannot lose sight of the fact that we are always equally a part of creation and therefore contingent beings. We are not only subject to change but ultimately dependent on an external source for our existence. The God who revealed himself to Moses as "I Am"[2] is the only being in existence with the capability to simply "be" apart from any dependence on an externality. Genesis makes clear that God is the only self-referent and self-existent being.

2. Exod 3:14.

The refusal to allow this to be our reality is what has always produced humanity's dilemmas. The first three chapters of Genesis endeavor to picture a good act of creation, resulting in a state of perfect flourishing, and at the same time explain why the world does not look the way it should today. The loss of connection to the idyllic condition of Eden through the attempt to become self-referent is what is meant by the desire for knowledge which brings about the dissolution of creation. Genesis 2–3 indicates the presence of the tree of the knowledge of good and evil in the midst of an otherwise ideal paradise.

My current interest is not to dive into the intricacies of theories on the physical or figurative accounting of the tree or why such a potentially destructive element was present in Eden, but to examine how astute biblical writers were in indicating the tree as they did. As the promoters and builders of America have often invoked the idea of the garden, one would expect an equally cautious reflection on the tree which is rarely forthcoming. The figure of the tree, however, is perhaps more clearly reflective of our modern condition than that of the garden. As Murray Jardine writes,

> [T]he term "knowledge of good and evil" means knowledge of everything. Thus, in saying that humans are not permitted to eat from the tree of the knowledge of good and evil, the story is saying that humans cannot claim to have absolute knowledge. This, of course, follows from the situation of humans. We are creators, but we are also creatures. As such, there are limits to our creative capacities, and limits to our knowledge. But because we are creators, we will have a powerful tendency to forget, or willfully ignore, the fact that we are creatures, and we will frequently try to be only creators—that is, to be God. This behavior is what is meant by the term *sin*, and its paradigm is attempting to claim absolute knowledge, which of course only God can have.[3]

As hard as we work at building or restoring Eden, the fact is we simply cannot get there from here. It matters little whether we are the designers and builders of our technological society or merely the consumers of those products, it is all about the effort to reestablish our dignity and in so doing enact human redemption. These are clearly religious themes which Daniel Bell had identified as the ultimate sources that undergird our society. The cultural condition in which we find ourselves, the shaping beliefs as well as the resultant physical infrastructure, implicates the Christian and the non-Christian, the religious and the irreligious, equally because we exhibit in our efforts the attempt to rise above our condition of createdness. We would

---

3. Jardine, *Making and Unmaking*, 186 (emphasis original).

like to think that we are on the verge of unlocking the mysteries of existence through the efforts of our best and brightest.

This is a specifically modern phenomenon that stands in deep contrast to the ways meaning was previously pursued. This is certainly due in part to the ways in which we press our own cultural realities onto the otherwise compelling nature of the biblical categories of meaning. In so doing, Western culture aspires to rise above as opposed to living within the created order—specifically, our own createdness. As Wendell Berry points out,

> Until modern times we focused a great deal of the best of our thoughts upon [the] rituals of return to the human condition. Seeking enlightenment or the promised land or the way home, a man would go or be forced to go into the wilderness, measure himself against the creation, recognize finally his true place within it, and thus be saved both from pride and despair.[4]

Our "way home" lies precisely in our return to an understanding of our humanness revealed through creation in contrast to our efforts to buy our way in through misapplied knowledge.

Part of our struggle to realize and live in this tension as created/creative beings on this earth stems from the foundations of Enlightenment and scientific thought conceived in what has been termed "The Cartesian Turn." When Rene Descartes formulated his own existence in the solitude of his home he declared, "I think, therefore I am." It was a profound attempt to make himself self-referent and assure his self-existence which has shaped Western thought since the sixteenth century. Regardless of Descartes's personal religious underpinnings, everything from this point is referenced from an "I." The problem is that we do not have the capacity to be self-referent in any aspect of our being. Our existence as cultural beings and our spiritualness is the internal state of external realities. This is what forms the landscape of the soul. The uniqueness of that something added by the Creator—the breath of life—ties it to creation and gives the soul, the seat of our spirituality, a state analogous to the created, external landscape. Our inner life has its own heights and depths and storms and the reality of the exposed and terror of the hidden. It contains a wealth of noise as well as silence, and can be either sublime and rich with flourishing or equally desolate.

This is to say, our spirituality—as the center of our internalized and accumulated meaning—does not occur in a vacuum. It is never self-created or merely self-referent. We respond to the external environment as the shaping function of the internal "us." Our culture, in all of its physical artifacts, values, expectations and bestowal of meaning along with the specific

4. Berry, *Unsettling of America*, 99.

environment we inhabit, is internalized to formulate what I am calling our spiritual selves. We realize, of course, that the way we internalize—reflect on, become conscious of—the external can shape us in ways that either aid our humanness or harm it.

The formulative sources of meaning that dominate Western thought and subsequent action are embedded in a specific physical environment which comes to give fuel to our ways of being. We respond to a physical landscape and the values that landscape perpetuates. For example, we may conceive of the landscape as a source of untapped and unlimited resources which responds to our efforts to extract wealth, which for us is meaning. We in turn reshape that landscape, which further serves as an additional shaping context. This, then, is the primary contention of this book: the increasingly built-by-us environment cannot help but become internalized to form a particular spirituality which further contributes to a humanity already paying a too-high price for our adherence to the source of meaning we ourselves have constructed. "Extensive interference with *outer* nature creates of necessity disorder of the *inner* nature, for the two are intimately connected."[5]

The way our internal landscape functions to supply meaning, and value takes many of its most important cues from the external landscape we expose ourselves to. Environmental writer Barry Lopez sees the "interior landscape" as a set of relationships consisting of "speculations, intuitions, and formal ideas," whether obvious or impenetrably subtle:

> The shape and character of these relationships in a person's thinking, I believe, are deeply influenced by where on this earth one goes, what one touches, the patterns one observes in nature—the intricate history of one's life in the land. . . . The interior landscape responds to the character and subtlety of an exterior landscape; the shape of the individual mind is affected by land as it is by genes.[6]

If our exposure is only to a paved-over, climate-controlled, noise-laden world of our own making, we may at some point be surprised to find a soul that yet contains heights and depths and sublime beauty alongside stretches of arid desolation.

At issue is the question of whether our contrived, humanly construct-ed landscapes that most of us inhabit on a daily basis can adequately serve as a formulative context for the spiritually produced landscape that inhab-its us as a creative act of the breath of God. While we have demonstrated

5. Meier, *Testament to the Wilderness*, 2 (emphasis original).
6. Lopez, *Crossing Open Ground*, 65.

incredible abilities to bestow order and accomplish production, are these efforts capable of impinging on the depths and intricacies of the soul in a more than superficial manner?

Until recently I was working as a wind technician on an eighty-five-turbine wind farm in southeast Wyoming. These nearly 300-foot towers that my co-workers and I climbed, sometimes multiple times a day, are monuments to technical ability and production. Wind turbines are intricate, computerized machines designed with countless internal monitoring systems that function in endless feedback loops to maximize the transferal of wind into useable electricity. A central computer, in continual communication with each turbine, displayed every turbine's operation and alerted the crew to any problems occurring in a vast cooperative system of electrical, mechanical and hydraulic components. Computer boards filled innumerable cabinets within each turbine, connected by miles of large and small cables relaying information and power. A vast number of parameters, all inter-related, had to be met before any one turbine could orient its enormous blades to capture the relentless Wyoming wind. It was a world of intricate and precise order that I inhabited and worked on almost daily. In a testament to engineering prowess, these machines actually worked as designed the vast majority of the time.

If that becomes the model of value and the highest form of meaning, I think most of us would confess that life does not actually reflect these clear-cut, ordered operations. While these intricate and highly efficient machines occupy straight lines on a landscape, designed by surveyors and technicians to maximize production, our own interior landscape too often resembles a chaotic menagerie of confusion and inefficiency. In the fall of the third year of my work on these turbines, my daughter suffered a devastating fall while rock climbing that resulted in a concussion, stitches, and destroyed her tibial plateau. Reconstruction required multiple surgeries in nearby Fort Collins and a great deal of follow-up care and therapy. The entire incident thrust my daughter, my wife, and I into a season of disequilibrium. We experienced disharmony in poor rest, poor diets, and very worried hearts. I was off-balance, unordered, unsettled—in a world very different from the contrived order in the context in which I worked.

I carried this sense of dissolution of order into the San Rafael Desert of Utah later in the winter. As I hoisted my pack and started up a narrow canyon alone, it felt as if I were wandering into a dark abyss. My travels over four days would consist of rarely encountering a trail in the midst of temperatures that never reached above twenty-five degrees. I worked my way through the San Rafael Reef, ascending a canyon obstructed often by dryfalls that had to be climbed or worked around via steep slopes. At the end of the first day the head of the canyon emerged in a vast bowl rimmed by cliffs of red and towers of white rock, covered by recent snows, and rising steadily to the south from where deep washes flowed, cutting the plain into a maze of depressions.

The following day I climbed another thousand feet between rock formations, at the head of multiple deep canyon walls, through a maze of gashes in the earth one might be tempted to think had never been visited. Near dusk I was pressed to find my way off a narrow mesa in a broken country of little more than pure vertical rock. A too-steep, narrow, boulder-filled gully requiring careful downclimbing was the only conceivable way off the top, dropping me by ridges of free-standing pinnacles perched like giant chess figures on long, unapproachable fingers of land, separating me from yet other canyons. The third day was yet more of the same: an ascent up a trailless canyon, bypassing unclimbable dryfalls, and still another day of an arduous climb up a much-too-steep broken slope which would place me back on top of the reef for a long descent back to my vehicle. The trip was long, hard, cold, lonely and often frightening.

We all tend to gravitate to a specific environment. But does that environment have any sense of actual connection with the realities of life? Most of us would naturally shy away from the chaotic and inhospitable terrain I confronted in the San Rafael Swell that winter. Conditions were harsh and travel was so difficult as to make progress seem miniscule. Yet that is the very environment—the landscape—that possessed a deep resonance with my soul at that time. Therein lies the value of such nonbuilt landscapes: Our contrived, human-oriented landscapes may seem more comforting and productive, but at the same time lack any connection with a spiritual condition we all know too well. If we derive meaning and value from a particular landscape, as I undeniably did in the San Rafael that winter, then a purely engineered and built landscape can cause us to ignore some of the unsettled depths and chaos (and even, I would contend, the corresponding beauty) of our souls in order to somehow convince us that all is right with the world. Wallace Stegner rightly observes that, "Any earth I have moved around with a bulldozer will be impotent to stir me. The more power I have and use, the less likely I am to submit to anything natural, and the less spiritual power natural things will have over me."[7]

While endeavoring to clean up and eliminate the less-than-straight and -smooth aspects of our world, we may actually be doing more harm than good. Bob Gouzwaard observes that our intertwined problems are intimately "related to the technically and economically oriented progress

---

7. Stegner and Stegner, *American Places*, 96.

of the West." It produces environmental and resource problems, but equally inflation, unemployment, alienation, and loneliness. For some interpreters of culture, the theme of progress is responsible for notions of fatalism and feelings of profound impotence.[8] This is also the conclusion developed by Bill McKibben in his book *Enough*:

> Since the mid-1950s pollsters have annually asked Americans if they are happy with their lives. The numbers who say yes have declined slowly but steadily for four decades, even as technology has dropped more and more conveniences from the sky. The researchers have found that people expect material progress to increase and also expect "inner happiness" or "peace of mind" to decrease. "The results of such surveys indicate that in fact a substantial majority of people believe there is a negative correlation between progress and happiness."[9]

The fact is, our uniquely American faith, and by extension our American experience of landscape, is unsustainable because it robs us of elements integral to true humanity and it also misshapes both our perception and procurement of value.

Our cultural attachment to progress, industry, and technology—pursued in part I—is unsustainable firstly because it serves to deprive us of some of the crucial elements which are basic to our humanness. In our struggle for a return to the conditions of the garden we have been fighting against our condition as created beings and would like to think of ourselves as little gods. If the return is indeed barred, as the Genesis story indicates, we will then endeavor to establish a new garden—certainly cleaner and more efficient than the one we were expelled from. This is a perpetual problem for the Western mind: a practical dissatisfaction with the messiness and inefficiencies of being human. A paved-over world of our own making cannot but distance us from some of the qualities that lie at the core of being a created being, and as such, deprives us of access to a right and humanly appropriate sense of being. As Howard Zahniser notes, "[T]he wilderness is essential to us, as human beings, for a true understanding of ourselves, our culture, our own nature, our true place in all nature."[10] If the exterior landscape forms the interior person, then we need places that exist as we do—the creations not of ourselves but of another—in order to relearn what it means to be a created being.

8. Gouzwaard, *Capitalism and Progress*, xxiii–xxiv.

9. McKibben, *Enough*, 122.

10. Harvey, *Wilderness Writings of Howard Zahniser*, 164.

Some of these essentials stripped from us by a world of our own making include humility, compassion, receptivity, complexity, mystery, and the very oughtness of creation. It appears as if by our science and technology we would just as soon take the humanness out of being human in the same way we have sought to remove the mystery and unpredictability from the natural world. Human qualities such as compassion or humility or the posture of receptivity are viewed as demeaning to human dignity, inefficient, and, at their worst, unprofitable. It simply does not propel one forward to cultivate basic human consideration, so these qualities are dismissed as relics of a pre-industrial age. Most importantly, our current way of being in the world does not allow for the critical and basic human quality of any sense of *limits*.

When I was in high school, I was especially close to three other guys. Each day for lunch we would rotate to one of our houses, descending on the kitchen like a swarm of locusts on a green, harvest-ready field. After a number of weeks of devouring whatever we could find, at times even an evening meal cooking in an oven, we were greeted at one friends' home by a note on the refrigerator: "You may have one sandwich, not all the sandwiches. You may have one serving of chips, not all the chips. You may have one soda, not all the sodas," and so on through a typical teenage diet, concluding with a list of items that were strictly off limits. We laugh about this list to this day, but the parent was simply trying her way of humanizing what was otherwise functioning as a pack of hyenas. I was being acculturated in a basic and critical form of being: limit.

Limits may be basic to our humanness, but American industrial culture has historically acted as if it could transcend any limits. Our builders shaped and extracted and redirected as if there were *un*limited water and minerals and oil and clean air and empty land. If a limit were ever encountered it would simply be bypassed by new technology. The corollary is the modern pursuit of unlimited growth and progress and profit available for those smart enough and industriousness enough to procure it. The expectation is for (mostly) easy and unfettered growth and progress as a whole expression of being—including what we might term the spiritual life. If one isn't growing or seems to have stagnated, simply apply unlimited human ingenuity to the problem and try harder, work more, read more, sweat a little bit. Growth should be seen, experienced, quantified. There is no room for periods of the obscure or arid or silent. This, in fact, is the paradigm this book is confronting as it has bearing on our participation in the repair of the world.

Wendell Berry has long confronted what it means to be essentially human again throughout his long career as a small-farm owner in Kentucky and modern prophet of American culture. In *The Unsettling of America* Berry writes,

> Much as we long for infinities of power and duration, we have no evidence that these lie within our reach, much less within our responsibility. It is more likely that we will have either to live within our limits, within the human definition, or not live at all. . . . The knowledge that purports to be leading us to transcendence of our limits has been with us a long time. It thrives by offering material means of fulfilling a spiritual, and therefore materially unappeasable, craving . . .[11]

To live within the created reality of our limitations is to embrace a beneficent aspect of the design of our Creator. The unwillingness to accept the limitations of being created beings requires us to transfer our faith from a wise and benevolent creator to a faith in the creations of our own hands. In order to actually be able to transcend limits means that our technology must always be out front, solving any crisis we are confronted with. We have in essence created our own gods in order to maintain the façade our culture foists upon us. Bill McKibben writes about recognizing the humanizing effect of acknowledging limits when he points out that "the larger society at the moment has a primitive and superstitious belief that we must accept new technologies, that they are somehow more powerful than we are." McKibben continues: "In [Noel] Perrin's words, we sometimes think of 'progress' as 'something semi-divine, an inexorable force outside of human control.'"[12] The divinity of the machine will keep us from having to acknowledge the uncomfortable and inefficient reality of being human within all of our limitations.

The second thing that makes our American landscape unsustainable as a source of deepest meaning is the way it taints both our understanding of value and the ways we go about increasing the fund of that value. Just as we internalize an external landscape, so we internalize the sense of what possesses value and meaning in the culture at large and act on that definition. Our humanness, constituted by that something extra which forms us also as conscious, spiritual beings, means we don't simply use and consume things, we derive meaning from their use and consumption. The things we come into contact with become charged with religious significance and identity-forming properties. What this means for those of us internalizing an American landscape is that value inheres in the instrumentality of a thing or in its ability to serve as a commodity. The categories of meaning promoted by the

---

11. Berry, *Unsettling of America*, 94.

12. McKibben, *Enough*, 168, 123.

kind of culture we are building constrain our definition of what is worthwhile. In terms of building a meaningful life, then, including but certainly
not limited to our spiritual selves, we will avoid elements that cannot serve
as instruments for advancing or acquiring, as well as anything that doesn't
have exchange value so we may trade for what we desire. We don't understand any other condition—silence, solitude, simplicity, dark and therefore
unproductive periods—as possessing anything of actual value.

What we ascribe worth to inevitably determines the ways we go about
increasing our own sense of worth. I mentioned earlier our restlessness and
sense of dissatisfaction which keeps fires fervently burning and engines forever revving. This is the only way to increase value. Keep in mind that we
have made the transition in this chapter to addressing the landscape of the
soul. For the stores of our deepest inner life to increase their value (utility,
to us) we will apply ever-increasing forms of labor in order to assure our
redemption as worthwhile human beings. Just as certain spiritual conditions lack any perceived value in themselves, so many exercises are deemed
worthless as they don't appear to increase the possibility of a return on our
efforts. So, space and silence and not-doing are not nearly active and labor-
intensive enough to increase our sense of the value of our spiritual selves.

The biblical account of creation is a compelling narrative because
it identifies a creator who can declare the condition of the creation "very
good" and also because it explains humanity as a part of the very stuff of
the earth even while acknowledging the something extra—the spirituality
that allows us to self-reflectively process the meaning of the physical world.
This is undoubtedly the reality that has allowed humankind the ability to
manipulate the physical world to the degree that we have, both for good
and for ill.

This point forces reflection on a second compelling element in the
Bible's sense of reality: that things are not as they should be. The goodness
or rightness of creation is a theme developed by biblical authors who place
this reality alongside the full acknowledgment that things are not right in
our world as we experience it today. Because humankind somehow seems
unable to live within the proper limits of being created beings, the grasping after absolute knowledge and unlimited ability disturbs the balance and
order of the good creation and results in the dissolution of that creation we
are now experiencing.

Beyond creation and an explanation of the fall, my own attraction
to the biblical narrative resides in a third compelling theme developed
throughout its pages: the vision of how the world could be righted and
how humanity, with all of its capabilities, could be a part of the restoration
in whatever limited way. This idea of repairing the world to a condition

more appropriate to its intended state will be explored more in depth below and in the following chapter. But I need to take a moment to introduce the theme of *shalom* because we require the idea as a biblical category in order to understand what has gone wrong in our world. Theologian Cornelius Plantinga Jr. presents a concise sense of a rich idea:

> The wedding together of God, humans, and all creation in justice, fulfillment, and delight is what the Hebrew prophets call *shalom*. . . . In the Bible, shalom means *universal flourishing, wholeness, and delight*—a rich state of affairs in which natural needs are satisfied and natural gifts fruitfully employed. . . . Shalom, in other words, is the way things ought to be.[13]

An idea of flourishing wholeness is embedded in the very goodness of creation. The reality is clear in the figure of Eden. But we all intuit that the world as it is today is most certainly not reflective of flourishing wholeness—of *shalom*—which is why the garden has so long been an important idea to strive for. In biblical terms, *shalom* was disturbed by humanity's willful rebellion against their human, created condition. That willful attempt to usurp the designed order of harmonious relationship between God, humanity, and creation is contained in the out-of-vogue idea of sin. As Plantinga again writes, "God hates sin not just because it violates his law but, more substantively, because it violates *shalom*, because it breaks the peace, because it interferes with the way things ought to be . . . we may safely describe evil as any spoiling of *shalom*, whether physically, morally, spiritually or otherwise. . . . In short, sin is culpable *shalom*-breaking."[14]

It is the height of irony, at the very least a mysterious tension present in the biblical narrative, that our unique possession of the breath of conscious spirituality may actually serve to be the source of creation's dissolution and our own undoing. As Miroslav Volf writes:

> In his *Systematic Theology* Wolfhart Pannenburg has suggested looking for the root of sin in the desire for identity—the instinctive will to be oneself—that is written in to the very structure of our selves. Though essentially healthy, the will to be oneself carries within it the germs of its own illness. Pannenburg describes the germ as the tendency of the self 'in fact to become the infinite basis and reference point for all objects, thus usurping the place of God.'[15]

13. Plantinga, *Not the Way*, 10; emphasis original.

14. Plantinga, *Not the Way*, 14

15. Volf, *Exclusion and Embrace*, 90.

This indicates an end toward which we have been moving all along: our incredible and unique capabilities which have taken on a life of their own and marred the landscape of the soul by redirecting our confidence toward what we think we have the ability to accomplish.

The consideration of the dissolution of creation, that things are not as they should be, prompts a decision on our part. On the one hand we can do as much of modern American Christianity demonstrates it is willing to do and simply live with the condition of the world. Because we can understand ourselves as standing above the rest of the created world, we can refuse any responsibility for it and simply wait for our redemption in some kind of life to come. In the meantime, it behooves us to apply our intellect and labor to make this existence as productive and comfortable (and hence, to this mind, as meaningful) as possible. We can maintain our attempts to build bigger and better machinery in order to insulate us behind a technological façade within a self-enclosed world and spirituality. This is a kind of landscape I have been arguing becomes a certain quality of the soul.

On the other hand, we can allow the unique features of our being human, created beings—in all of its glory and infamy and limitation—to compel us to cooperate with the Creator in the repair of the world. This is the vision of the biblical narrative and that which causes Christians to at least provide a nod of acceptance to a desire to move things toward where they ought to be. The question then becomes that of "how?" Does the desire to cooperate with a Creator bent on redemption require us to revert deeper into our grand attempts to build better machines and engineer better systems? This, I contend, is the heart of our spiritual crisis. Part III will address some of the categories which the repairing of our spirituality and our world would entail. But lest we rush too quickly into another ill-informed, heroic effort to work out our own sense of meaning in this regard, we first need to attend to two intertwined crises which our ethos has produced.

These two crises have to do with our *being* and our *acting*. Inevitably, there will be some crossover between these two elements as we act from our sense of being and our actions further define our being; the lines separating the categories will naturally be blurred. In our current landscape we lack the necessary personal resources to even be as we ought, having for so long prioritized our own built environment. Our personal paradigm and resources—our crisis of being—will be the focus of the remainder of the current chapter. The following chapter will seek to address how our way of being in the world, from a biblical perspective, too often negates our acting in truly redemptive ways. Our demonstrated unwillingness to operate as created beings reduces the cooperation necessary to move in small steps back to *shalom* and its New Testament corollary, the kingdom of God. If we confront our broken ways of being and acting in creation, perhaps the resources for repair we introduce in part III can then aid us in realizing a restored spiritual and physical landscape.

We begin the examination of our crisis of being in what is likely the oldest document in the Bible's Old Testament: Job. It is not necessary to have been raised in the church or even exposed to much biblical thought to be familiar with the basic flow of the story; Job's reach exceeds the confines of biblical scholarship. The story is often cast in terms of suffering and what to do—and what not to do—when things seem to have unjustly beset one. The book appears to be prompted by some rather universal questions regarding prosperity, justice, guilt and innocence, suffering, and ultimately meaning—most of which the story fails to directly address or adequately answer. The bulk of Job's forty-two chapters consists of an increasingly tense debate between Job and his three friends who all endeavor to produce a reason for Job's suffering. Job relentlessly asserts his innocence while the friends contend this simply cannot be: a man innocent in the eyes of God does not simply lose his oxen, donkeys, sheep, camels, servants, and family in one day, only to be followed by the loss of one's own health. A transgression has most certainly occurred in order to warrant such misfortune.

The book of Job has many layers for theologians to discuss and many questions for anyone to mull, most of which don't concern our present purpose. We can simply note that Job has been denied the flourishing wholeness and delight which indicate *shalom*. At issue, then, for Job and his counsellors, is what would constitute the way back to *shalom*. If the innocent (which the author affirms in the opening chapters definitively include Job) can be made to suffer and—as Job affirms—the guilty are frequently treated to prosperity, where is the sense of any kind of order in the world? How can a proper conception of the way things ought to be be formulated?

Job appears to struggle with the discrepancy more honestly than his friends who appear to already have figured out the ways of man and God in the world. At heart, the book of Job describes a spiritual crisis which, like all variations of our specific dilemmas, has at its core the question: How are we to understand and balance life in this world as both creators (in however limited a sense) and creations? The answer for Job's three friends is obvious: do something; take action; act in the ways the conventional wisdom of society and history have declared will alleviate the crisis. Even Job's wife encourages him to action—anything to eliminate the suffering. The encouragement to set the record straight by admitting fault demonstrates that "Job's friends believed that God's calculus was their own, that he made his plans with regard to our very human ideas of justice and fair play."[16] The intent—as our efforts always are at their deepest level—was to affect a realignment of the whole of life through some kind of action.

The biggest surprise in the book of Job, and hence likely its most profound lesson, is how some of the most crucial questions of existence are *not* answered and seemingly not even acknowledged by God. When God finally enters the debate in chapter 38, he directly addresses Job out of the whirlwind and launches into a long soliloquy on creation. God demands that Job account for his presence at the forming of the earth's foundations, the sea, daylight, snow, rain, and all variety of created beings. Of course, the demand is sarcastic and rhetorical: Job had nothing to do with the act of the creation of the earth. In fact, creation is affirmed as being accomplished regardless of humankind's presence:

> Who has cleft a channel for the torrents of rain,
> And a way for the thunderbolt,
> To bring rain on a land where no man is,
> In the desert in which there is no man,
> To satisfy the waste and desolate land,
> And to make the ground sprout with the grass? (Job 38:25–27)

God satisfies the waste and desolate land, the land which humankind doesn't even occupy. The image is closely related to the Western image of making the desert blossom which we frequently encountered in chapter two. But in Job, there is no sense that humans even have the capacity to accomplish such a task. This is something God affects apart from any human occupation or utility. God's speech is actually directed *against* such confidence in our efforts to establish meaning. As Bill McKibben writes in a small booklet about Job, "God seems untroubled by the notion of a place where no man lives—in fact, God says he makes it rain there even though it has no human benefit at all. God makes the *wilderness blossom*—what stronger way could there be to make the point, what more overpowering fact to resist the notion that we are forever at the center of all affairs."[17] We are treated here, in God's speech and Job's response, to the exposure and remaking of a soul's landscape in terms of the creator's intended order. Humanness, in this light, is contrasted with the judgment of Job's three friends who could only adhere to their culture's conventional wisdom.

As one of the world's ancient texts, Job communicates that, first and foremost, existence is not about what we do, how much we accomplish, or how we labor. It is not about Job's perfect attendance record which opens

16. McKibben, *Comforting Whirlwind*, 25.

17. McKibben, *Comforting Whirlwind*, 28; emphasis original.

the narrative nor about some kind of contrived repentance he is encouraged to engage in in the midst of his suffering. We cannot control the ebb and flow of life by how well or how much we apply ourselves. Job was not told what to do in order to restore life to the way he perceived it ought to be, he simply oriented himself away from human speech and knowledge and the self-reinforcement of picking and choosing what we see and hear. As McKibben concludes regarding Job: "Why are we here? At least in part, or so God implies in his answer to Job, to be a part of the great play of life, but only a part. We are not bigger than everything else—we are *like* everything else, meant to be exuberant and wild and *limited*."[18] This is about the fundamental sense of our *being*, not as capable creators or little gods, but as those who can only stand in silence and embrace the unknown.

There is a significant scale to the human questions posed in Job, just as there is to the caution presented in Genesis 11. Just as the story of Job surpasses the boundaries of his own time and situation, the account of the Tower of Babel reveals a long-standing problem with our conception of technology. This tower, regardless of when or where it may have been conceived, is emblematic of the efforts and accomplishments of humanity and thus plays an important role as warning. In the context of biblical history, the events recorded in the eleventh chapter of Genesis are laid down in a crucial moment of humanity's developing sense of being. In the flow of the biblical narrative, the Genesis chapters following the transgression of limits in chapter 3 have been recording one scene of dissolution after another: Cain and Abel, increasing corruption, the devastation of the flood. Coming to chapter 11, we are at the verge of a watershed because, "The Tower of Babel story is the last great judgment that befell mankind in primeval times."[19] The opening of chapter 12 in Genesis crosses a significant threshold as it establishes the Abrahamic covenant through which all nations on earth are to be blessed. For many Old Testament scholars, chapter 12 seems to be the point to which the author of Genesis has been hurrying all along.

This means that the first nine verses of Genesis 11 stand on the doorstep of the reason for the biblical narrative in the first place. This crucial placement should heighten our interest in the scene of humanity gathering on the plain of Shinar to begin their first major building project. There are at least three crucial aspects to this story which impinge on our purposes here: First, this is an intentional act of human effort to regain something that was lost in the fall at the garden. "Come, let us make bricks, and bake them thoroughly. . . . Come, let us build ourselves a city and a tower with its

18. McKibben, *Comforting Whirlwind*, 66; emphasis original.
19. Wenham, *Genesis 1–15*, 1:242.

top in the heavens . . ." (Gen 11:3–4). As human beings become more aware of their inherent creative capabilities, they reason that effort can accomplish their most significant end, thereby anticipating the Enlightenment thought by many millennia. This is not a haphazard occurrence: the bricks are made and baked in order to temper them, to give them permanence. And just as American Western settlement was always about the garden, this city and its tower are to reach the heavens—the dwelling place of God. This is but the first of countless applications of technology as a way back to Eden.

The second thing to note is that the purpose of building is to "make a name for ourselves." For ancient and what we often (disparagingly) label "primitive" cultures, "naming" is an especially critical act. To name is to actually bestow identity and therefore meaning on someone or something. Until this effort to build a monument to human ability, we get the sense of a wandering people, undoubtedly trying to reestablish a sense of the way things ought to be following the estrangement from their Creator. This purpose reveals a central problem with all of human technology, which for us has become technological determinism: it stems from created beings as an attempt at a path to meaning. Our identity is not something *given*, in this line of thought, but something built as we apply ourselves to more and better techniques with an eye toward permanence. This continues to address our efforts at identity formation through personal accomplishment.

Finally, we should take note in this story that God intervenes to thwart the purposes of humankind because "this is only the beginning of what they will do. And nothing they propose to do will now be impossible for them" (Gen 11:6). We need to avoid the conclusion that God is somehow threatened by this construction project. The author of Genesis specifically notes that God had to "come down" in order to see the city and tower that were supposedly high enough to reach into his realm. This is actually an act of mercy; an act to preserve the truth of what it means to be a created being. In the Babel account, humanity "is seen organizing and arrogating to himself essentially divine prerogatives."[20] We simply do not have this capacity and the results have always been, and can only be, a bastardized form of *shalom,* which is always but a poor reflection of the Creator's intended order. "[S]o building the tower, an arrogant undertaking in itself, may be the forerunner of yet further trespasses on the divine prerogative. . . . Only God may plan without limit. Man is not supposed to emulate his Creator in this way."[21] If nothing we propose is impossible then we simply hasten down a path in the *opposite* direction of the source of true being.

---

20. Wenham, *Genesis 1–15,* 1:242.

21. Wenham, *Genesis 1–15,* 1:240–41.

The protective thwarting of the Babel attempt is accomplished in Genesis 11 through the confusion of language. By way of contrast, Luke writes in Acts 2 of a bewildered multitude who came together to hear the early disciples "speak in his own language" (Acts 2:6). In listing a variety of language groups which are all able to hear and understand the same thing at the same time, Luke is figuring the reversal of the confusion and dispersal at Babel. Central to the Lukan account is that this reversal is accomplished not through human ability and ingenuity but precisely as the disciples *wait* and *receive*. The Creator thus reasserts his unique capacity to provide, unilaterally, a sense of identity as he here forms a new people.

It is not as if the scene on the plain of Shinar serves to forever solve the problem of the human inclination to prioritize their own efforts. As the final episode of a condition of the whole of humanity before biblical history begins to dial in on the establishment of a covenant people in Genesis 12, the Tower of Babel scene reveals much about ongoing patterns of acquiring identity and purpose in what we build. The pattern is further exemplified in the Israelites' building of the temple. For the Israelite people, the temple became the center of their identity as a nation and the "people of God." The temple housed their greatest national treasures, provided a point to which a dispersed population could converge, was the location of their most important national holidays. The temple was the very dwelling place of God and therefore the most sacred location in the world and the place to experience the restoration of order to creation: the forgiveness of sin.

But for all of these reasons and more, the temple became—like the Tower of Babel before it—problematic precisely because of the way a built environment would shape a people's understanding of and approach to God. When King David first proposed building a temple as a dwelling place for the Ark of the Covenant, the nation's symbol for the presence of God, he was rebuffed, with God essentially saying, "I never asked you to do this."[22] The temple, rather than the Creator, soon became an object of the people's confidence. The mere presence of the building itself caused a nation to believe that it could continue to contribute to the dissolution of creation with no consequences. The prophet Jeremiah had to warn the nation that their confidence in the built was misplaced: "Do not trust in these deceptive words: 'This is the temple of the Lord, the temple of the Lord, the temple of the Lord'" (Jer 7:4).

There is every indication that while the nation of Israel was oppressing the poor and ignoring the precepts of justice, further forming a world that was not as it was supposed to be, they were still active in temple worship,

22. See 2 Sam 7:7.

as if this structure somehow absolved them of any culpability.[23] When the disciples of Jesus—as good Jews were wont to do—marveled at the majesty of the temple in Matthew 24, Jesus quickly dismissed their admiration by telling them it was all about to come down. It is not that the temple itself was inherently evil; God's glory had actually inhabited Solomon's temple complex. It is simply that it shared the quality that all of our efforts to construct reality share: It became a source of identity not centered in the bestowal of a Creator but in the act of a created. Babel and the temple both share the qualities of demonstrating our confidence in the human-built environment as a source of identity; a condition I am arguing becomes the landscape of the soul which in turn requires ever-increasing effort by us in order to restore any sense of things as they ought to be.

We lack the necessary resources to meaningfully participate in the repair of the world because our way of being in the world has always been working in ways contrary to the source of *shalom*. We seem to have lost our capacity to orient ourselves to creation as a figure of our own createdness and limitation. As Wendell Berry so astutely observed, "Because of its inclination to be proud and greedy, human character needs the practical deference toward things greater than itself; this is, I think, a religious deference. Also, for reasons of self-interest and our own survival, we need wilderness as a standard. Wilderness gives us the indispensable pattern and measure of sustainability."[24] It is because we internalize the external in forming identity that the wilderness kind of environment can inform us toward a sustainability of *spirit* as well.

The situation faced by Job, the attempt at building Babel and the undue confidence placed in the temple as a source of identity helps direct us to a central biblical category critical for being: the idea of righteousness. At first blush, this may seem like a strange concept to come to as the idea of righteousness typically evokes a sense of adherence to an ethical standard which would somehow entail our efforts to demonstrate. At some point and at some level it would still have to come back to our abilities to think things through and apply those thoughts to certain actions. It is my belief that we understand righteousness much too narrowly and that this idea reveals much more than we realize about our way of being in the world and about our access to the necessary resources for transcending our prioritizing of human efforts to be our own sense of meaning.

23. See, for example, Isa 1:11–17; 58:2–14.
24. Berry, *Another Turn of the Crank*, 40–41.

The concept of righteousness litters the entirety of the biblical canon. God requires righteousness[25] and God is the very embodiment of the idea.[26] There is a form of righteousness conceived by religious authority which entails a strict adherence to the ethical and moral standards of Old Testament law. Especially in the prophetic writings of the Old Testament, we sense a focus on the priority of *being* righteous. But Jesus upends much of the conventional thought when he appears to prioritize the sick and sinful over the righteous,[27] emphasizes a longing for rather than a strict possession of righteousness,[28] and proclaims that on some level God treats the righteous and unrighteous in similar ways.[29] Confusion is multiplied when Jesus tells his audience that access to the kingdom of God requires a righteousness that *surpasses* the strict observance of the Pharisees, and yet informs those same Pharisees that tax collectors and prostitutes—the exact opposite of righteous law-abiders—are the very ones entering the same kingdom.[30] It is not always easy to sort out in a way which is helpful and instructive for our way of being in the world.

The biblical notion of righteousness does not appear in the ancient world out of a vacuum. The idea actually has a history of development which supplies a conceptual framework for us to understand why this is such a central idea and how it resources our sense of being. The Greek term is *dikaiosune,* which for Plato defines the basic structure of both the state and the human soul so that his idea of utopia is grounded in the concept.[31] Righteousness is "anchored in the soul of man, who inwardly comes to what is *proper to himself, in inner order* and the *harmony* of spiritual virtues" and is thus a state of spiritual balance or harmony.[32] The Jewish philosopher Philo, writing much closer to the time of the New Testament, reflects this idea of righteousness by claiming it has its origins in the soul and comes into being when the three parts of the soul (intellect, will or desire, and emotion) act in harmony.[33]

Modern Christians are inclined to view righteousness as simply adhering to a standard of law and ethical conduct. The concept is much deeper

25. See Gen 18:19; 1 Kgs 10:9; Isa 35:15–16.

26. See Ps 71, which is a celebration of the righteousness of God, and e.g., Isa 45:24; Jer 23:6.

27. Mark 2:17; Luke 15:7.

28. Matt 5:6.

29. Matt 5:45.

30. See Matt 5:20 and Matt 21:31.

31. Kittel, *Theological Dictionary of the New Testament* (hereafter, *TDNT*), II:183, 192.

32. Kittel, *TDNT* II:183, 193; emphasis added.

33. Kittel, *TDNT* II:154.

and richer than this simplistic formula. It is not primarily a standard or law that is imparted upon the world, but is inherent in the very nature of being. Righteousness is the axiomatic, unshakable foundation of all human life, and so speaks to the created order—to the way things ought to be.[34] The idea of a basic rightness and harmony is illustrated by the way the term can be applied to correct weights and measures: there is a certain inner integrity or rightness in the accurate measurement of an ounce or a mile; what one might call that measurement's righteousness. Likewise, it is used to designate a quality which is fitting to the earth: its being fertile—basically, what is fitting or proper.[35] So while righteousness certainly issues in certain acts, those acts are not extraneous to us, a law we have to come to understand and obey through long years of hard practice. Righteous acts are acts which epitomize harmony and which emerge from a rightness of the created order in a full-orbed political, legal, social, and religious sense.

Righteousness is given its fullest expression and deepest understanding by being applied to God as the Creator of all being. God's action is a perfect whole, and from God's whole and consistent state of being which issues in an integrity of his acting, "righteousness" emerges in the very existence of humanity as well as the assurance of humanity's ongoing place in creation.[36] To call God righteous is to refer to the "one who is infallibly constant in the normative self-determination of his own nature."[37] To speak of the concept as something fitted to its nature and purpose, something appropriate or conforming to order, is to invoke the realization that God in himself as Creator operates from and therefore establishes the only fully consistent rightness or proper functioning of creation. For this reason, the Bible further connects righteousness closely to the concepts of *shalom*, salvation, and covenant—qualities that flow from the very "isness" of God the Creator. God himself, and therefore all of his acts—specifically creation— are righteous because they fit into a harmonious whole, stemming from a certain ground of being.

What we need to realize from this brief and perhaps wandering survey is that, at its core, righteousness designates that which is proper or right according to the fundamental ordering of the universe and the ground of its very being. Righteousness certainly entails certain acts, but it is first and foremost the harmony, inner order, and fitness of creation because these

34. Brown, *New International Dictionary of New Testament Theology* (hereafter, *NIDNTT*), 3:353.

35. Kittel, *TDNT* II:184, 185.

36. Kittel, *TDNT* II:176.

37. Kittel, *TDNT* II:185.

emanate from the kind of Creator who is himself righteous. This state has to inhere in a capable Creator and could never be produced by the creation itself, of which we are a part. *Thayer's Greek Lexicon* concisely defines righteousness as "the state of him who is such as he ought to be."[38] The quality is therefore one of existing in the condition in which we ought to exist according to the pattern or state of being which undergirds the very reality of creation. The apostle Paul shows no hesitation in claiming that no one exists in this condition of ought or rightness because they trade the harmony inherent in the Creator for a poor substitute of their own making.[39]

What is proper or right and therefore in balance and harmony with the ground of being—righteous; the realization of our own ought—cannot be attained through any effort on our part. This is difficult for even North American Christians to fully embrace due to the American ethos that surrounds us. Most of us continue to strive to achieve our own ought because we exemplify all the ways which ascribe meaning and value to progress and production. Righteousness, that which undergirds and explains what we pursue in salvation and *shalom*, is actually built into the very fabric of creation as right being, not right doing. This in part explains God's immediate move to invoke the creative act in the midst of Job's issues. This is also why Paul writes about "religious outsiders" attaining righteousness in contrast to the "religious insiders" who fail to attain their ought. The first did not pursue it or work at it like the second.[40] We cannot create our own existence or world as we think it ought to be. We are simply not creators with that capacity.

Our task is to be rightly oriented to the source of rightness, not work harder at producing it. A repaired, restored world has its source in the Creator, not the accumulated wealth and progress of the created. Righteousness—our rightness, our ought—is *created* apart from effort.[41] This is the point realized by Job and figured in the Tower of Babel as a formulative story. Until we learn to stop functioning as if we could create our own well-ordered world and existence we will continue to languish in a wasted landscape of our own making—as a reality of both the earth and the soul.

Our tendency is to limit righteousness to the realm of a religious concept, holding significance only for those interested in cultivating a specifically religious life. It gains its proper depth, however, when we recognize that is has more to do with the harmony inherent in the entire substructure of the creation as the act of God which declared it "very good." In direct contrast to

38. Thayer, *Greek-English Lexicon of the New Testament*, 148.

39. See Rom 3:10-12.

40. See Rom 9:33.

41. See Rom 4:3, 6, 13.

this original state of being, we have established the tenor of our culture as one bent on grasping for our own most significant dignity and meaning through the human-built and humanly achieved. This grasping through productive progress cheapens and negates the creation in the way it was designed to exist. We simply do not have the capacity as members of creation to in turn create on a meaningful enough level. Our acts cannot flow from a self-determinative nature. As Old Testament scholar Walter Brueggemann points out,

> We can't secure our own existence by our productivity and hustle. . . The capacity to secure our existence has not been turned over to us. The Lord has retained that. That, of course, is what we do not like. How convenient if it had been turned over to us. What has apparently been turned over to us is the capacity to destroy ourselves. But the Lord has not placed within our hands the comparable power to make our lives safe, whole, free. This is kept by God. . .[42]

I earlier introduced the idea of the faith exchange. What it appears we have now exchanged is the reality of the way things ought to function for the basic unreality of our humanly constructed environments—socially, physically, environmentally, economically, etc. Our modern form of Christianity disparages the world we inhabit through an attempted focus on a transcendent spirituality bent on the afterlife. In a somewhat paradoxical condition, due to a lack of understanding concerning the ground of being that undergirds all of reality and the oughtness which is the creation's harmony, Christians are daily invested in the very acts of production which perpetuate their own growing unreality and further distance them from utter reality which would turn a true spirituality into an interest in the repair of culture and creation.

Ours is a culture which has learned to ascribe a certain permanence and importance to what we can or have built. In so doing, we often attempt to bring the unreal into the realm of the real. At issue with such acrobatics is how the unreal—the contingent, temporary creations of contingent beings—then becomes ultimate (an ought) to us and eventually serves to damage the sense of what is actual reality. The dissolution and confusion that becomes our world, as for Job and Babel, then issues in an angry, frustrated, broken soul which has difficulty sorting out the real—our being—from the unreal. Our world bases reality on technology and economy: what we build and accomplish and what we earn and consume. These become the elements of the real world. Individually, it is often manifest in image, reputation, honors, respectability—what we've done with our lives. Reality

42. Brueggemann, *Living Toward a Vision*, 57.

for Western culture is exemplified by our progress, which is internalized, our being fundamentally religious animals, as a similar reality of the soul.

Before turning in the next chapter to the ways in which our crisis of being impinges upon our crisis of acting as we turn our attention to involvement with the repair of the world, I want to conclude this chapter with some of the perspective possible in what we call *wilderness*—those small portions of land still available in which humankind is but a temporary visitor and which continue to exist in an undeveloped condition. "Wilderness areas depict the story of a people deciding to slow themselves down before taking everything, to engage the world with humility rather than just desire."[43] A wild and isolated canyon or lofty mountain peak has repeatedly brought me out of myself and the dark thoughts that I have somehow missed life as it ought to be. The wild and unengineered-by-us provide the necessary components to provide the perspective that this is something made by another who is not, nor ever could be, myself. It is the reality beyond our capacity to create which causes to fall to the wayside our paltry and limited creative efforts to define meaning and existence. It is the scale of such places, their silence and solitude and sublimity, that surpasses the smallness of life. The contrast between a great canyon or high peak and the things we form through technology or economic processes highlights how the latter work in our lives to create a basic *un*reality at odds with the rightness and oughtness of a creation of order. But this is anticipating our work in part III.

---

43. Hausdoeffer, "Wild Partnership," 245.

Chapter 5

The Repair of the World

A PRIMARY CLAIM WHICH I have been pursuing is that life is embedded in and affected by landscape, regardless of what that particular landscape might entail. We are shaped by the world around us to intuit certain value judgments based on that which we are exposed to. As is probably clear by this point, my own landscape during my formative years embodied the tension of the two sides of this book: an experience steeped in humanly constructed settings of industrial extraction while being immersed in an immensity of untrammeled natural environs. This was simply a reality of growing up in the rural West. While our fathers spent their days in the underground or strip mines and drilling fields of southwest Wyoming, we all spent weekends and holidays fishing, hiking, floating, climbing, hunting, and backpacking in what were still uncrowded and wild areas. It still seems rather contradictory that Westerners can place such a high value on enjoying their natural surroundings while they earn a better than average living tearing its heart out. The West has always been of two minds.

By the time we were old enough to drive, my friends and I would travel the nearly 100 miles to South Pass along the Continental Divide where we would fish, hike, camp, and which we later utilized as a convenient jumping off point for backpacking in the high wilderness of the Wind River Range. There is even now a small historic mining ghost town at South Pass City which serves as a tourist attraction, playing on the nostalgia of the Old West. South Pass is a relatively well-watered and easy crossing of what has been called the "Spine of the Continent," the Continental Divide, which separates two of the primary western watersheds: the Colorado and Missouri Rivers.

THE REPAIR OF THE WORLD   113

Generally lacking the steep ascents over the divide which are typical of Colorado and Montana, the crossing at South Pass comes at the end of generally friendly gradients from both the east and the west. For this reason, its discovery in 1812 by a fur-trading party became monumental in the period of western expansion.

In his Pulitzer Prize-winning history of western expansion, *Across the Wide Missouri*, Bernard DeVoto describes in colorful detail a momentous crossing of South Pass that occurred on July 4, 1836. The crossing on that day was important because it was likely not only the first time a wagon was pulled across the Continental Divide on the way west, but the crossing party contained the first white women who had come to the mountains. Missionaries bound for the Oregon Territory, the Reverend Henry Hart, his wife Eliza Spalding, and Marcus and Narcissa Whitman, were greeted on the fifth of July by a rowdy band of fifteen mounted Indians who came at the party at a full gallop, whooping war cries, and firing what turned out to be welcome shots to their trading friends who had led the party and were headed for the rendezvous at Horse Creek.

In characteristically lucid language, DeVoto wrote:

> There are significant scenes in Western history but few so significant as this moment of uproar and wonder in a sagebrush sea. A Sioux chief is supposed to have once said that his people were not alarmed till they saw plows in the emigrant wagons and his remark has served innumerable chroniclers who may forget that the Sioux had no way of knowing what a plow was. A truer symbol for the chief would be these two women surrounded by Indians and men in buckskin, in Oregon, west of the Continental Divide.[1]

The rush to the farther West would soon begin and millions of settlers would cross the Rocky Mountains through this very opening. Oregon in the far northwest, nearly as far as one could get from the settled culture of the east, would become a state just twenty-four years later. South Pass on the Continental Divide, part of the setting for my own western experience, still exists as both *idyllic* and *iconic*: It continues to border the wild, unoccupied Wind River Mountains to the north and a vast expanse of high desert running for 100 miles southward; and it still marks a critical opening in time for the progress of a nation on its way to the riches of Oregon and California and the Deseret Kingdom of Utah.

The divide at South Pass serves as an appropriate figure for us as we find ourselves at a sort of divide in this current chapter as we endeavor to

---

1. DeVoto, *Across the Wide Missouri*, 247.

participate in cultivating a meaningful condition of being, which will issue forth in actions that promote rather than further detract from the repair of the world. Part I represents a climb through the Western cultural conception of meaning accrued through progress and effort to the point of crisis—internally and externally—in which we currently find ourselves. The previous chapter ended with a conception of the ought, or rightness, of the world which would flow from a people who are such as they ought to be, understood as a foundational harmoniousness embedded in the very nature of being. The current chapter begins with a deeper dive into the vision of the condition of *shalom* as a defining category of rightness: peace, order, and harmony on a cosmic scale. As was previously emphasized, how one conceives of *being* determines how one *acts*. Rightness, ought, *shalom*, is either inherent in the ground of creation, being embedded there by a capable Creator, or it must be built and established by the efforts of human ingenuity.

Our location in this book can be envisioned as standing on a high ridge between two watersheds, separating the flow of water into the lowlands of activity. From this dividing point where we are developing a vision of a whole and flourishing condition for safe and meaningful existence for the whole of the created order, the sources of life divide to flow one way or another. Part I represents one side of the divide, where we continue to enact a heroic vision of accomplishing and producing more under our vision of progress in order to make the world as we think it ought to be. Part III will represent the other side, a different watershed which I believe embraces an alternative way of realizing a vision of rightness and *shalom* which is embedded in, and therefore realized from, a reality as created and superintended by Another.

The figures exploring the way around and off this divide are Job and the inhabitants on the plain of Shinar. Both find themselves in a world of dissolution where things are not as they should be. Both Job and the builders of the Tower of Babel desperately *want* things to be made right; to experience a context of flourishing wholeness where life can find a sense of value and its corresponding meaning. So, one undertakes a purposeful effort to build a way back to restoration while another discovers a restored life through a vision of the rightness of the Creator and his works. This is about a right ordering in the midst of things falling apart; a correspondence with the way things ought to be. And just as righteousness is rooted in the proper ordering of the world, so the idea of *shalom* speaks to a way of being—an *ought*.

Hebrew *shalom*, most often rendered "peace," is a biblical theme which, like the concept of righteousness, was much richer in its application than the simple idea we today tend to associate with its one-word translation. Unlike our modern conceptions of peace, *shalom* is not primarily used in reference to a relationship between people but indicates a state or condition from which flows everything necessary for both land and people to flourish, and which can thus be identified as the supreme good. *Shalom* is "a general expression of a very comprehensive nature," pointing to general well-being, which would therefore encompass all of cultural life together.[2] So the rabbinic vision of the usage of *shalom* in Israelite culture maintains that the very continuation of the universe depends on the condition.[3] We are dealing in this concept with features inherent in and necessary for creation to be ordered as it was designed and intended to be. *Shalom* is that which corresponds to the normal (intended by the condition of creation) state of things and it extends to the universe as a whole.[4]

We can begin to see how we can minimize the idea of this peace and rob it of its richer significance when we limit it to referring only to an individual as describing the absence of conflict with another or a mere inward feeling. The idea is far more frequently used of groups as an emphatically social concept which draws our attention to what should be a culturally formative idea. As communally and socially conceived, *shalom* speaks to well-being in a material, political, and social sense.[5] As Walter Brueggemann points out in his reflections on the theme, "*Shalom* is the substance of the biblical vision of one community embracing all creation. It refers to all those resources and factors which make communal harmony joyous and effective. [It is] security and prosperity granted to a whole community—young and old, rich and poor, powerful and dependent."[6]

Because *shalom* extends to universals and is fixed in the rightness of the created order, like righteousness it is not within the capacity of human beings to bring it about. *Shalom* as a state has its impetus in the perfection of creation which is the direct result of a self-referent Creator who elicits *shalom* from chaos. For the Hebrew prophets, then, the word is the final signifier of the relation between the Creator and creation, which is the result of his initiation of a covenant relationship: the relationship in which the Creator (Yahweh) recruits humanity to participate in the repair of the world. Yahweh is the source of covenant, and covenant inaugurates a relationship of *shalom*. The goods and values associated with *shalom* are thus always referred to with Yahweh as their source.[7] When Gideon named his

2. Kittel, *TDNT* II:400–2.

3. Kittel, *TDNT* II:409.

4. Kittel, *TDNT* II:412.

5. Kittel, *TDNT* II:406, 402.

6. Brueggemann, *Living Toward a Vision*, 16.

7. Kittel, *TDNT* II:403. See Isa 54:10; Ezek 34:25; 37:26. The entirety of Ps 85 is a

altar "The Lord is *shalom*" in Judges 6:24, the "confession embraces all that the pious tried to say about Yahweh."[8] The prophetic vision of a repaired and restored world condition was exemplified by the use of *shalom* as a formative concept and signified their hope of the future, which is what made the prophetic office what it was.[9]

Hebrew culture and language provided a concept for something as all-embracing as how the world ought to be, but it is an idea certainly not limited to this specific ancient Near Eastern people. This vision of life and the world we inhabit has threads which are apparent in the fabric of many diverse cultures. The idea is not merely biblical; it is deeply human. We can consider two such examples which are especially revealing in that they stem from indigenous peoples which inhabit the same setting as that which propelled the Western paradigm of progress: the ideas central to Cherokee and Navajo tribal peoples. Randy Woodley is a Professor of Faith and Culture at George Fox Seminary, as well as a member of the Keetoowah Cherokee Tribe. From his own indigenous experience, he describes the Cherokee concept of well-being as represented by the word *Eloheh*: "*Eloheh* is one of several Cherokee words describing the concept of the Harmony Way or a *shalom*-type construct."[10]

Woodley indicates the parallels with the biblical concept of *shalom* by pointing out that the Cherokee term refers not only to their religion but is a much broader concept that includes land, history, law, and culture. "*Eloheh* is translated as 'balance' or sometimes as the 'Harmony Way'. . . . The Harmony Way is also said to be a way of *Duyukta* which means something close to justice or righteousness."[11] For ancient Hebrews, righteousness epitomizes harmony through a correspondence with what is fitting in creation. The close resemblance between *Eloheh* and *shalom* provide a sense of a vision of human existence which transcends time and culture to address basic ways of healthy being in the world.

In the American southwest, the Navajo concept of *hozho* resonates closely with both *shalom* and *Eloheh* to demonstrate how we are addressing categories of meaningful and healthy existence not as a specifically religious experience but a quality sought by virtually every culture throughout history. According to anthropologist Clyde Kluckhohn, who provided some of the most exhaustive studies of Navajo culture, *hozho* "is probably the central

---

celebration of Yahweh as the source of *shalom*.

8. Kittel, *TDNT* II:403.

9. Kittel, *TDNT* II:405. See Isa 11:1–9; Hos 2:20–23; Amos 9:13–15.

10. Woodley, *Shalom and the Community of Creation*, 71.

11. Woodley, *Shalom and the Community of Creation*, 71.

idea in Navajo religious thinking. . . . In various contexts it is best translated as 'beautiful,' 'harmonious,' 'good,' 'blessed,' 'pleasant,' and 'satisfying.'"[12] It is not primarily a theoretical idea which exists only in an ephemeral realm, as the prefix *ho-* refers to the environment as a whole. The idea thus refers to a positive ideal environment which is all-inclusive.[13] To be in *hozhoji* is to walk a path of beauty; a path of peace and harmony.

The idea of a world where things are as they ought to be envelopes all of human culture. Randy Woodley recognizes close parallels between Hebrew *shalom* and indigenous constructs of the Harmony Way throughout the world as emphasizing a holistic and integrative worldview. By way of contrast, "Western worldviews tend to be less integrative and more reflective of modernity's extrinsic categorization, as well as having an emphasis on the individual at the expense of the community."[14] On the one hand, we can recognize in our culture's ways of acting that this vision of reality is what we have been building toward. At the same time, we have to be honest with the ways our view of meaning and value actually serve to push us away from *shalom*. In the words of English theologian Colin Gunton, "Modernity is the realm of paradoxes: an era which has sought freedom, and bred totalitarianism; which has taught us our insignificance in the vastness of the universe, and yet sought to play god with that same universe; which has sought to control the world, and yet let loose forces that may destroy the earth."[15]

In our inherent and natural desire for a whole and flourishing life— *shalom*-like—the real failure of Western culture is the fact that we cannot get there from here. Being embedded in creation as we are, we do not have the capacity to design or create our own ought. To function on the basis of a religious adherence to progress in order to build a world of ought through human ingenuity and ability is to hasten a move away from a path of harmony. A rather bold contention, to be sure, but one that is borne out by the actual conditions of our built society, which contains little resonance with the vision of righteousness and *shalom*. It is perhaps ironic to consider that a full sense of *shalom* can actually be gleaned from viewing some of the elements of contemporary culture which are in stark contrast to that for which we actually desire as the ought of existence.

Colin Gunton identifies one such reality in our contemporary culture as that of *disengagement*: "Disengagement means standing apart from each other and the world as external, as mere object." This means that "we use

---

12. As quoted in Farella, *Main Stalk*, 159.
13. Farella, *Main Stalk*, 159.
14. Woodley, *Shalom and the Community of Creation*, 74.
15. Gunton, *One the Three, and the Many*, 13.

the other as an instrument, as the mere means for realizing our will, and not as in some way integral to our being." Gunton sees this as the heart of our current technocratic attitude wherein the world exists to do with exactly as we choose, with the result being that "we do not seek in the world for what is true and good and beautiful, but create our truth and values for ourselves."[16] The primary problem with the disengagement of the modern ethos is the way in which humanity and the world are torn apart as a result of the narrowing of all claims for knowledge to the narrowly scientific. From Gunton's—and others'—perspective, we are left isolated in a world empty of personal meaning because "human living is good, appropriate to the way things really are, when it conforms itself to the source of all being, the form of the good."[17] Our current efforts are precisely acts of *non*conformity to that which is otherwise inherent in the created world.

A corresponding condition which follows from disengagement and further illustrates what *shalom* would entail by way of contrast is *displacement*. While unable to displace religious belief per se, the modern project has succeeded in displacing God as the focus for the unity and meaning of being. What once would have been sought from the Creator of the condition of *shalom* has been relegated to the realm of human reason and ability. God as the ground of being and source of the rightness of the world has been displaced as redundant, leaving us only the self-referent point of the rational mind which, in Berry's words quoted earlier, shakes more than it can hold. "God was no longer needed to account for the coherence and meaning of the world, so that the seat of rationality and meaning became not the world, but the human reason and will, which thus *displace* God or the world."[18]

The displacement of God as the source of a flourishing condition for individual and social life means that Western culture has been forced into an attempt to build a culture out of the resources of its own technology. While we are continually convinced that the experience has been largely successful, it has in reality resulted in conditions that bear little resemblance to a meaningful existence. "Modernity promised us a culture of unintimidated, curious, rational, self-reliant individuals, and it provided . . . a herd society, a race of anxious, timid, conformist 'sheep,' and a culture of utter banality."[19] In distinction from a context of wholeness, delight, and the fulfilling sense of individual giftedness and contribution, we have instead the coercion of a homogenous culture which has unleashed forces that grind us

---

16. Gunton, *One, the Three, and the Many*, 14.

17. Gunton, *One, the Three, and the Many*, 16.

18. Gunton, *One, the Three, and the Many*, 28; emphasis original.

19. Robert Pippin, quoted by Gunton, *One, the Three, and the Many*, 13.

into a conformist herd. As Walter Brueggemann points out in contrasting contemporary culture with a vision of *shalom*, "We are driven, controlled, manipulated people, and we spend our lives doing what we must and what we do not choose." It doesn't sound like the way things ought to be when we recognize "that the powers that coerce us are powerful and alive, and for some reason we are not free to live our lives toward joy. We spend our time crying, satisfying others, measuring up, meeting quotas."[20]

Brueggemann's assessment is that *shalom* consists of "a massive protest against the central values by which our world operates. The world depends on coercion. The world depends on fragmented loyalties."[21] The power and centrality of cultural values which mitigate against *shalom* place humanity in a rather tenuous position because, while the vision of *shalom* appears fulfilling on one level, there is still the sense that we prefer not to relinquish our own sway over the processes leading to a full and meaningful life. "It is no wonder that we resolve boldly to change toward *shalom*, and at the same time we refuse with equal fervor to change at all. It has always been so with the vision. We have not yet decided whether or not we want uncoerced, unfragmented lives."[22] We therefore find ourselves in a not-entirely-unique position in twenty-first-century America as humans have historically been drawn to alternative visions of *shalom* which depend on human definitions and abilities.

It was a condition present even in ancient Israel. While the Hebrew prophets attached themselves to the vision of a time when *shalom* would be the world's reality, they also inherently recognized those instances when this hoped-for condition was the false posturing of human efforts to build up a world of rightness. Writing early in the sixth century BC, the prophet Jeremiah found himself in the midst of a prophetic and priestly leadership who had determined that their fasting and sacrifices would secure them the sought-after *shalom*. Yahweh assures Jeremiah that there is no such peace which stems from "a lying vision" and "the delusions of their own minds."[23] Later, in chapter 28, Jeremiah must again publicly confront another prophet who was assuring the nation of Israel of peace when there was no peace forthcoming. A late contemporary of Jeremiah, Ezekiel also confronts a humanly contrived vision of *shalom*. In what could serve as a commentary on our own recent culture, Ezekiel invokes an image of false prophets

20. Brueggemann, *Living Toward a Vision*, 42, 43.
21. Brueggemann, *Living Toward a Vision*, 50.
22. Brueggemann, *Living Toward a Vision*, 52.
23. Jer 4:12–14.

proclaiming peace as those who "whitewash a wall."[24] The image applies to any culture bent on achieving its own ought which justifies actions under a thin veneer of progress and profitability. A century earlier, the prophet Micah confronted a peace that was not *shalom* but instead consisted of a false condition of safety because it existed in the midst of a people who, while confident in their relatedness to Yahweh, were actually distorting a right order of things through accumulation, bloodshed, and bribery.[25]

Vivid contemporary parallels can also be drawn from the New Testament confrontation of both Jesus and Paul with the false peace of their condition under the Roman Empire. In the century before the arrival of Jesus as a new prophetic voice, Rome's most celebrated poet, Virgil, invoked the worldwide condition of *shalom* under the reign of Augustus. The *Pax Romana* (*pax* being Latin for "peace") was supposedly an era of absolute security. In Virgil's celebration of the Roman Peace achieved by Augustus there are "strong echoes of ancient longings for redemption, so pacification is achieved by the strong hand of the Emperor, so that this is haloed as the Golden Age."[26] Jesus establishes his role in direct opposition to this then-widely accepted vision of *shalom* when he tells his followers that the peace he brings is not the peace of the current world system.[27] When Paul opens each of his letters to the early churches by pairing "grace and peace" he is associating the condition of *shalom* not with a humanly contrived social order, but specifically with a gift of God. *Shalom* surpasses human abilities to fully understand and therefore to appropriate by effort.[28]

The contrast between the vision of *shalom* and the way in which modern Western culture would have us achieve that vision is granted particular clarity by Walter Brueggemann in his small book of reflections on *shalom*: *Living Toward a Vision.* Brueggemann draws from the events leading up to the Hebrew exodus from slavery in Egypt, an event which later formed the centerpiece of the Hebrew conception of Yahweh as their God. Specifically focusing on Exodus 5, where the oppressive conditions for the Hebrew slaves building pyramids for Egyptian pharaohs are at their height, Brueggemann contemporizes this people's plight in terms of their labor in the "brickyard." The image invokes the idea of "a place of competent production where the production schedule is taken with great seriousness." Production in these conditions naturally breeds coercion, unhappiness, a single-minded focus

---

24. Ezek 13:8–16.
25. Mic 3:5–12.
26. Kittel, *TDNT* II:402.
27. John 14:27.
28. See Phil 4:7.

on profit, oppression, enormous hostility, and ultimately hopelessness: "There will never be enough bricks to meet the quota. There will never be enough profits to satisfy the regime. There will never be enough power to get rid of the pressure and demand."[29]

Contemporary culture is implicated by this narrative because "we are all of us caught in a way of life that yields only frantic hostility and desperate effort, which cannot finally pay off." It matters little whether we are on the bottom of the scale as laborers "never having a zone of freedom," or the owners of the brickyard, obsessed with production, "always being inventive to find new ways of being anxious. It is a system that is obvious in public life, but which invades the dark recesses of our *piety* and our *morality*."[30] This is the very context in which the ancient Hebrews experienced the opening of *shalom* as Yahweh stepped in to secure a change which they were hopeless and helpless to produce. Brueggemann emphasizes, "Above all: this was not a change of attitude, nor simply of perception. This is a real change of power, a decisive redistribution of power, an abrupt disruption of political, economic arrangements." At the same time, it is not a change effected by more production and greater progress. "The supreme fact about us . . . is that our well-being, our salvation, our *shalom*, is hidden in God's holy mystery, which none of our best efforts can penetrate or explain."[31] We will revisit this idea of mystery in the next chapter.

Because the vision of *shalom—Eloheh, hozho*—as a figure for the repair of the world is so compelling, we must be continually vigilant to guard against our best efforts to build it into existence. I return again to the argument that we cannot exalt the built environment at the expense of the natural world as a way to *shalom* because *shalom* is itself embedded in the created order. In the words of Christopher Dawson in his work *Progress and Religion*,

> No civilization, however advanced, can afford to neglect those ultimate foundations in the life of nature and the natural reason on which its social welfare depends, for even the highest achievements of science and art and economic organization are powerless to avert decay, if the vital functions of the social organism become impaired. Apparent progress is often accompanied by a process of social degeneration or decomposition . . .[32]

---

29. Brueggemann, *Living Toward a Vision*, 54.

30. Brueggemann, *Living Toward a Vision*, 55; emphasis added.

31. Brueggemann, *Living Toward a Vision*, 56, 57.

32. Dawson, *Progress and Religion*, 62.

Exposure to the natural environment is critical precisely because of the way it mitigates against the false forms of identity our culture foists upon us. As Joseph Wood Krutch wrote, "No man in the middle of a desert or on top of a mountain ever fell victim to the delusion that he himself was nothing except the product of social forces, that all he needed was a proper orientation in his economic group, or that production per man hour was a true index of happiness."[33]

As we move further down from the divide on the other side of our attachment to progress, we can now begin to engage with the Creator's alternative vision for enfolding the world in *shalom* once again. A critical category for such reengagement is one I introduced in chapter 2: sabbath. As with the idea of righteousness, which was examined in the previous chapter, the idea of sabbath is often dismissed as a specific exercise of an antiquated religion which has little consequence in our modern, progressive, technology-paced culture. In so doing, however, we miss a category central to life as it was designed to be. While rarely understood and adequately practiced, the idea of sabbath maintains a prominent position in the Creator's design of the world.

We are at odds with the order of creation when we consider the category of sabbath as a mere sidenote to healthy spirituality. Unlike many of the Old Testament laws which had ethical stipulations that were paralleled in other cultures contemporaneous with the development of Israelite religion, the meaning and content of sabbath cannot be explained by any other non-Israelite model. It is something unique and exclusively controlled by Yahweh.[34] Sabbath expectations are found in all of the sources of the Mosaic law and has a broader witness than *any other* Old Testament command.[35] In the law's summary statement of the Decalogue (Exod 20:3–17; Deut 5:7–12), the commandment regarding sabbath serves as a bridge between expectations regarding Yahweh and responsibilities to the human community, thereby encompassing duties to *both*, and also elicits the longest explanatory justification of any command. The centrality of the idea of sabbath is further established in contexts where it is tied to the foundational Israelite experiences of creation and exodus. "The sabbath commandment is thus the heart of the law."[36]

The verbal root of sabbath simply means "to cease activity"[37] and actually refers to a whole host of days and even years in which Yahweh's people

33. Krutch, *Desert Year*, 127.
34. Kittel, *TDNT* VII:3.
35. Kittel, *TDNT* VII:2.
36. Kittel, *TDNT* VII:8. See Exod 20:11 and Deut 5:15.
37. Kittel, *TDNT* VII:3.

were expected to stop working and rest and celebrate. This was an expectation not only for those specifically identified as Israelites, but extended to everyone—animals and people alike—within their sphere of influence. The benefits of a weekly day of rest extended to servants, domestic livestock, and even travelers in Israel. In addition to a weekly day, every seventh year the land was to lie fallow for the express benefit of the poor (Exod 23:10) and all loans were to be remitted in this year (Deut 15:1–11). There was an early recognition of the spiraling nature of indebtedness for those facing poverty, drought, or the loss of one's livelihood, so provisions were made to assure a socially flourishing condition for the entire society by periodically resetting the economic baseline. Following seven of these seven years of sabbath, Israel was to observe an additional sabbath Year of Jubilee when all slaves were freed and any individual or family who had been forced to sell their family plot of land was allowed to return and begin again on the original allotment.[38]

The point of the sabbath regulations was to create a people who would recognize that accumulation was not the point. Endless productivity, unceasing effort, ongoing collection of land and wealth, always striving after something more was never the model of either creation or redemption; it was early on rejected by Yahweh as a means to *shalom* and was recognized as actually detrimental to a state of communal health. Herein lies the problem with sabbath: It detracts too much from our natural ability to perform and therefore robs us of too much return for our labor and intelligence. The idea verges on the offensive. This explains why the Israelite response from the beginning was as ours likely is: this is too much. Despite the uniquely central nature of the entire sabbath complex, there is every indication that the Year of Jubilee was never actually practiced. For a nation on the rise, experiencing their own progress, this practice was simply too costly. As early as Leviticus 26:34–35, the author predicts the Israelite loss of their lease on the land (as Yahweh maintained ownership of all of creation anyway) due to a failure to properly observe the sabbath expectation.[39] For the prophet Ezekiel, the sabbath was specifically a sign of the goodness of Yahweh, which makes the rejection of the practice all the more glaring.[40]

An early transgression of sabbath occurs shortly following the experience of release from Egypt in Exodus 16:22–30. The scene is centered on a desert environment where the newly emancipated Hebrews are being

38. See the Year of Jubilee stipulations in Lev 25:8–55.

39. See also: 2 Chr 36:20–21 as the historic explanation from the far side of this loss, and Jer 25:11 as the prophetic perspective.

40. Ezek 20:12–13.

provided a daily supply of food miraculously supplied by Yahweh. In deference to the sabbath, the people are expected to gather enough manna on the
sixth day in order to supply them for a day off. As we might expect, a day off
from striving and struggling for sustenance seems like so much wasted time
and some members of the tribe venture forth in an attempt to accumulate a
little more. It draws a swift rebuke from the Provider of all that is necessary
for life. Such apparent wasted potential and wasted productivity is always
fought against. Eventually, even the sabbath would be propped up with a
tremendous weight of religious paraphernalia and additional rabbinic stipulations in order to somehow make it appear like a worthwhile endeavor.

The issue of sabbath becomes an important source of controversy Jesus
has with the religious leadership of his day. Every early biographer of Jesus
devotes space to the conflict over the sabbath which serves to demonstrate
its ongoing centrality.[41] The sabbath was never intended to be about more
effort to prove one's place in the religious order but about protecting land,
animals, strangers, the rich, and the poor from the too-heavy cost of endless building and accumulation. Jesus felt compelled to stand against any
additional sabbath regulation which would rob it of its intent to remind
a people from where their existence and freedom stemmed. Jesus actually
reinvigorates the core ideal of sabbath when he invokes the image of Jubilee
in his inaugural address to the synagogue in Luke 4:16–21.[42] To understand sabbath as a formulative concept is to recognize that our productivity
and hard-won progress does not secure our highest form of being. Sabbath
stands against the disengagement, displacement, coercion, and fragmenta-
tion which the belief in and effort toward progress of the Western order
foists upon us.

It is no accident that Luke identifies the text read by Jesus when he
entered the synagogue in Nazareth on that particular sabbath as being the
anticipation of Jubilee from the prophet Isaiah. The idea of the freedom
and restoration figured in the Year of Jubilee provided a resounding back-
drop for the message of Jesus and he concludes his reading in Luke 4 by
proclaiming that, "Today this scripture has been fulfilled in your hearing"
(4:21). Through this statement, Jesus takes upon himself the responsibility
of restoring an intended order to creation. The idea is embedded in the core
of the message of Jesus: the kingdom of God. Dominating the themes of the
Synoptic gospels—Matthew, Mark, and Luke—the message of the kingdom
is the key to sorting out our role in the repair of the world.

41. See: Matt 12:1–4; Luke 14:1–6; John 5:1–16, as well as parallel passages throughout Mark.

42. The passage is drawn from Isa 61:1–2, which is itself a recasting of the expectations from Lev 25.

The invocation of the idea of the kingdom of God occurs near the beginning of each of the gospel accounts of the life of Jesus.[43] Matthew 4:23 stands as a summary statement about the entire work undertaken by the public ministry of Jesus: "and he went throughout all Galilee, teaching in their synagogues and proclaiming the gospel of the kingdom and healing every disease and affliction among the people." The kingdom indicates everything Jesus talked about and the acts he performed on behalf of the people. When Jesus sent out his twelve disciples in Matthew 10:7 he charged them with the same task: to proclaim the presence of the kingdom and heal the sick. The idea is the centerpiece of the life of Jesus and formed the self-understanding of his earliest followers.

A full understanding of New Testament themes depends on a recognition of Old Testament roots. If the idea of *shalom* embraces at root all one tried to say about Yahweh, then the weight of the presence of the idea of kingdom, especially in the life of Jesus who was so self-consciously sent from Yahweh, relates these two themes closely together. The word "kingdom" occurs 120 times in the Synoptic gospels with the specific designation "kingdom of God" or "kingdom of heaven" used 108 times, the majority of these usages being found in Matthew's account. While Jesus refers only twice to the idea of church, he specifically mentions the kingdom of God/heaven ninety times.[44] What Christians often refer to as the gospel is more appropriately the good news of the kingdom, which holds a significance far deeper than one's destination in some other realm of existence.

We can conceive the idea of the kingdom of God in its most basic form as God's agenda for the return of *shalom* to his creation. The life and activity of Jesus emphasizes this agenda which consists of, first, the recognition of the reign of the Creator over the earth, and second, the actual embodiment of what such a reign looks like when enacted in creation. An understanding of the kingdom of God as demonstrated by Jesus and embraced by the early church must also acknowledge what virtually every New Testament scholar recognizes are the tensions in the idea as developed by the gospel narratives. As was emphasized in the previous discussion about the biblical themes of creation and dissolution, there is not the Western concern in these narratives to make the accounts straightforward, scientific treatises.

Early Christian thought was comfortable with a both/and condition which grants the idea of the kingdom of God a breadth and richness our

---

43. Matt 4:23; Mark 1:14–15; John 3:3, 5. While Luke 4:18–21 does not specifically utilize the term "kingdom," the Isa 61 passage quoted by Jesus was commonly understood in Israel as referring to the condition that would predominate at the time God established his kingdom on earth. See Fuellenbach, *Kingdom of God*, 68–69.

44. Fuellenbach, *Kingdom of God*, 4.

more narrowly conceived categories can at times find contradictory. The kingdom is *at the same time* an internal, spiritual reality *and* an external, physical condition meant to embrace society as a whole.[45] It is equally local or particular and universal in its application.[46] The kingdom is presented as a fully future reality while it is also present in creation.[47] These tensions indicate the pervasiveness of the idea of kingdom without narrowing its nature to a single condition. The kingdom of God transcends our Western conceptions of time and the separation of an internal and external life.

In his work on the kingdom of God, John Fuellenbach emphasizes that by the close of the Old Testament period the idea of the kingdom had already developed to the point that it could encompass the whole intent of the biblical narrative: "It is this conception of the kingdom, and the story of God's work in history to establish it, that gives unity to the Bible and significance to its various parts."[48] This is why the New Testament idea of the kingdom of God can encompass the vision of *shalom* and indicate how a repaired order of being does and does not come about. The relationship between the kingdom of God and what we have already viewed about *shalom* is clear. Fuellenbach quotes Belgian theologian Edward Schillebeeckx to demonstrate just this point: "The hermeneutics of the kingdom of God exist especially in making the world a better place. Only in this way will I be able to discover what the kingdom of God actually means." Fuellenbach adds that, "what really is at stake here is the world-transforming dimension of the kingdom of God. . . . the kingdom of God implies a revolution of the human world."[49]

"Making the world a better place" recalls the theme of part I, where the Western program of progress was launched on this very idea. We have also seen how that program has gone so dramatically wrong in our midst. We will touch on the alternativeness of the vision of the world's repair imbedded in the kingdom momentarily. But it is essential that we get the sense that the kingdom is fully the figure of *shalom* which touches every aspect of created reality and therefore cannot be relegated to a future condition of a narrowly defined spiritual existence. New Testament scholar George Eldon Ladd has probably done more to advance the reality and relevance of properly understanding of the kingdom of God in the teaching of Jesus

45. See Luke 17:20–21 and Matt 9:35.
46. See Matt 15:24 and Matt 6:5–13.
47. See Luke 23:42 and Matt 12:28.
48. Fuellenbach, *Kingdom of God*, 53.
49. Fuellenbach, *Kingdom of God*, 58, 60.

than any other writer of the past century. I quote Ladd at length to give us a sense of the weight of the concept. Ladd points out that the kingdom of God

> is a total, global and structural transformation and revolution of the reality of human beings; it means the cosmos purified of all evils and full of the reality of God. The kingdom of God is not to be in another world but it is the old world transformed into a new one. . . . The kingdom of God cannot be reduced to the reign of God within the individual soul or modernized in terms of personal existential confrontation or dissipated to an extra-worldly dream of blessed immortality. The kingdom of God means that God is king and acts in history to bring history to a divinely directed goal.[50]

The point of world transformation is advanced by understanding that the kingdom Jesus inaugurated was never intended to be limited to his physical presence and activity. Jesus indicated that the realities that were to come about as a result of the presence of this good reign were granted to his followers to perpetuate the condition. There is a derived nature to the kingdom initiated by Jesus: "And I assign to you, as my father assigned to me, a kingdom" (Luke 22:29).[51] It may be this aspect of advancing a hope for a new kind of world that stands behind two millennia of heroic efforts to build the kingdom and reform the world as it ought to be. It can be, and often has been, construed as permission for the Western cultural paradigm of progress.

This is where the vision of God's *shalom* reignited in the New Testament reality of the kingdom of God must part ways from too much of the Western attempt to build the world's ought into existence and implicates even much of modern Christianity, which is complicit in a failed effort. The emphasis surrounding the repair of the world indicated by the figure of the kingdom of God is directed at the reality that the kingdom is *God's*, and it therefore comes in terms very different from the ways in which human beings too often endeavor to make it happen. John Fuellenbach emphasizes the distinct way of the kingdom when he points out that Jesus was absolutely convinced that a new social order could be brought about only through God's intervention: "This absolute confidence in God's ability alone to bring about the new order gave Jesus a kind of detachment from the type of activity of the revolutionists who made the final coming of God dependent on

---

50. Ladd, *Presence of the Future*, 53, 331.
51. See also: Matt 16:19; 18:18; Luke 12:32; John 20:21–23.

their strategy."[52] The larger point has to do with not just armed struggle but with *any* of the strategies we feel are crucial in our own context.

This is a primary point of this book and the reason for spending so much space considering the nature of the kingdom: we cannot build our own best life or world through human effort because we do not have the capacity to effect change on that level. For me, this also forces a reassessment of even American Christianity's demonstrated attachment to progress on the terms established by Western categories of meaning and value. We seem to have misplaced some of the key images utilized in reference to the distribution of the cultural renewal meant by the kingdom, two of the central images being the cup and the basin.[53]

Jesus' talk of the kingdom led the mother of two of the disciples to request positions of authority and therefore power in the new reign, a scene which we find in Matthew 20. Jesus' response is to ask a strange question about a cup: "Are you able to drink the cup that I am to drink" (20:22)? Later in the garden of Gethsemane, prior to his crucifixion, Jesus specifically prays for the *cup* to pass from him three times (Matt 26:36–44). The cup obviously stands as a figure of the impending suffering Jesus will endure in the crucifixion the following day. Jesus also clearly acknowledges that there is no other way for the kingdom to be manifest than through his suffering (Matt 26:42). It is an experience (minus, perhaps, being hung on a Roman cross) that the followers of Jesus would indeed be expected to emulate (Matt 20:23).

In a similar way, John pictures one of the final, and therefore critically important, acts of Jesus as being an embodied parable of the way the kingdom would be perpetuated. In John 13, knowing that time was short, Jesus "poured water into a basin and began to wash the disciples' feet" and informed the disciples that, "I have given you an example, that you also do just as I have done to you" (John 13:5, 15). The kingdom of God renews the world through a cup and a basin; specifically, through suffering and the kneeling posture of a servant. By our cultural standards and according to the ways we have learned to operate and control every aspect of our lives, these images are not only offensive but seem a colossal waste of potential and are inherently inefficient. We might be tempted to think that God has no idea what he is doing.

52. Fuellenbach, *Kingdom of God*, 129.

53. There are certainly other such images, not the least of which is the cross which is basically offensive (see Gal 5:11). Other "lost" images include: a childlike reception (Matt 18:3), jars of clay (2 Cor 4:7), weakness (1 Cor 1:27), poverty (Matt 5:3), and even foolishness (1 Cor 1:27). I focus on the cup and the basin for their stark imagery and the way in which these images confront our Western paradigm.

The entirety of the life of Jesus as presented in the New Testament is related to the what and how of the kingdom as God's model for the world's repair. Matthew indicates the beginning of the public activity of Jesus in chapter 4 of his writing and immediately precedes Jesus' message of the kingdom with the account of the temptations in the wilderness. The scene is not only especially relevant as we consider the value of natural space to instill in us a sense of how things ought to be, but equally because it so clearly demonstrates the ways in which the restoration of the world would *not* occur, in contradistinction to many of our cultural inclinations. In brief, the three temptations demonstrate that the kingdom would not come through, or as an expression of, personal provision or what we would today refer to as wealth (Matt 4:1–4); the kingdom would not require—and likely not be associated with—an outward display of power or authority (Matt 4:5–7); and, perhaps most importantly, the kingdom of God would not be subject to any shortcuts of ingenuity which would bypass the difficult way of struggle and ultimately the cup (Matt 4:8–10).

I find one of the most revealing scenes about both the nature of the kingdom and its exercise in one of the many difficult sayings of Jesus: Matthew 11:12. The English Standard Version reads: "From the days of John the Baptist until now the kingdom of heaven has suffered violence, and the violent take it by force." The difficulties for grasping Jesus' point hinge on the understanding of the two ideas "suffer violence" and the "violent" who somehow take the kingdom by force. Various translations are little help as they tend to wander over too many possibilities. The point of this hard saying and its relevance for the Western church becomes clear when we pay attention to both the central terms and the larger critical context of chapter 11, which enfolds Jesus' claim.

The two words or phrases, "suffer violence" and "violent [people]," are Greek cognates which means that they derive from the same root word. The first word is a verb while the second word is the noun form of that verb. This relationship causes most translators to attempt a consistent sense for both words; either the negative connotation such as that implied in the ESV, or the more positive sense of the NIV rendering of "forceful advance" and the "forceful" (perhaps "enterprising") people who then perpetuate the kingdom. In his commentary on the book of Matthew, D. A. Carson does a remarkable job of sorting out the dilemma. Relative to the verbal form of the word, Carson points out that the sense of a forceful advance, without any negative connotation, is a considerably more common usage of the word. The second, noun form of the word, "is rare in Greek literature (only here in the NT), but where it occurs it almost always has the negative connotations of violence and rapacity." Furthermore, the noun is followed by a verb, "take by force," which "almost always has the same evil connotations."[54] We can thus render the statement, with Carson, as indicating that "from the time of John the Baptist until now, the kingdom of heaven has been forcefully advancing; and violent and rapacious men have been trying to plunder it."[55]

This is not meant as a mere academic exercise into the obscure, but has profound implications for our understanding of the kingdom as the context of Matthew 11 bears out. The verses preceding verse 12 in this chapter serve as a celebration of the present experience of *shalom* in the world. Not only does John the Baptist appear as a manifestation of the prophetic hope for one to announce the coming of the kingdom, but the present reality of the blind seeing, the lame walking, the leprous being cleansed, the deaf hearing, and the poor being exposed to restoration have all been open and visible manifestations of the movement of the kingdom in real time and space. Hence the kingdom's "forceful advance." The tenor of the chapter takes a dramatic shift in the middle of verse 12. Jesus indicates his audience ("this generation") is like the children who complain that they have done all the right things, played all the right tunes, but did not in so doing elicit the response they expected (vv. 16–17). John and Jesus acted in countercultural ways (though in ways opposite of one another) and are both vilified for failing to toe the party line (vv. 18–19). Jesus, in fact, reverses anticipated roles when he denounces the cities which form the center of religious piety, while exonerating the pagan cities of nearby Tyre and Sidon (vv. 20–24), and claims value for children and the heavy-laden laborers (vv. 25–30).

As Carson summarizes the point, "Not the aggressive zealots will find rest for their souls, but the weary, the burdened, the children to whom the Father has revealed the truth."[56] The establishment of the kingdom, which is itself the restoration of *shalom*, is something the Creator has always intended to bring about. He has made possible the repair of the world in the message and life of Jesus. The problem then becomes our doing damage to this movement as we attempt to engineer the reality and, in so doing, rob it of its intended purpose by continuing to prioritize our own narrowly established sense of conventional value and wisdom, thereby denigrating the noninstrumental and those who stand most in need of *shalom*. The kingdom Jesus offers upends typical Western ways of approaching the death and decay of the world and therefore elicits this warning about those who would damage the kingdom through overconfident human effort.

In his essay collection *Home Economics*, Wendell Berry opines that,

54. Carson, *Expositor's Biblical Commentary*, 266–67.

55. Carson, *Expositor's Biblical Commentary*, 267.

56. Carson, *Expositor's Biblical Commentary*, 268.

The worst disease of the world now is probably the ideology
of technological heroism, according to which more and more
people willingly cause large-scale effects that they do not foresee
and that they cannot control. This is the ideology of the profes-
sional class of the industrial nations—a class whose allegiance to
communities and places has been dissolved by their economic
motives and by their educations. These are people who will go
anywhere and jeopardize anything in order to assure the success
of their careers.[57]

Rather than achieving a society of flourishing wholeness characterized by harmony, ours too often demonstrates an increasing divide between
the rich and the poor, the proliferation of gun violence and hate crimes,
a growing polarization in the divide between political ideologies, and an
ever-higher price tag attached to a deteriorating environment. We have apparently failed to live by the vision of the kingdom, *shalom*, and sabbath.

Interestingly enough, there is actually a third way off the divide which
opened this current chapter. Less than ten miles south of the crossing at South
Pass, the Continental Divide actually splits in two, with one arm trending
south and the other generally east before making their way back to a single
divide about twenty miles south of Rawlins, Wyoming, where the divide once
again moves as a single ridge into the alpine settings of Colorado. The now
two Continental Divides create a large, somewhat rectangular natural depression known as the Great Divide Basin. As the high divide in the middle
west, this ridge running from Mexico to Canada generally separates water
into the Pacific or Atlantic watersheds. Covering nearly 4,000 square miles
with a floor at 6,500 feet, the Great Divide Basin collects whatever scarce
precipitation falls over the Red Desert and confines the water that would
otherwise flow west or east. It is not as if this water has any discernable effect,
however, as the basin is characterized by sand dunes, dry bluffs, alkali flats,
and a sparse growth of sagebrush buffeted by nearly continuous high winds.

If the divide serves as a figure for our options to move either toward
more intensive technological determinism or, alternately, toward a vision
of *shalom* and repair, I would offer that too much of American Christianity
appears to have chosen the no man's land of a closed basin. Our world bears
little resemblance to the harmony of creation or the inclusive restoration
embodied by Jesus. The Christian confession stands as an acknowledged
dependence on a Creator, and yet appears unwilling to give up the desire
to secure meaning through accomplishment, consumption, power, or the
constructed world. We have generally failed to maximize the ancient and

---

57. Berry, *Home Economics*, 150.

compelling vision of repair and have largely become a mere sideshow of the larger cultural realities explored in part I.

Martin Luther King Jr. made just such a point in his "Letter from a Birmingham Jail" in the midst of the Civil Rights Movement. King points out that there was a time when the church was powerful precisely because of their joy in suffering which made an enormous impact on the political structure of the first-century world. He looks back to a time when "the church was not merely a thermometer that recorded the ideas and principles of popular opinion" but served as a "thermostat that transformed the mores of society." Through conviction and commitment, the church, in its smallness and marginality, disturbed the people in power. But, as King explains,

> Things are different now. So often the contemporary church is a weak, ineffectual voice with an uncertain sound. So often it is an archdefender of the status quo. Far from being disturbed by the presence of the church, the power structure of the average community is consoled by the church's silent—and often even vocal—sanction of things as they are.[58]

I believe this largely explains the waning of Christianity in America. In a recent article published in *The Atlantic*, Derek Thompson points out that "in the early 1990s the traditional tether between American identity and faith snapped. . . . By the early 2000s the share of Americans who said they didn't associate with any established religion (also known as 'nones') had doubled. By the 2010s, the grab bag of atheists, agnostics, and spiritual dabblers had tripled in size."[59] This change was a notable historic occurrence because it was not slow, subtle, and cyclical, but *exceptional*. Thompson further concludes that, "The rise of the nones shows no signs of slowing down. In fact, the religious identity that seems to be doing the best job at both retaining old members and attracting new ones is the newfangled American religion of Nothing Much at All."[60]

In 2016, the Public Religion Research Institute (PRRI) published the results of a nationwide survey on religious affiliation in America which discovered that the one quarter (25 percent) of Americans who claimed no formal religious identity constituted the largest "religious group" in the US. The trends for the future indicate even more dramatic changes when one compares the 13 percent of Americans age sixty-five and older who are religiously unaffiliated with the 39 percent of those between the ages of eighteen and twenty-nine who claim this status. There is further a substantial

58. King, "Letter from a Birmingham Jail," para. 36.
59. Thompson, "Three Decades Ago," para. 4.
60. Thompson, "Three Decades Ago," para. 20.

gap between those over the age of fifty—15 percent—and those under the age of fifty—33 percent—who identify with no religious tradition. "Younger Americans raised in nonreligious homes are less apt to join a religious tradition or denomination than young adults in previous eras."[61]

Sociologists offer many explanations for the waning of religion in American culture, including general institutional mistrust, the antagonisms to religion presented by capitalism and the internet, and the changing dynamics of the American family. Derek Thompson offers that "religion has lost its halo effect in the past three decades, not because science drove God from the public square, but rather because politics did."[62] Thompson's view addresses specifically the marriage of Evangelical faith with conservative politics, which has had the effect of disenfranchising younger Americans from both. The PRRI study found that two-thirds (66 percent) of religiously unaffiliated adults agree that "Religion causes more problems in society than it solves."[63] Apparently, Christianity in America has come to be associated more with the seats of power and wealth as a source of dissolution than with its role in the ancient vision of repair and the restorative principles of Jesus' kingdom of God.

My primary conclusion is that faith in America has traded a compelling vision of creation and *shalom* for a culturally recognizable and therefore acceptable adherence to the principles of Western progress, wealth, and power. I do not believe our culture has moved away from the Christian confession out of any particular spite. I simply think that the church in America is not all that distinctive and therefore not very compelling as a people. Our faith, for the most part, simply does not reflect things as they ought to be and has little resonance with the ground of being, which in the end results in little impetus to embrace this movement. I quote the following passage from Wendell Berry's essay "Christianity and the Survival of Creation" at length because of his unique eloquence in framing our issue:

> Despite its protests to the contrary, modern Christianity has become willy-nilly the religion of the state and the economic status quo. Because it has been so exclusively dedicated to incanting anemic souls into Heaven, it has been made the tool of much earthly villainy. It has, for the most part, stood silently by while a predatory economy has ravaged the world, destroyed its natural beauty and health, divided and plundered its human communities and households. It has flown the flag and chanted

61. Jones et al., 'Exodus," para. 9. See also: Jones, *End of White*.

62. Thompson, "Three Decades Ago," para. 13.

63. Jones et al., "Exodus," para. 23.

the slogans of empire. It has assumed with the economists that 'economic forces' automatically work for good and has assumed with the industrialists and militarists that technology determines history. It has assumed with almost everybody that 'progress' is good, that it is good to be modern and up with the times. It has admired Caesar and comforted him in his depredations and defaults. But in its de facto alliance with Caesar, Christianity connives directly in the murder of Creation.[64]

I am convinced our path to repair lies in the exposure to a different landscape which is not dominated by that which has been humanly constructed. This will also require us to become comfortable with a certain amount of tension and additionally move past the familiar and habitual. It is these three alternatives to our current way of being that I offer as a way out of the closed basin as we anticipate moving into part III.

The first step is a reengagement of the natural world as noninstrumental and as not merely a commodity to supply increased wealth. Near the end of his meditations on the book of Job, Bill McKibben writes,

My heart tells me that the environmental destruction we see around us, if we allow it to continue, will be the prelude to a similar convulsive crisis of faith even more profound than the crises of faith that we have already experienced. . . . Overcoming the orthodoxy that places us at the center is, I think, necessary not only for our individual souls, but also for the collective future of our churches.[65]

Unless we can humbly, and within limit, approach a landscape not of our own making, then it is unlikely we will be able to cooperate with the Creator because we will simply be unable to recognize his way in the world. According to Randy Woodley,

Human beings make up just a small part of life on earth. It seems that from the Almighty's purview, heaven and earth are the primary witnesses to God's pronouncements. Could it be that, the further removed from creation we become, or the more interested in the power of human [ingenuity], the less we notice the importance of the things of God?[66]

This conclusion leads to the second alternative of learning to embrace a certain amount of tension. The most profound tension in the gospel, I

---

64. Berry, *Sex, Economy, Freedom and Community*, 114–15.

65. McKibben, *Comforting Whirlwind*, 63, 66.

66. Woodley, *Shalom and the Community of Creation*, 26.

believe, is the expectation to engage in advancing the kingdom as the means of restoring *shalom* even while we fully acknowledge that this is the work and responsibility of the Creator. Advancing the kingdom is the task that we more often than not damage by our heroic efforts to return to Eden. As Jacques Ellul frames the tension:

> We must give up believing that we can 'improve' the world, that at least we can make man better, even if we cannot make him happy. At the same time, we must refuse to further the disintegrating tendency of the world. We must not say to ourselves, 'we cannot do anything about it.' . . . On the one hand it is impossible to make the world less sinful; on the other hand, it is impossible for us to accept it as it is.[67]

Tension is obviously uncomfortable to a scientific, progress-oriented culture such as ours. But it is also integral to the gospel, and, as I hope to make clear in the following chapters, a unique heritage of the lessons of wild places.

Finally, it should be fairly apparent at this point that we stand in need of a new paradigm which will facilitate a move away from our conventional ways of being and acting, even as a church. In writing about the move from what he identifies as the "first half" of life with its concerns of identity formation and financial security to the maturity of the "second half," Franciscan Friar Richard Rohr points out that sages and medicine-men and -women have always had to respond to an invitation to "something more" and have had to do so by grace and daring:

> None of us go into our spiritual maturity completely of our own accord, or by a totally free choice. We are led by Mystery, which religious people rightly call grace. . . . The familiar and the habitual are so falsely reassuring, and most of us make our homes there permanently. Most of us are never told that we can set out from the known and the familiar to take on a further journey. Our institutions and our expectations, including our churches, are almost entirely configured to encourage, support, reward, and validate the tasks of the first half of life.[68]

We move now into what may be unknown, and at the very least unpracticed, territory in an effort to participate in what is still a compelling vision for meaning, value, and a world of ought.

67. Ellul, *Presence of the Kingdom*, 17.
68. Rohr, *Falling Upward*, xvi–xvii.

Chapter 6

Soil

FOR SOME TIME, I have maintained the idea that if I were to write the story of my life, I would have to borrow the title of Malcom Muggeridge's own autobiography: *Chronicles of Wasted Time*. Muggeridge's purpose in choosing his title certainly differs from my own, and I would not be so presumptuous as to claim any correlation with either the fullness of his life experience or his mastery of the English language. Nevertheless, the title would serve well to indicate how much of my life seems to have been conducted relative to what has been said thus far about our Western context. When measured by the standards of progress, my life both vocationally and recreationally can be construed as a grand waste of time. While I would certainly argue otherwise, from all appearances, my own path lacks the necessary inventory of successful endeavors.

For the past decade, I have especially been attracted to regions far from the settings of our iconic, if overcrowded, national parks. Of late I have been moving further from the majesty of the great peaks and the verdant green of forested mountain slopes and deeper into what are still construed as "wastelands." There is a reason why these areas still have few trails through them: they consist of little more than rock, sand, and sagebrush; there is little grass and less water; everything here seeks to poke, scratch, bite, and otherwise expose blood otherwise hidden in the veins. The deserts of the Colorado Plateau are cut by deep canyons that have to be climbed in and out of nearly continuously, adding to the strain of travel in an aridness either too hot or too cold through most of the year.

It moves against the traffic of much of our culture to consider that beauty and renewal might be most readily discovered in landscapes of non-utility. Those expanses which do not exhibit a usefulness due to the presence of a grand viewpoint or the practicality of wealth extraction still maintain their value in instructing us in the ways of stopping, receiving, and becoming friendly with space. American poet and former Professor of English at the University of Colorado, Reg Saner, wrote,

> Our grand Western spaces are an empty plentitude. On the thoughtful person they confer depths beyond any *thing* humans can ever put there. The middle of nowhere is a power, a moving unity of spirit in us, that habitation can only break up, never enhance In such a midst, we've our best chance of sensing what this world is, and ourselves.[1]

The sentiment is one which resonates with the colorful natural imagery of the stories of Jesus and helps us make the transition to experiencing a different landscape of the soul.

Jesus has long been regarded as a profound teacher, a sage. This recognition has proved to transcend the time and cultural context of his own life in the first-century Middle East. Leaders of other world faith systems have expressed their admiration of the wisdom of this marginal Jew from what was at the time the backwaters of the Roman Empire. The ongoing appreciation of Jesus as a teacher, regardless of religious confession, is partially associated with his ability to bring important religious concepts down to earth. Jesus was not concerned with joining the ranks of philosophers by using esoteric language, instead telling short stories laced with the natural elements surrounding his listeners at the time: soil, wind, birds, sheep, and trees, among others. This approach certainly built his appeal as he was able to speak not only to the learned or those occupying the positions of wealth and power, but equally to the level of the peasant population of his day.

Beyond simply being understandable, the intentional use of these images from nature serve to ground the perspective of Jesus to the very order of creation. Jesus connects right ways of being with the created world which is visible for his audience in the everyday experiences of their lives as farmers, shepherds, fishermen, and those generally intimate with agriculture and the outdoors. Lessons of the natural world are lessons for any human as we are all a part of the created world. This recognition plays a central corrective role in our confrontation with the more insidious aspects of our Western approach to meaningful being. If many of the biblical images of human technology and ability are negatively hued, the natural order of the

1. Saner, *Four-Cornered Falcon*, 283.

created world serves as a source of alternative wisdom for how life ought to be conducted in order to be truly human.

The movement toward a corrective paradigm for the church and society, which makes up this third part of the book, will utilize as an organizing structure the earthy and natural parables of Jesus about the sower (or more appropriately: the soil) and that of the growth of the seed from Mark 4. These are two short stories told by Jesus, the first followed by an explanation which is unique for most of his parables, which are steeped in everyday and basic natural elements. Because of the way these particular parables stand in opposition to human ability to build meaning, they are especially relevant to my aim in pursuing a healthy landscape of the soul. All of Jesus' stories are in one way or another related to his message of the kingdom of God, so these brief scenes from Mark point us to a way to *shalom* and our participation in the repair of the world.

The first nine verses of Mark 4 have generally been designated as the parable of the sower. The one who appears to be indiscriminantly sowing in this scene is undoubtedly an important figure, but in Jesus' explanation of his story in verses 14–20 the seed appears to be an equally critical component. I believe that a case can also be made for designating this as the parable of the soil, as the soil appears to have more to do with the productive growth or nongrowth of the distributed seed than anything else in the story. The lesson embedded in the image of the seed will serve as the subject of chapter 7 and the peculiar growth of the seed in good soil, Jesus' parable in Mark 4:26–29, will be my focus of chapter 8. Prior to the seed, however, soil serves as a fundamental and basic element which stands as foundational for whatever else happens in Jesus' story.

Mark 4:1–9 mentions four types of soil, only one of which is designated as good. We don't know anything about this soil other than it is a soil of the condition that is rightly ordered to receive the seed, which then takes root and accomplishes its purpose by producing grain. The other three soil types are given more detail in their condition of being compared to the one good soil. The basic deficiency of the three types of unusable soil is their inability to adequately receive the seed because they have been given over to other uses, apparently for prolonged periods of time. Soil is a fundamental part of the earth, critical for the production of life-giving sustenance, and therefore basic to life itself. But Jesus' point is that a good soil condition is not something to be assumed. Not all soil types or usages are a good setting for a seed.

In Mark 4:1–9, Jesus goes into specific detail about three types of soil which are incapable of either receiving the seed or promoting its growth. Jesus could have simply designated bad soil in contrast to good soil, but he had an important point to make about the conditions of receptivity. The first soil is actually a path. It is earth that has been trod over for years, perhaps centuries, hardening it into an impenetrable condition. This is probably ground often walked over because it served as the easiest transition from one point to another. Paths are established and reinforced as products of culture, and become a soil turned over to a use other than agriculture. The second soil mentioned by Jesus isn't really a soil at all, as Jesus calls it "rocky ground" which "did not have much soil" (4:5). There is an apparent lack of organic material; a ground which basically lacks natural, soil-like qualities. The final unproductive soil type actually has things growing on it, but not things necessarily beneficial for human consumption. This soil is not good soil simply because it is overcrowded with too much unuseful stuff.

We are treated to an unusual explanation of Jesus' intent in the parable of the soils in verses 14–20, something we are not always privileged to have. Off the top Jesus says "the sower sows the word" (4:14). For the biographers of Jesus "the word" is another designation for the good news of the kingdom we examined in the previous chapter.[2] This is at heart a story about properly responding to the full depth of that good news. We go too far if we think that Jesus is advocating running a plow over the earth or through our lives in an effort to make everything productive—good—soil, as if more purposeful activity is the answer. Jesus is simply contrasting a condition for *shalom* with what are the conventional, cultural ways of being already in place. Soil is a condition for how one receives—responds to—the message of how God intends the world to be. Hence, in this parable there are conditions which preclude that message of our *shalom* from growing into a reality. Those conditions depend on a type of vision for how life ought to be lived. The point is the soil of being: three types of being which act against the proper reception of the seed of good news.

The first soil, or way of being, was likely good earth at one point which could have received a seed, but it had been trodden over through patterns of movement for so many years that it had been transformed into a hardened surface which facilitated easier and more efficient movement. Paths often become roads, and we noted in chapter 3 that roads serve as cultural signifiers which demonstrate our ability to build meaning and move our society toward greater productivity and efficiency. A pathless or roadless region lacks the avenues for adequate use. Because paths tend to evolve and harden over time, they are especially vivid as designators of conventional, cultural routes toward activity and meaning. Cultural paths of meaning are for us centered on utility: What is most efficient for progress and wealth

2. See Luke 1:2; John 17:8, 14, as well as Rom 10:8, 1 Thess 2:13, and 1 Pet 1:25.

accumulation and the good life? We trod along this path through part I and Jesus does not affirm such places as being especially receptive to the message of the kingdom.

The second unresponsive ground stems from its basic detachment from what soil should actually be. The absence of organic material, always in the process of decomposition, change, death, and life, is the result of the presence of too much hardened material. Our own soil of being, especially that which is the product of the scientific mindset and technological determinism, has little room for mystery and requires the solidity of assured answers; not a welcome setting for the tensions inherent in the gospel. A root issue I have been pursuing is that our separation from the natural—the organic—compromises our ability to respond to the Creator who maintains the only viable perspective on being truly and fully human. Desert writer and naturalist Joseph Wood Krutch wrote of the deficiencies wrought by separation from the natural:

> Not to have known—as most men have not—either the mountain or the desert is not to have known one's self. . . . It is to forget too easily that the question of the good life—both the question what it is and the question how it can be found—has to do, first of all, not with human institutions, but with the human being himself.[3]

A third type of soil serving as a contrast to good (and therefore a receptive way of being) soil is the ground choked with thorns. This soil elicits the longest explanation by Jesus in verse 19, where it is designated as a life centered on "the cares of the world and the deceitfulness of riches and the desires for other things." "The cares of the world" indicates those elements which the culture prioritizes as essential to defining our ways of being. When we are completely subsumed under the Western paradigm of progress and the value of the built environment as we have defined our culture in part I, it follows that the possibility of embracing the vision of God's *shalom* appears as far too countercultural. Jesus found it necessary to explicitly mention wealth accumulation, which is a central reality in our way of approaching life, but it additionally encompasses all of our desires, which we recognize give rise to all of our actions. Good soil—the soil of being—is thus contrasted in a full picture with the conventional forms of world meaning and value.

Jesus opens our recognition to the ways in which the natural environment can shine a light of perspective on broken ways of being. Because this is about an element as fundamental and basic as soil, which is actually about

3. Krutch, *Desert Year*, 126.

our way of showing up in our world, I want to briefly pursue what might serve as a modern parallel parable about soil which I hope is illustrative of the larger cultural problem I am pursuing.

The nature of the soil has always been a pivotal reality for settlement in the western United States, so it comes as somewhat of a surprise that it has seemed to be so roundly ignored. Chapter 2 delved into the agrarian vision which accompanied the Latter-day Saints into the Salt Lake Valley and subsequently into the heart of the Colorado Plateau, endeavoring to make the desert blossom as the rose. The Mormons were a people theologically tied to agriculture in a region consisting of soil not especially conducive to large-scale agricultural pursuits. Not only is the plateau a region of high altitudes, cold winters, and especially hot summers, with most areas receiving less than ten inches of rain per year which most often falls in huge concentrations during summer months, but additionally "much of the soil is 'aridisol,' or very dry and possessing a low concentration of organic matter with salt accumulated at the surface."[4] In 1930, Secretary of Agriculture Henry Hyde identified millions of acres of western lands as "submarginal lands" which ought not to be farmed because of "location, soil exhaustion or natural infertility," many such lands lying in Utah.[5]

The possibility that soil conditions could be inconducive to agriculture "clashed with the Mormon spiritual conviction that with irrigation water, dry farming techniques, and a faith in divine providence the desert would 'blossom as a rose.'"[6] Throughout the late nineteenth century, regional flocks of sheep and herds of cattle were growing far beyond the carrying capacity of the land while careless logging practices denuded slopes of timber. "By the 1890s people across Utah were documenting flash floods, arroyo cutting, and landslides on mountain slopes that had always seemed stable." Native grasses which had held a tenuous soil in place for centuries were soon replaced by sagebrush, rabbitbrush, shadscale, juniper, and after 1900, cheatgrass and Russian thistle overtook many pastures.[7] It serves as a picture of ignoring the qualities of native soil and an illustration of the ways in which we pursue identity along culturally defined paths which can be utterly destructive.

The pursuit of a way of being in the midst of an ignorance of natural systems leads inevitably to ruination and loss. On the American Great Plains, a region of high wind and low rainfall, native grass was indispensable

4. Frehner, "People Cannot Conquer the River," 178.

5. Cannon, "There are Millions of Acres," 204–5.

6. Cannon, "There are Millions of Acres," 205.

7. Nichols, "Before the Boom," 171.

in holding the soil in place. As nineteenth-century western settlers discovered a region on which they could make a good profit growing wheat they began turning the native sod over. In 1879, 10 million acres of land on the southern plains were plowed under. Fifty years later, that figure would be 100 million acres.[8] The tenfold increase was partially empowered by the Federal Bureau of Soil which had proclaimed that, "The soil is the one indestructible, immutable asset that the nation possesses. It is the one resource that cannot be exhausted, that cannot be used up."[9] History knows different. Following half a decade of drought and devastating winds, 1935 alone witnessed the loss of topsoil on 100 million acres. Eight hundred and fifty million *tons* of topsoil were blown off the plains and, in some cases, fell on streets as far away as New York City.[10] The cultural ethos dictated that when wheat prices began to fall in 1929, the solution was to maintain a profit margin by simply planting more acres. An additional round of plowing cut up even more of the Great Plains following World War II as commodity prices once again encouraged rampant production. The lesson embedded in soil is that we have a difficult time walking away from production or adequately learning from our past, thereby losing what is basic to life.

For a culture such as ours, the obvious answer to these dilemmas of keeping and rendering productive the soil is to engineer solutions which rarely take into account natural processes but which instead demonstrate how capable we are as humans. The sentiment was pursued with genuine earnestness in much of the western United States in areas of problematic soil. When farmers and ranchers began to recognize how overgrazed valleys and heavily logged slopes were pushing water at increasingly devastating volumes down watercourses, removing even more precious soil from stream banks, efforts to hold soil in its place included the purposeful introduction of nonnative Tamarisk and Russian Olive. Tamarisk in particular took to its new home with a vengeance, displacing more than a million acres of native vegetation and sucking up an estimated 1.6 *trillion* gallons of water annually in an already-thirsty land.[11] A recent online article from *National Geographic* highlighted plans by the Bureau of Land Management to utilize ship anchor chains dragged between two bulldozers to remove the vegetation on 1,021 square miles in southern Utah's Grand Staircase Escalante National Monument. The program is designed for "the benefit of sustainable agriculture," even though the BLM's own management plan found that the method

8. Egan, *Worst Hard Time*, 267.

9. Egan, *Worst Hard Time*, 51.

10. Egan, *Worst Hard Time*, 223, 254.

11. Wilshire et al., *American West at Risk*, 86.

irreparably harms the landscape. Scientists point out that "heavy equipment use on fragile desert landscapes threatens to increase erosion, encourage flammable invasive species, and destroy biomes already compromised by climate change."[12]

Jesus encourages a look into our own inner condition too often hardened by routes defined by cultural inheritance, a separation from natural rhythms, and crowded with too many concerns which direct us away from created design. Still a principal element of life, these modern pictures of good vs. abused soil serve as reminders that we have much to learn by paying attention to our natural environment. The condition of the natural world reflects the values and priorities of the soul. This has been central to my thesis throughout this book: we too often ignore our natural setting and likewise the condition of our own spiritual life as created by another, risk losing and ruining its proper anchor points, and respond by inadequate attempts to apply our own methodologies to repair what has been broken.

Our way back to *shalom* starts by understanding the soil of being. We ignore this fundamental element to our own peril. Soil is an elemental reality and Jesus uses it as an image in Mark 4 because it is so utterly basic not only to the earth but to our own humanness. "Adam," as a figure of humankind, is a derivative of "*adamah*," ground. We are made from the very soil of the earth. A basic grasping of this idea means in part to be prepared not to first build, but to *receive*. If a good soil of being is contrasted with cultural conventionality, then we need to start by first stopping. The way forward is the way back. This first figure of the soil from the parables of Mark 4 calls us initially to suspend effort in order to touch the *real*—the organic, the natural—buried beneath our contrived and choked surface. Harder work and more effort will only add to an already overcrowded and hardened life.

If it takes good soil to properly receive the seed of the message of how the Creator might repair his creation, then we are committed to consider how we might pay adequate attention to this condition of the very dirt and dust which form the foundational basis of our being. I see this occurring in three ways which will form the remainder of this chapter. The first is our willingness to be exposed to a context which enables us to distinguish the real from the unreal. Following close on the heels of this exposure is our need to suspend language and to a certain degree even thought—ancient spiritual practices which were once a vital part of Christian experience. Finally, there are models of practices which entail the suspension of an agenda; practices distinguishable from all that has been said thus far about

12. Oldham, "Forests on Utah's Public Lands," paras. 5–13.

our pursuit of progress because these are notably counterintuitive acts of nonacting.

When Edward Abbey wrote in his journal that, "In the desert one comes into direct confrontation with the bones of existence, the bare, incomprehensible absolute is-ness of being,"[13] he was making a statement about the difference between reality and unreality. For Abbey, and many other writers and travelers through what we have seen were long considered "waste spaces," there is a striking difference between a desert or wilderness reality and the chimera of our cultural constructs. It is partially the inability to distinguish between the utterly, fundamentally real, and a self-created and basic unreality which so plagues modern society.

I developed the point in chapter 4 that our context—our landscape—becomes us. The built environment as our reality, as our source of being, begets ever-more-frantic and prolific building, mining, drilling, driving, flying, paving, purchasing, and accumulating. Jesus indicated that these cares, established as the rule of our culture, compact and choke our existence over time, robbing us of a vital depth and richness which would otherwise characterize a healthy soil of being. The landscape we immerse ourselves in and take our cues from is of vital concern relative to how we distinguish the real from an unreal life. I believe this is especially true for our spirituality.

There is a marked difference between, say, an untracked desert expanse and the world we surround ourselves with on a daily basis. For a number of years, I worked as a roughneck on a natural gas drilling rig in western Colorado. Unless the rig is in the process of moving from one drill pad to another, it is in a continuous state of busy activity, twenty-four hours a day, seven days a week, straight through the year regardless of holidays or weather. I spent twelve-and-a-half hours a day, fourteen days at a time, alternating hitches between days and nights in a near-continuous state of noise and movement. I mixed drilling fluid, wrestled hoses, swung sledgehammers, twisted pipe wrenches, repaired massive pumps, and pushed and pulled 100 feet of iron pipe over long hours high in a derrick. A boiler and long series of hoses and heaters kept the rig running through sub-zero winter nights. Countless lights flooded the location with daylight on a continual basis.

Many days during my weeks off were spent in a very different environment. I frequently ventured into the soundless deserts of western Colorado and eastern Utah where I might rig multiple rappels into the underground labyrinth of a slot canyon where nothing lived, sun barely shone, and noise was absent. Sometimes I would walk miles through an empty basin beneath a wide sky or climb to sprawling plateaus where the only footprints were

---

13. Abbey, *Confessions of a Barbarian*, 197.

left by desert bighorn sheep. Rarely frenetic activity; simply a daily routine of walking and at times scrambling or backtracking over a lost way. Most of my trips have been solo trips, bathed in silence and stillness, spent under a blue expanse or a night beneath the darkness of skies free from the artificial. In contrast to the half of my life spent on the drilling rig, in the desert I was fully subject to the natural rhythms of sunset and sunrise; to freezing temperatures and boiling sun. My many long walks were not about accomplishing anything. In all the miles I have traveled, I have still barely entered even a fraction of a vast wilderness.

This kind of exposure is a balance in an otherwise built, programmed, and artificial world, and therefore an important source of reality in the otherwise unreal. In a collection of essays about the desert, Frederick Turner poses the question, "What is it that has drawn humans to the desert and that has made desert dwellers sages and metaphysicians?" Turner responds to his question:

> In its apparent inhospitality to humankind, the desert is nonetheless a unique expression of the life force, more evident in such stripped conditions than in smiling lands or in the weltering centers of civilization. Perhaps it was this fact that made the desert-dwelling Arabs such deep thinkers, speculators, tellers of tales; that drew the ancient desert fathers out into Egyptian sands. In the desert you see that life force in all its undifferentiated, impersonal power. And it might just be what draws us still to spots such as this.[14]

It basically comes down to what we tie ourselves to, what we anchor our identity in: whether it is the merely self-constructed or the real. Furthermore, can we distinguish between the two in the social setting in which we find ourselves? Our culture ascribes a certain permanence and importance to what we can build or have built. Our world bases reality on technology and economy: what we build and accomplish and what we earn and consume. These become the elements of the real world. The real, at least for our Western culture, is what we build and grow and advance and manufacture; and this kind of story of reality is internalized as the similar reality of the soul. This is not to say that our homes and vehicles and tools and instruments of technology lack a certain solidity. We simply need to be reminded that as limited and hemmed-in, temporal and contingent beings, anything we construct must by necessity be permeated with the same limitations and temporary contingency.

14. Turner, *Of Chiles, Cacti, and Fighting Cocks*, 63.

The problem is our housing developments, powerplants, computer networks, webs of highways, and savings accounts are no longer merely physical storage containers for those things that make life easier and more comfortable, but instead have become reservoirs of *meaning*. These products of human ingenuity hold our conceptions of significance for us. My view is the constructs of contingent, humanly derived systems have taken on purposes never within their capabilities because they dictate not only how we live but how we construe value and purpose. The key ideas here are "contingent" and "derived": we ourselves are a part of the created order, so anything we are privileged to design and then build become of an even lesser order of reality, too far down on the scale of the real to provide any substantive value. Our culture deals basically in chimeras. A "chimera" is an illusion or fabrication of the mind. Western culture is fundamentally built on ways of being derived from philosophers and scientists who had recast human ability as capable of fabricating meaning from the operation of the mind, which in turn issued in the actions which characterize our belief in progress.

I believe we have some resources to aid our sorting out the real from the unreal. Fortunately, we still have access to untrammeled space, even in its rapid diminution, where perspective can be found, and an important connection to ancient wisdom from others who confronted a confusion about reality similar to our own. "To the deserts go prophets and hermits; through the deserts go pilgrims and exiles. Here the leaders of the Great Religions have sought the therapeutic and spiritual values of retreat, *not to escape but to find reality*."[15] It is not uniquely a function of our modern society. Jesus told stories about people stuck in the unreal constructs of society. And later desert fathers and mothers applied the distinction by first *ceasing* to try to say or do anything constructive, lest it leads one further to living in an unreality.

A properly ordered landscape of the soul, a healthy soil of being, requires exposure to a standard—to a baseline of meaning not established by our own building prowess, but instead gained through a meeting with a reality beyond our contrivances. If a first step is learning to recognize the difference between the real as created and the unreal as secondarily derived, it follows that we must be careful in any next step not to continue to add our own concepts and language which might diminish the real. We do best at this stage to stop and limit our words, our concepts, and our efforts. This is the way of apophatic theology promulgated by the desert hermits of the fourth and fifth centuries in the deserts of Egypt and Palestine.

15. Shephard, *Man in the Landscape*, 44; emphasis added.

Early in the fourth-century Roman world, Christianity suddenly found itself in a very different position relative to its culture. What had grown up as a marginal religious movement, holding meetings in secret and trying to stay out of the mouths of lions, was now embraced by the ruler of the Western world and thrust into the centers of wealth, security, and power. When the Emperor Constantine became a Christian and ended persecution, new prestige and prosperity was available for mainstream Christianity. In what could be said about our own cultural context, "Christianity after Constantine had become a major means for obtaining economic, political, and social advantage. It lent itself increasingly to competition, to climbing the ladder of success, acquiring influence and making oneself look good. All this became possible as Christians enjoyed the prerogatives of established power." Many thoughtful Christians observed in the new cultural ascendancy not a return to *shalom* but a loss of earlier Christian zeal.[16]

The surprising change in the church's position drove a group of concerned Christians, those now identified as the desert fathers and mothers, to isolated and uninhabited corners of wild and arid earth. These men and women recognized the basic unreality of a cultural system which had captivated the church and endeavored to immerse themselves in a simple, bedrock existence. Desert monks did not inhabit the desert in an attempt to first design or build a better culture. They walked into the spaces of Egypt to be first stripped and emptied of any agenda of their own. It was an act demonstrating an understanding of the kingdom of God not unlike what we developed in chapter 5: not as a heroic act of human persons but as a gift of the self-referent Creator.

In these solitary spaces, desert saints developed their reputation for what they *stopped* doing: proliferating plans, programs, answers, and even language about who God is and what he wants done. The result was the beginning of a long tradition in Christian thought known as apophatic spirituality. Belden Lane, a professor of Theological Studies at Saint Louis University, explores desert and mountain spirituality and the value of the apophatic tradition in his book *The Solace of Fierce Landscapes*. He says, regarding the movement, "Emphasizing the importance of reaching 'beyond' (*apo*) every 'image' (*phasis*) one might use to speak of God, the movement emerged as a prophetic critique of theological presumption."[17]

The idea that we should limit what we are able to say about God arose in a climate where the Christian faith suddenly sensed a need to act on and articulate its newfound sense of security and power. The desert movement

---

16. Lane, *Desert Spirituality and Cultural Resistance*, 50, 53.

17. Lane, *Solace of Fierce Landscapes*, 62.

hence serves as a corrective for any era bent on imposing its own vision of *shalom,* as if humans could possibly grasp the full will of the Creator. The source of the tradition reached back to the experience of Moses on Mount Sinai, where he met Yahweh, who dwelt in thick darkness, hidden behind an impenetrable cloud, only glimpsed as a passing shadow from a hiding place anchored in rock.[18] The apostle Paul likewise emphasizes the utter mystery of a God beyond human sight and comprehension.[19] A prominent word of Paul's appears to be "mystery," which designates something hidden in God, attainable only through God's self-disclosure and never through human activity.[20] Christians went to the desert primarily to *listen.*

Belden Lane points out that the apophatic tradition emerged both as a theological response to fourth-century heresies that claimed to be able to grasp the entirety of the divine nature as well as a spiritual check on a growing, muscular faith which was being developed contrary to the explicit vision Jesus had promoted with his disciples. As a *via negativa* (the way of negation), desert monasticism reduced life and language to the bare essentials. The tradition appears to be experiencing a recovery as a check on the presumptions of theologians as well as a "summons to the simplicity of life that flows from the relinquishment of language." It serves to emphasize abandonment as well as a recognition of limits,[21] two conditions which, as has been noted throughout this book, are particularly difficult for the modern mind. As Lane writes,

> God cannot be *had,* the desert tradition affirms, if this means laying hold of God by way of concept, language, or experience. God is a desert, ultimately beyond human comprehension. . . . It is only as we abandon every effort to control God by experiencing God, relinquishing even the grasping self (always anxious to add the deity to its store of personal acquisitions), that the mystery of meeting God beyond experience even becomes possible.[22]

This tradition was reinvigorated in the sixteenth century by Saint John of the Cross who penned the still widely read *Dark Night of the Soul.* John of the Cross emphasized the need to "experience the deprivation of all other

---

18. Exod 20:21; 24:15; 33:21–33; Lane, *Solace of Fierce Landscapes,* 63.

19. Rom 11:33; 1 Tim 6:16.

20. See Rom 16:25; 1 Cor 2:7; 4:1; Eph 1:9; Col 1:26–27. The following chapter will further explore the idea of the self-disclosure of God as establishing our primary posture as receivers, especially through the theological work of Karl Barth.

21. Lane, *Solace of Fierce Landscapes,* 64, 67.

22. Lane, *Solace of Fierce Landscapes,* 12 (emphasis original).

things we may have depended upon for comfort, security and self-esteem." because, "knowledge of God is not found in 'spiritual delights and gratifications,' but in 'the sensory aridities and detachments referred to by the dry and desert land.'"[23] While such imagery and approach to spirituality grates against our modern sensibilities and, by all appearances, the very things most American Christians want from their faith, this apophatic approach to the inner life serves as a necessary correction to "a God without thunder, having been thoroughly housebroken and made presentable to the cultural elite" of the day.[24] The point of embracing an apophatic spirituality extends beyond our own narrow experience of the renewal of the inner life because we are ultimately and compellingly called to participate in the repair of the world. As Lane writes of the deeper implications, "My fear is that much of what we call 'spirituality' today is overly sanitized and sterile, far removed from the anguish of pain, the anchoredness of place. Without the tough-minded discipline of desert-mountain experience, spirituality loses its bite, its *capacity to speak prophetically to its culture*, its demand for justice."[25]

My sense is that it is perhaps especially difficult for American evangelical Christians to grasp the importance of this step of first stopping in our talking and doing because this is a group who appear especially self-assured in what they say about God and in the actions they would undertake on his behalf. As I have sought to emphasize, that self-assurance stems from a society continuously surrounded by the apparent and self-referent benefits of our built environment. We would do well to reevaluate the source of our self-confidence because too much of our God talk appears as little more than a projection of and self-justification for our own aims, culturally defined. The generations of youth disillusioned by the Christian faith recognize in too much evangelicalism a feeble attempt to assuage our internal longings for a God who would simply think like us and happily send us on our way with a blessing to do what we had planned to do in the first place.

The apophatic serves as a much-needed corrective tradition to move us into a more vibrant and honest spirituality. To embrace mystery, the unknown, is to counter the tenor of a society in which everything is over-engineered, programmed, dialed-in, and sanitized. As long as such a society serves as our only defining reality, our spirituality languishes from too much human-driven control. Immersion in a different landscape—a wild, perhaps desolate, and at the very least uninhabited landscape—produces a different kind of soul with a greater resonance to the ground of being. In

23. Lane, *Solace of Fierce Landscapes*, 73–74.

24. Lane, *Solace of Fierce Landscapes*, 187.

25. Lane, *Solace of Fierce Landscapes*, 20; emphasis added.

wild mountain, plains, or desert environments we still have an opportunity to become intimate with mystery and that which is beyond our control. These are the landscapes that form an entirely different understanding of the gospel.

This is precisely why I seek any opportunity to escape into an untrafficked, unpopulated wilderness, especially where mystery resides thick on the land. To trade a contrived security for a long walk into the unknown is a small act of protest against a built world which believes and acts as if its products constitute the elemental reality of existence. Many such small acts accumulate to cultivate a different soil of being. Our built environments serve to comfort and coddle us, but thus far have proven inept at producing the flourishing harmony of *shalom*. We require the unknown and uncomfortable in order to connect us with an inner life capable of understanding the rightness of being which transcends the narrowness of too much of contemporary life.

When I spend days wandering the deserts of the Colorado Plateau, where trails are rare and visitors rarer, I don't often get lost but I rarely know exactly where I am. It is an enlivening and deepening experience. I frequently ascend vast systems of canyons with no idea if I can find a bypass around the next dryfall or discover a way through the caprock of cliffs guarding the plateau above. I descend slot canyons with no idea of what kind of squeezing drop lies around the next blind corner or how much deeper the freezing water will get or how long it might be until I once again experience the warmth of the sun. Always the unknown: Is the spring still running up ahead? Will my water hold out another day? Can I maintain this pace or have the energy to ascend what I just have just slid and scrambled down? Will I find a place to camp in this narrow canyon bottom choked with brush or on this slickrock dune tumbling toward an abyss before it gets too dark to see? These are solid realities and connection points to participation in a kingdom we don't get to control.

While a world of technology and industry can provide many things, it is incapable of meeting the heights and depths to which the human soul is capable of traveling. The unpredictability of emotional responses to an untamed setting is far more reflective of the realities we swim in than the leveled and insulated environments which seem to be built against the dark, different, and uncomfortable. I have experienced emotions as sharp as cactus spines, as solid as house-sized boulders on these trips, encompassing elation and utter broken frustration, often in the same canyon. I can be reveling in color and scale and beauty a mere moment before a missed canyon exit adds wearying miles to a trip and the water runs dry. Not a few of my most memorable trips have ended in utter exhaustion, on the verge of dehydration, at times bitten by bitter cold. It's not always an experience of idyllic joy and refreshment. These aren't always safe environments, but after all, we didn't make them. And it's precisely because of that reason they can enliven, deepen, and expand our sense of the real.

As the desert dwellers of the fourth century discovered, natural spaces such as these serve as a baseline for being. They produce good soil, rich and deep with organic material, not the hardened paths of conventional ease. This is true even if a wild visit seems to do nothing but produce a lack: the suspension of our knowledge and tendency to be problem-solvers. This peculiar lack is something I have learned to expect and has often rolled over me in what I identify as a state of nonthought.

Several years ago, I was working a night shift on the rig when I experienced a fall onto a handrail shortly after midnight, breaking two ribs and lacerating a kidney. The doctors determined that the kidney would repair itself, but only if I significantly limited physical activity for a number of weeks. When I was finally given the green light to resume activity, it was still with some limitations. I would not be doing any climbing or any long trips that could be considered strenuous, and under no terms was I to risk some kind of impact or fall. Needing a few days away after being laid up for six weeks, I hoisted my pack and headed to Colorado's Flat Tops Wilderness for a long walk through high mountain parks on Forest Service trails; a decidedly nontypical trip.

I generally carry a small notebook with me on trips to the backcountry, jotting notes in the fading light of the evening about what the landscape is infusing into my soul through varying landforms, weather, and the efforts involved in traveling through a region. I have come to anticipate important perspectives on a sense of being in the world, but was taken unawares by what would be the perspective developing over these few days in the Flat Tops. For many of us, wilderness trips have served as an important role in pushing our reset button; a chance to slow down, reflect, simplify, and hopefully connect with a more natural rhythm which we hope can inform a life back in civilization. Part of the problem with our paradigm, however, is that we tend to live by an agenda and can approach any time in creation with a sort of vigor in the soul, hoping to accumulate enough rest to carry us to the next outing. Additionally, we don't carry our life's struggles and perspectives into a remote location and unload them under a tree or in a cave. We are inevitably waiting for ourselves at the trailhead.

This is part of the perspective I later realized through the paradoxical experience of nonthought. I was camped by a small lake and sitting outside my simple, one-person tent, holding my pen and notebook in the fading light of a late August evening. For a later-recognized length of time, as I gazed across a meadow at water and a forest and rounded hill tops, my thinking simply ceased. I was fully awake, but my recognition of anything and processing of any thought and consciousness itself seemed to come to an end. At the time I could not have recorded a single perspective on existence or even have remembered a sentient thought. A later reflection in my journal reads:

> The setting may be sublime, but not produce any life-altering revelations. It's as if at these moments all the world and all your intellect in the midst of this swirling reality simple ceases for a time. It's not that you cease to exist, but conscious thought ceases and brings nonthought. There is nothing to write down and ruminate on later; just the absence (or cessation) of your always figuring and guessing and planning. The value of nonthought.

I anticipate that for some readers this will sound far too Eastern in its orientation. But the fact remains that the Christian faith was not born under a Western paradigm. Contemporary monastic writers like Thomas Merton have demonstrated the resonance between Eastern forms of meditation and early Christian faith.[26] I see a clear connection with the corrective perspective cultivated in the apophatic tradition of early monasticism. The value in considering the idea lies in the way it counters an accepted way of being which we have come to accept as natural and therefore real.

I noted earlier that we operate as a restless culture, driven by a lack of confidence that we ceaselessly try to build against; grasping to somehow create the security of a sense that things are as they should be. Progress is the mantra, the pursuit of which is hardening a path to unforeseen consequences that we then have to endlessly apply ourselves to in an attempt to solve, placing us on an endless treadmill. We are uncomfortable with, and therefore attempt to remove, sources of tension from life in order to facilitate the easiest procurance of health and security and emotional stability and wealth and even spiritual vitality. The result is a natural devaluing of those who don't achieve the same standard in *any* category, marginalizing people and questioning their general competence.

Even for Christian spirituality, there is the mindset which identifies an ought—a sense of the kingdom, of *shalom*—and follows with an agenda of what we need to be vigilant about doing: agendas which books and seminars seem to endlessly promote. We rarely pause to consider that the kingdom of God is a gift granted in waiting and receiving.[27] Nonthought is about a however-brief cessation of the restless operation of the mind, with its tendency to endlessly create problems for which it is forced to create solutions.

26. See, e.g., Merton, *Asian Journal of Thomas Merton.*
27. See Acts 1:4; 2:1–2.

It is one way to address what is too often a bankrupt spirituality which follows the patterns of dependency on the less-real world of the-built-by-us. Nonthought is a basic form of suspending an agenda so life can return to the natural soil of being created by another; a soil in a condition to receive seed.

The apophatic tradition and the corollary of nonthought serve to counter our addiction to ceaselessly design and act as if we could secure our own rightness. In *The Unsettling of America*, Wendell Berry reminds us that

> we need places that we do not use at all. We need the experience of leaving something alone. We need places that we forbear to change, or influence by our presence, or impose on even by our understanding; places that we accept as influences upon us, not the other way around, that we enter with the sense, the pleasure, of having nothing to do there; places that we must enter in a kind of cultural nakedness, without comfort or tools, to submit to rather than to conquer. We need what other ages would have called sacred groves.[28]

Berry points us to the foundational realization of limits in our words, thinking, and acting. Truly biblical spirituality as the soil from which *shalom* grows develops a pattern in each of its forming historical epochs, which demonstrates the indispensable posture advocated by Berry of ceasing to impose an agenda in order to first be influenced by an externality.

The identity of the Jewish people as demonstrated in their laws and celebrations anchors itself in the experience of the exodus from Egypt. It was a centrally formative period in their history which shapes their understanding of Yahweh and how human responsibility is enacted on earth as a response to the acts of a redemptive God. Sabbath is certainly a core of this responsibility and is characterized specifically by *not* acting. Equally revealing and closely related to the sense of the value of inactivity for a period of time is the experience of a forty-year journey through the desert.

It would be tempting to ascribe the forty years only to a punishment meted out for disobedience[29] if the time frame of forty did not figure so prominently in other important shaping eras. Exodus 13:17 indicates that God did not lead the Hebrews out of Egypt to Palestine by the way of the closer, shorter, and easier northern route along the Mediterranean Sea, but instead led them over a circuitous route through a desert wilderness. The word "although" in the verse has been argued over by rabbis for centuries due to the fact that it can also mean "because." "God doesn't lead them along the northern route *because* it is closer and shorter and easier. God leads

28. Berry, *Unsettling of America*, 30.
29. See Num 14:34; Heb 3:17.

them instead to the south, deep into the desert toward Mount Sinai. God *intentionally* chooses the more difficult landscape."[30]

There is the sense that what was occurring was a sort of offloading, a process of undoing, of cessation, a *via negativa,* in order to facilitate a new reality that would replace the unreal. An old culture steeped only in restless production had to be replaced by a process of learning a new way of being. It mirrors the very explicit and purposeful act of Moses entering the dark unknown of the cloud engulfing Mount Sinai for forty days and nights, returning with the expectations of Yahweh for the creation of a new culture.[31]

Another historical epoch, the prophetic era, was again empowered by a forty-day period, this one experienced by Elijah. In 1 Kings 19, the prophet Elijah is coming off one of the most successful and productive runs in prophetic history: fed by ravens, the miraculous never-empty flour jar, the raising of the dead, the defeat of 850 false prophets, and a role in ending a severe drought three years running. In an age-old story where success and production are never enough, Elijah flees to the desert under the threat of a tyrannical Queen Jezebel. Elijah is treated to a renewed perspective by the voice of God speaking out of a thin silence, but not before he has had his own forty-day experience of undoing in the desert.[32]

Prior to his announcement of the kingdom of God, Jesus repeats the forty-day pattern when, as Mark tells us, he is *driven* into the wilderness (Mark 1:12–13). There is nothing especially magical about the number forty other than its repetition in decisive transition periods indicate an important pattern relative to individual and communal spirituality and subsequent kingdom-oriented acts. The first need in these instances is always pictured as a kind of not-doing. As French writer Antoine de Saint-Exupéry wrote early in the twentieth century, "In anything at all perfection is finally attained not when there is no longer anything to add, but when there is no longer anything to take away, when a body has been stripped down to its nakedness."[33] The apostle Paul indicates that following his meeting with the risen Christ, he went first to the desert of Arabia which was undoubtedly a period of offloading all of the successful trappings of a full and productive (if ill-conceived) life.[34]

The *via negativa* consists of the paradox of moving forward by non-movement. It highlights the peculiar value of acts which are characterized by nonacting. The negative and apophatic practices of silence, solitude, and

---

30. Lane, *Desert Spirituality and Cultural Resistance,* 20; emphasis original.

31. Exod 24:15–18; 34:28.

32. 1 Kgs 19:12, 8.

33. Quoted in Nichols, *On the Mesa,* 30.

34. See Gal 1:7; Phil 3:4–11.

simplicity are most notable in their lack: the absence of noise, the comforting and reinforcing presence of others, and the trappings of an overcrowded life. This is an absence which becomes a Presence, just as a basin and cup are the sources of a kingdom. It is difficult for us to grasp just how empowerment can come from first disempowering our voice, community, and accumulation. The nonact of silence is practiced against our self-justification (our own conceived rightness), solitude against our reputation, and simplicity against our accomplishments. Such practices are called for by Jesus' expectation in his parable in Mark 4 that we evaluate both the soil we live in and the soil that is ourselves. An effective evaluation must have the capability of sorting out the real from the unreal; it must make a judgment about whether or not the context we inhabit is the only or even the best way to conduct life. Silence, solitude, and simplicity serve as the means to empty our reliance on modern forms of meaning in order to create the space for a critical appraisal of our Western paradigm.

Noise is ubiquitous in our culture which is not always a mere function of sound or volume. We experience a near continuous bombardment of "noise" through a variety of media outlets and the general, never-ceasing industrial environment. Our culture depends on the continuous proliferation of messages in order to maintain production and consumption patterns. Mobile devices mean we are never far from the noise of sounds and images. The various messages that dominate our waking hours are about naming. As we noted earlier, naming is about identifying value. Modern news, entertainment, advertising—they are all voice, and therefore aimed at establishing gradations of worth. Silence then becomes an especially important means of sorting out relative importance.

The experience of true, actual silence can be unnerving and perhaps even terrifying because of the way it separates us from the voices which we depend on to reinforce or even establish meaning and purpose. A few years ago, I was deep in Utah's San Rafael Desert during an unusually cold few days in late November. The cold had driven all life—mammal, insect, even bird life—into a protective silence or a friendlier climate. As darkness fell, the sky was clear and free from even the distinct overhead sound of jet traffic. The air was as dead calm and cold as I have ever experienced, without the breath to even move the blades of yellow grass near my head as I lay in my sleeping bag. It was an absolute and complete silence which I was reticent to disturb by even the slightest movement. It was a kind of silence in which one can almost hear the blood coursing through the veins; a frightening silence, as if the world itself had stopped turning.

If one has never experienced such a pure lack of sound, it might be difficult to understand how such a quality of silence contains its own clear voice, a voice of a different quality, of an unsettling negation. Silence has its own tonal quality, a distinctive pitch not otherwise discernable in our world of continuous, manufactured messages. And for those of us listening to the cacophony of messages which are always about identifying and naming value, these different notes can frighten us as they challenge our inherited ways of being. As humans, we are products of culture, so any silence which would help us sort out the real from the chimera must be deep enough and of a long enough duration for the soundtrack of the mind to run its course to the point that there is no sound left.

Solitude resembles silence in the way that it serves to dismantle the cultural scaffolding with which we protect the inherited ways of functioning in a society that we secretly fear may not provide the meaning for which we had hoped. Solitude is the purposeful separation from the group, the communal context which forms us, and so creates a distance from cultural constructs like progress. It has long been a practice of various cultures to drive their youth on the verge of adulthood into a solitary existence for a period of time in order to open the possibility of evaluating cultural constructs and question societal norms. This has been a challenge for Christianity in our modern North American setting because we have long believed our youth can only rightly be shaped to live as Christians if they are acculturated as good citizens and contributors to the ruling social order. By now I hope it is apparent that the dominant cultural values that we are so anxious about in our children may not have as much basis in God's *shalom* as we had hoped.

Most of my backpacking trips are designed to maximize solitude. I typically avoid trails or identifiable and popular landmarks that will potentially attract visitors, and I make every effort to travel in conditions which are likely to keep the majority of people safe at home. I am fortunate to live on the edge of a region where I can still identify enormous tracts of space with no trail or road. My concerns in walking through landscape have far less to do with experiencing an arresting view or stunning beauty—things I nevertheless encounter regularly—and more to do with the ways a silent and solitary landscape shapes the soul. This, of course, is often a source of primary concern for my wife of nearly thirty years, who at times worries about the repercussions if something were to happen. Not only am I most often alone, but it is not always clear where I might be within a massive expanse of no established route—no cultural pathway. We have both had to come to some sense that the reward is worth the risk.

Solitude has always been a risky endeavor, which partially explains its lack of favor in our historical situation bent on managing risk and the unknown. Solitaries have always been viewed with suspicion as they inhabit the margins of society. John the Baptist was considered possessed because of his eccentric desert solitude, and yet was instrumental in delivering the message of God's intended *shalom*. Those intimate with solitude are considered rebels, revolutionaries, eccentrics, crazy hermits, or just general outsiders. This is due to their access to different definitions of being. And while their answers may not be always beneficial, we cannot avoid the space for questioning. We live in a generally risk-averse culture because risk is antithetical to our priorities of control over both nature and the social order. I would argue, however, that the reward of solitude is worth the risk that it might produce a revolutionary because the life of faith itself is a kind of risk, and proper solitude may actually cultivate a soil of being receptive to the seed of the gospel.

If silence is unnerving and solitude is disparaged for its inherent risk, simplicity is simply untenable. The world of progress that is our landscape requires the constant restlessness of a mind always in need and never satisfied. The self-preservation of the Western order examined in part I depends for its success on opposing the very idea of simplicity, making this a difficult act of nonacting. It was partially the simplicity of Jesus which so challenged the ruling order of his day. He ignored the stratification of society and simplified the social order by emphasizing the value of even the unvalued of his day: women, children, lepers, the lame, the poor—anyone who was socially marginal. Jesus instructed his followers not to be concerned with what they ate or wore; refused to defend or justify his own reputation among the rich and powerful; prioritized time alone and with his small band of followers over against an appeal to the crowds.

This lies at the heart of how we understand and develop the landscape of the soul. As we move from the shaping context of our built environment into a landscape of reality because it is one not of our making, we are forced into considerations of simplicity. Trips deep into the silence and solitude of natural environments are a purposeful way to dismantle the supports that artificially prop up our lives. When one must account for the fact that he or she will only have what one is able to carry, it forces an accounting of what can be dispensed with. It may surprise us all what we can happily do without.

There is a point at which silence becomes voice, solitude presence, and simplicity a kind of wealth. Thomas Merton once wrote, "The value of our weakness and of our poverty is that they are the earth in which God sows the seed of desire."[35] Our starting point is our stopping. The *via negativa* of the apophatic, nonthought, and the acts of nonacting are the points at which the soil of being is softened and cleared from the cares of the world. Perhaps now we are ready for the seed.

---

35. Merton, *Thoughts in Solitude*, 48.

Chapter 7

Seed

LIKELY AT THE BOTTOM of the to-do list for any of us is an exposure of weakness, inability, or need. We are conditioned to generally avoid situations in which a lack of perceived competence could come to the fore, and to tell a story revealing one's own shortcomings is almost as painful as the experience because of the way we become exposed to other people. One winter I attempted an obscure and less-than-well-defined trip along a section of the spine of the Waterpocket Fold in southcentral Utah. The fold is a hundred-mile, enormous uplift of domes and rocks cut deeply by canyons that can appear abruptly and force long detours. Trails are nonexistent and the trip reports provided by others are notoriously difficult to reconcile with the actual features on the ground; a perfect recipe for things to go wrong.

Thanks to the bitter cold I encountered any potholes of water I might otherwise have used were frozen solid and rendered useless for refilling my water supplies. I was forced to gather thin layers of snow to melt for water which not only contained as much sand as liquid, but too-quickly burned up my stove fuel. On one high ridge on the third day I missed a critical exit and eventually found myself on a high point of land surrounded on three sides by hundreds of feet of sheer cliff. Having no idea where I had gone wrong, I was forced to backtrack off the ridge to my starting point of the day. I was reduced to crossing low hills carved by innumerable washes, slippery with gumbo mud that coated my legs to mid-calf. When I eventually reached Pleasant Creek, the batteries on my water purifier were dead and I was forced to drink my fill of unfiltered water. I ended the trip in the growing dark and plummeting temperatures with a twelve-mile bike ride back to my vehicle.

It certainly was not one of my finest hours and revealed not a few of my own weaknesses and lack of foresight in preparation. Nonetheless, I will most assuredly venture to undertake a similar trip again and again. In just such a context which reveals our lack of control and utter mastery, we are thrust into a position where we can be powerfully worked on by an externality. There is an uncomfortable benefit to being exposed in such a manner: the disarming realization that at some crucial level our position in the universe is one of utter dependency. This certainly shapes my own reading of Jesus' parables in Mark 4.

In my mind, the parable of the soils in Mark 4:1–9 and Jesus' interpretation in verses 13–20[1] is one of the most important stories Jesus told to his earliest followers. This short, yet richly endowed parable steeps the meeting point between Creator and the created in natural imagery while addressing the issue of cultural formation, which is a uniquely human phenomenon. We are reminded on the one hand of the order and coherence of natural creation pictured by the authors of Job and Genesis. There is an inherent goodness in what God designed the world to look like. On the other hand is the breath of consciousness granted to human beings which enables the additional creation of culture as we internalize the external creation to formulate purpose and human action. What we have seen thus far is that human uniqueness can also become the problematic issue when, instead of recognizing its condition as a part of creation, the human creative capacity seeks to become its own empowering end for a vision of existence, thus becoming self-referent, which is the soil in which we operate.

The conflict is embodied in this parable. Various types of human cultural constructs are contrasted with a rich soil of being which serves as the setting for the decisive act of the reception of the seed. This story warrants the explicit explanation of Jesus in verses 14–20 because it uniquely pictures the pivotal point at which humanity meets the full intention of the Creator for his world. Too often this parable has been narrowed to apply only to the ways in which individuals respond to a kind of personal invitation to some kind of paradisiacal afterlife. The exploration of the imagery of soil indicates this is instead a presentation of the larger issue of culture-wide meaning-making. The role of the seed likewise expands the intention of Jesus beyond the individual soul to encompass our whole way of being in the world. The parable is not at its core about another realm of existence, but instead what

---

1. Parallels are found in Matt 13:1–23 and Luke 8:4–15.

we do with this one, and therefore serves to counter the ethos I went to such lengths to develop in part I.

I briefly noted in the previous chapter that Jesus explicitly designates the seed as "the word" (Mark 4:14). Matthew's explanation of the parable provides greater clarity in the image when he says the seed is "the word of the kingdom" (Matt 13:19). The good news of the kingdom, what is often referred to simply (and too often narrowly, individualistically) as "the gospel," by now should invoke the whole imagery of *shalom*: of the way the Creator intends his world to look. Everything the New Testament says about gospel draws on the vision of a flourishing creation in both individual and communal terms. The message of the kingdom, the heart of the activity and words of Jesus, is about the repair of life, culture, and by extension the world we inhabit as members of creation. In the parable of the soils, Jesus is therefore directing attention to the ways this good news is received and acted on.

The reception of the gospel and our understanding of what that entails then comes down to the particularities of our cultural formation and value-establishment. This is simply part of what it means to be human. Jesus indicates that not all ways of receiving the good news and the way of life that emerges from a particular reception are equal. In each of the four ways of seed meeting soil, Jesus says, "and these are the ones" (vv. 15, 16, 18, 20). The seed is a message of the Creator's intention while it is at the same time *people*. We act on any variety of messages we receive in ways that reflect the value we ascribe to those messages. The point is meant to demonstrate how the message of created order—our ought, *shalom*—takes root internally and then is expressed in the formation of our culture. What do we *do* with the vision of the world as it ought to be? Apparently, it is one thing to contact the message of the vision of the Creator's intention, but another thing entirely to see that contact produce a different personal and communal experience which would bear the fruit of a world as it was designed to be.

For all of his other foibles, Peter seems to have actually received the message of the seed Jesus was emphasizing in this parable in Mark 4. In his first letter, Peter reminds his readers that their newly formed personal and social ways of existing in the world are the result of the proper reception of the "seed" (1 Pet 1:22–23). Furthermore, Peter explicitly contrasts a new cultural reality characterized by personal wholeness and "brotherly love" with the fleeting nature of the constructs of our own ways of being: "All flesh is like grass and all its glory is like the flower of grass. The grass withers, and the flower falls. . ." (1 Pet 1:24). The word—the seed—is the good news of world renewal which is progressing according to the terms of the Creator and stands in contrast to a supposed reality we ourselves can construct.

The foremost aspect of the nature of the seed in this critical parable is that the gospel is fundamentally something to be *received*. While the soil establishes our need to suspend our own constructive agendas, the seed is a reminder that the richness of all that the image of the gospel entails is given by Someone external to ourselves and thereby surpasses our best efforts and good intentions. The seed as that which is received, not produced, therefore confronts the cultural paradigm we live under laid out in part I, and informs the movement toward *shalom*, oughtness, and kingdom, all of which made up part II. The healthy and proper landscape of the soul is an organic soil cleared of the arrogant self-sufficiency of Western culture, and one which then stands ultimately in a receptive condition.

Herein is a key issue for us to grasp: We must come to terms with our own agendas, built up through centuries of progress through efforts to build our own best societies; agendas which establish us as primarily builders, not receivers. It should be apparent at this point the multiple ways in which our humanly derived and self-reinforced efforts frequently do more harm than good. The issue lies embedded in the context I have been at such length to describe because it is in so many ways antithetical to the very heart of the gospel. We are all-too-rarely capable of assuming a truly receptive posture because to do so is to relativize our own ability and accumulated sense of self-worth. Regardless of Christian protests to the contrary, we demonstrate a rather sparse understanding of the ways in which our condition as created beings places us first and foremost in a position to be acted on by another.

To allow Jesus' image of the seed as that which is given to develop in us a properly receptive posture, what follows in this chapter will draw from some of the categories of the theology of Karl Barth before turning to an exploration of the centerpieces of Paul's New Testament theology: faith and grace. I will then explore the ways in which the nonindustrialized portions of the natural world serve as a uniquely powerful context for restoring us to our condition as recipients. Only as we fully accept our position as those to whom something must be bestowed, in contrast to our ways of being that would produce our own meaning, can we discover the reality of the world as it ought to be.

I acknowledge a certain risk in turning to the theology of a figure such as Karl Barth. Born in the Swiss city of Basel in 1886, Barth has been somewhat of a polarizing figure in twentieth-century theological thought because he was long considered too conservative for liberals and too liberal for conservatives. In addition to the perception that Barth occupies theological margins, few would be so presumptuous to claim an intimate understanding of Barth's brilliance as a theologian and the breadth of his thought. I certainly claim no special insight into the depths of his at times inaccessible intellect. The sheer volume of his life's work—just the single masterpiece *Church Dogmatics* runs to nearly 8,000 pages in the English translation— precludes a full understanding of Karl Barth for all but a select few Barth scholars. Still, it is the opinion of not a few contemporary theologians and church leaders that, "there is little doubt that Karl Barth will tower above the others as the most prominent and influential theologian of his time."[2]

While it is true that Barth was educated in the most prominent liberal theological climes in Europe in the early twentieth century, he became disillusioned by the failure of liberal Christianity to say anything meaningful about God. He later approached his position teaching Reformation theology at a German university with an honesty and thoroughness sometimes lacking on both sides of the theological spectrum, and in many ways was able to formulate a theology that surpassed the narrow human concerns of *both* liberal and conservative thought. Barth's importance for our current conversation additionally lies in his confrontation with a German church experiencing cultural realities oddly similar to those in our own North American context. In the end, Barth provides us with a refreshingly brutal honesty regarding the limitations of our speaking of God and our need to first be recipients of grace and revelation. Because I am no Barth scholar, I will rely in what follows on the accessible *Barth for Armchair Theologians* by former Biblical Theological Seminary professor John Franke, and the summary of Barth's *Church Dogmatics* provided in the *Introduction to the Theology of Karl Barth* by former Fuller Theological Seminary professor Geoffrey Bromiley.

Karl Barth's break with the leading scholars of the European Christian church came to a head on the verge of World War I in 1914 and serves as a clear connective point regarding my own contention that too much of the twenty-first century North American church is simply a reflection of our own Western cultural paradigm. Some of the most prominent German theologians had signed a declaration of support for the Kaiser and the war which disturbed Barth because of "the way in which the love of the Fatherland, the assumption of the legitimacy of war, and the Christian faith were brought together in hopeless confusion across Germany."[3] The German church's open support of World War I demonstrated its limitations in speaking about God in ways that could challenge the ethos of a given culture. In the climate of 1900s Germany, and equally so in 2000s North America, it appears to much of the wealthy and fully programmed church an inconceivable notion that God might oppose "the values, ideals, and aspirations" of

2. Franke, *Barth for Armchair Theologians*, ix.

3. Franke, *Barth for Armchair Theologians*, 29.

our particular cultural setting. For Barth in 1914, and I would contend he would see the situation similarly today, God served "to function as one who simply sanctioned the values and norms that society had established and certified them with a divine seal of approval."[4]

A similar situation occurred in 1934 when Barth was largely responsible for drafting the Barmen Declaration in the context of the rise of Nazi Germany. The signers of the initially unpopular declaration became known as the Confessing Church during World War II, and included the likes of the martyr Dietrich Bonhoeffer. Barth, along with the other signatories, refused to support the nationalistic aims of Nazi Germany and were forced to do so against the German Lutheran Church of the day. The Nazi party had successfully married the promise of economic recovery and political stability with the emergence of a national German identity and did so aligned closely with the German Lutheran Church. Barth's refusal to equate God the Creator with narrow, culturally determined ends resulted in his dismissal from his teaching position in Bonn, Germany and his return to Switzerland.

This background is important because it not only forms Barth's theological categories but additionally serves to challenge our own situation in which it is all too easy to justify our current God talk and busyness on the basis that this is surely what God would have done. Rather than the good news of the kingdom being a seed that is received, it is instead something to be pursued through effort, growing wealth and influence, and political power. For Barth, this is essentially the "domestication of God" because it establishes God's will as "merely an improved continuation of ours that can be easily ascertained from our situation."[5] God is instead Wholly Other, and therefore Barth openly criticized "the all-too-ready assumption that God could easily be annexed to the desires, goals, and aspirations of human interest."[6] As John Franke summarizes Barth's seminal thought in this regard: "When human beings talk about God in such a way as to make their beliefs and aspirations the locus of ultimate truth or to claim divine sanction for institutions that are all too human and flawed, they become guilty of idolatry and ungodliness."[7]

In order for God to be the Creator and not contingent on us as created, plans, purposes, and even language must come from outside our own cultural constructs. This places us in the position of being recipients of anything God would say or do. This is perhaps the single greatest emphasis in

4. Franke, *Barth for Armchair Theologians*, 30–31.
5. Franke, *Barth for Armchair Theologians*, 35, 37.
6. Franke, *Barth for Armchair Theologians*, 45.
7. Franke, *Barth for Armchair Theologians*, 46.

the theology of Karl Barth. God is never subject to our cultural formations of meaning, but rather unilaterally distributes seeds which indicate the intended form of the world. "As creatures we cannot presume upon God, we cannot 'have' God. Instead, we are always in a place of need and dependence on God for our knowledge of God, our speech about God, and our relationship with God."[8] God does not exist to affirm the way we already view the world, but according to Barth invades and disrupts what we take for granted as the order of reality by speaking on his own terms as the one who establishes the ought of creation.

The too-often unacknowledged dependency on culturally determined systems of value which predominate in much of American spirituality, such as those indicated by our belief in human forms of progress, mark this era as one especially needful on the thinking of Karl Barth. Regardless of where we might place Barth on the theological spectrum, his writing and, perhaps more importantly, his acting, was centrally focused on the otherness of God and how that chief quality confronts a people whose daily activity is far more emblematic of human-oriented cultural definitions of being than it is the kingdom of God. To understand the fundamental difference between the Creator and the created is for Barth the basic starting point for suspending unexamined assumptions and thereby placing one in a position to receive the restoration of a kind of humanity more in accordance with the intent inherent in God's design.

Near the opening of his massive *Church Dogmatics*, Barth goes to lengths to emphasize that knowledge of God can never be independent, self-grounded, or self-controlled.[9] This might appear to be stating the obvious, but the church and her theologians too often correlate the knowledge of God with the categories of personal meaning already established in human culture. While there is a *relative* difference among all creaturely objects, one I emphasized in the Genesis image of the breath of life, there is an *absolute* difference between the Creator and the created. This leads Barth to the natural conclusion that "God is known through God and God alone,"[10] and places us firmly in the position of recipients first and foremost.

While this might seem as a rather elementary point of Christian theology, a confession most would readily give ascent to, Barth emphasizes that the idea too seldom serves to actually form Christian identity because of the way it sets itself against the universal tendency toward self-sufficiency. Humankind demonstrates a basic resistance to God, regardless of the ways in

---

8. Franke, *Barth for Armchair Theologians*, 51.

9. Bromiley, *Introduction to the Theology of Karl Barth*, 11.

10. Bromiley, *Introduction to the Theology of Karl Barth*, 58–59.

which we might consider ourselves receptive. This resistance has always led to the alternative pursuit of an inauthentic knowledge of God which "has no true object" because it is in actuality the desire to create our own ultimacy based on our own being and nature.[11] The problem for the religiously inclined is that this alternative and secondary kind of pursuit makes one just happy and secure enough to think that the "God" category is covered when there is actually no reality present. Apart from God's self-revelation as a gift, we have only a poor and dim reflection of the reality, a reflection that has its origin in human thought. One of the most significant issues with a secondary knowledge is that "even in the church, even in the context and doctrine of grace, man will always jump at this possibility."[12]

We are reminded that the soil which receives the seed is one in which agenda and language are first suspended, lest our experience of the otherness of God becomes merely the self-projection of our own sense of what is valuable. When we self-project, we end up with a church and spirituality that accepts its own busyness and productivity as marks of a successful religious life. Barth emphasized that we do not acquire authentic words and concepts merely by repetition of those we already have. What we comprehend we resemble, control, and possess, which is to emphasize the incomprehensibility of God.[13] The mystery of God is basic to the distinction between Creator and created which places us in an absolute dependence of God's self-unveiling, and which, "may then be described as an act of wondering awe, the sense of an overcome incongruence, inadequacy, and distance, in which we let the overcoming grace be truly grace. . ."[14]

Joseph Pieper echoes Barth's categories and illumines our conception of the seed when he writes that, "Human knowing has an element of the non-active, purely receptive seeing, which is not there in virtue of our humanity as such, but in virtue of a transcendence over what is human, but which is really the highest fulfillment of what it is to be human, and is thus 'truly human' after all."[15] The whole project of this book is to renew in us the position of reception where something is poured into us; something we did not have nor could ever produce. This must be something that comes from

---

11. Bromiley, *Introduction to the Theology of Karl Barth*, 61. In the sometimes-difficult language of Barth, we pursue "an inauthentic knowability in the self-originated movement of thought which has no true object but simply takes the form of an absolutizing of his own being and nature." Such is a basic "encroachment on God" and a resistance to revelation.

12. Bromiley, *Introduction to the Theology of Karl Barth*, 63.

13. Bromiley, *Introduction to the Theology of Karl Barth*, 65, 66.

14. Bromiley, *Introduction to the Theology of Karl Barth*, 66–67.

15. Pieper, *Leisure*, 12.

without and therefore not based on applying ourselves more diligently to making things happen. This posture lies at the heart of the gospel and, while it is often emphasized and acknowledged, our efforts to produce greater mastery, wealth, and ever-expanding growth betray a basic allegiance to a very different reality. Our soil of being—the landscape of the soul—is too often given over to too many other purposes and enveloped in an environment frequently unconducive to the adequate reception of the seed.

It is critical to keep the image of receiving invoked by Jesus' use of the figure of the seed ever before us because of our human tendency to be restless and so to subvert the process of God's self-unveiling which cannot depend on our schedule of production. The temptations of Jesus referenced in chapter 5 demonstrate his refusal to use any other ability as a shortcut to the purposes of the Creator. Our failure to depend on the self-disclosure of God is evidenced by how hurriedly and obsessively we undertake efforts to secure our own ought, even in the church, and especially in our individual lives. This forces a consideration of the ideas of faith and grace, two necessary and interrelated themes explored by the apostle Paul in his New Testament letters to churches struggling to form a new identity in the midst of an absolutizing cultural reality.

When Paul writes to the Christian church in Rome reminding them that "Abraham believed God, and it was credited to him as righteousness" (Rom 4:3), he was making an important statement not about Abraham's ability, but about his orientation to the self-revelation of God. In Genesis 15, God's self-disclosure to Abraham consisted of a promise that Abraham would be the father of many nations despite the fact that Abraham was already over seventy-five years old. Obviously, this was something that came from outside Abraham and would completely reformulate not only Abraham's entire cultural reality, but even definitions of human ability. Paul indicates that "faith" brought about the state of Abraham as he ought to be ("righteousness," Rom 4:5). For Paul, this condition of faith becomes definitive for anyone who would be similarly oriented to the utter reality of a reformulating God (Rom 4:16).

We are meant to understand Paul's explication of faith in Romans 4 (and similarly, Gal 3) as indicating a receptive posture to the self-disclosure of the ultimate reality of God redefining the sense of the possible and the real. If our unique capacity for spirituality entails the internalizing of the external,[16] then faith is a unique expression of internalizing the unseen and previously unknown. For the writer of the New Testament book of Hebrews, faith is the "assurance of things hoped for and the conviction of things not

---

16. See ch. 4.

seen" (11:1). Faith directs an attention to our hoped-for ought and does so through a seeing of the unseen reality of God. Abraham oriented himself away from received cultural ways of being and toward a new form of life, despite not knowing where he was going (Heb 11:8), while Moses "endured as seeing him who is invisible" (Heb 11:27).

For the New Testament, faith does not consist in an easily voiced platitude which leaves an established and inherited order intact, but always comes about in response to the self-disclosure of the otherness of God which brings about a rightness of existence even while it reformulates one's cultural underpinnings. For Karl Barth, faith is at root a risky enterprise because of the unseen otherness of God: "If there be no gamble of faith, if faith be forgotten or for one moment suspended, or if it be thought of as anything but a hazard, this identity is no more than an entirely trivial enterprise of religious or speculative arrogance."[17]

Paul is adamant in his theology about the contrast between the receptive posture of faith and the efforts of human instrumentality.[18] His concern certainly stems from a recognition of human proclivity toward meaning-making and our tendency to then cast the Creator as one who sanctions what we ourselves have conceived. In order to maintain the otherness of God as self-existent and self-referent, any of God's self-disclosure—what Paul refers to as "the promise" in Romans 4—must maintain God's position as independent and establish the human position as receptive. To maintain the distinction, Paul emphasizes that the self-revelation of God which forces us into the receptive posture of faith must be predicated on *grace*: "That is why it depends on faith, in order that the promise may rest on grace. . ." (Rom 4:16).

Grace is an idea that potentially loses its impact through much overuse. While likely a more common *experience* than we might be aware of, a fully formed understanding of the idea appears to be lost in common usage. At its root, grace refers to God doing something that does not get done in any other way. When someone even flippantly proclaims, "But for the grace of God, there go I," the idea behind the sentiment is that if God had not intervened, things would have turned out quite differently. It is the unilateral and utterly self-determinative act of God as creator and sustainer of the world that lies behind the biblical presentation of the concept of grace. Perhaps more than any other category, grace establishes us as humans firmly in the receptive posture advocated by Jesus' parables in Mark 4 and thereby

---

17. Barth, *Epistle to the Romans*, 149.

18. See Rom 3:27–28; 9:32; Gal 2:16; 3:2.

dismantles the meaning derived from our own efforts to build a world of purpose.

In his farewell speech to the early church in Ephesus, Paul indicates that his single purpose in life was to present the message of "the gospel of the grace of God" (Acts 20:24). The gospel—the good news of the *shalom*-bearing kingdom of God—is here paired with grace as an indication that it is something only God can bring about. Anything of ultimate value in the life of one oriented to the Creator comes about by grace. The state of him who is as he ought to be is the result of the gift of grace (Rom 3:24). The right ordering of the world on both an individual and communal scale can only come about as the Creator does what only the Creator can.

The New Testament presentation of the decisive nature of grace counters a culture such as our own, convinced of the value and universalness of its own agenda. Grace stands in contradistinction to the efforts of our culture to work hard enough to produce anything enduring (Rom 11:6); it is in contrast to our accumulated cultural wisdom (2 Cor 1:12); and rather than the perceived strength which would render individuals capable, grace is centered on weakness (2 Cor 12:9). The very root of the idea centers worthwhile activity in the unilateral initiative of God.

It is not unusual in our context for individuals to understand grace as a necessary entry-point into a life of faith. It is also not unusual to then move forward in life as if little had changed because we believe that we have the rest of life's concerns covered. This is precisely what the framework of our built-up environment convinces us of. But Paul warned both his Galatian and Corinthian readers of the possibility of nullifying grace or somehow causing it to be in vain (Gal 2:21; 2 Cor 6:1–2). There is the sense, perhaps even more noteworthy in our contemporary cultural climate, in which one might respond to the Creator in order to begin a life of faith, but quickly revert to the categories valued so highly by modern progressive culture in order to pursue one's fitness of life. If grace is God doing what doesn't get done any other way, then to accomplish what we can in our own inherent talent or ability is to render God's intervention superfluous. This is not to say that we do nothing we are capable of, simply to remind us that *shalom* and the kingdom are the possession and distribution of the Creator and that with regard to the ultimate harmony and flourishing of intended creation, our basic posture is necessarily one of perpetual reception.

Grace, as the unilateral move of God, also served an important social role for Paul addressing developing churches. What are typically designated spiritual gifts in Romans 12 and 1 Corinthians 12 are literally "graces" (Rom 12:6; 1 Cor 12:4). These are acts of service or words of wisdom or incidents of healing in which it is clear that God has performed an action for which no individual could take credit based on natural ability. Separated from such acts of grace, the church is little more than another social club or civic organization, sometimes with good music and a talented orator. And while apart from grace churches may reflect having successfully perpetuated the cultural categories of progress in crowds of people and large budgets, they lack the capacity to reflect the way the Creator designed the world to look. It has become all too easy to justify our own busyness and the trappings of success as marks of vibrant spirituality when they may be little more than demonstrations of human ingenuity which do not require God to be anywhere near the gathering. By way of contrast, the early churches of Macedonia experienced severe affliction and extreme poverty, but in this very condition were evidence of God doing what would not otherwise get done as the churches overflowed in a wealth of generosity: a grace (2 Cor 8:1–7).

Each of Paul's thirteen letters written to New Testament churches includes the invocation, "grace to you and peace." It might be tempting to minimize this repeated greeting as merely formulaic, but this becomes unlikely when we keep in mind the first-century context in which Paul wrote. These early gatherings of Jesus followers lacked not only widespread literacy, but additionally did not have the full collection of religious texts or resources we are privileged with. The churches existed in a Roman imperial climate which viewed Christianity as an upstart political movement, which meant the church was not granted the tolerance and sanction typically afforded merely religious movements. The Jesus followers were openly opposed by the Jewish religion out of which they had emerged, straining family and community bonds. For the first three centuries of its existence, the church was poor, persecuted, driven underground, and generally marginalized.

The grid through which Paul's letters were received, therefore, had far more to do with the nature of God's design for creation as a whole than how smoothly individual life could be made to operate. The view of reality and the nature of the Christian faith had to entail a larger world concern, otherwise why sign up for the hassle? The few and far between letters from church leaders such as Paul would have to be read and reread and passed among congregations, so the themes of grace and peace would have been repeatedly encountered. These two closely related ideas would have been largely irrelevant in the first-century context if they were merely concerned about being in by grace or at personal peace. They could only sustain this marginal movement if they served as indicators that God had powerfully intervened in a broken world and was engaged in its repair. Grace and peace are themes of world remaking, especially in the ready recognition of the limitations of self-oriented activity and resources; limitations which would have sat heavy on the early church. Today, the very idea of limitation seems especially far from our own experience, continuously surrounded by the reminders of our own abilities in the enveloping, built environment.

What we have done in the contemporary church to minimize peace to a personal, internal state and shrink grace to a momentary need stems from the ways these categories oppose our narrow approach to a personally comfortable existence as well as confront the self-sufficiency of our efforts to engineer a meaningfully constructed life. Because we want the appearance of welcoming grace and peace without the implications of their attack on our adherence to self-confident effort, we end up, in the words of Jacques Ellul, subverting and perverting the core of faith. Grace and peace are comforting images for most of us, invoking a satisfied state of calm, inner tranquility and having a ledger littered with mistakes wiped clean. On the contrary, Paul's characterization of grace is the unleashing of a formerly unknown and uncontrollable creative power which wants to engage the messy brokenness of the world in a way that propels it toward *shalom*.

In his *Subversion of Christianity*, Ellul confronts the difficulty we have with being in the position to receive, as opposed to build, our own fitness. "Grace. Do you think it is acceptable? To learn that we are the recipients of grace. It does not depend on me; I can do nothing. . . . Grace is odious to us."[19] When we understand the full weight of our inability to establish our own oughtness and must respond to its bestowal by Another, "the worst possible injury is done to us. We are dispossessed of grandeur, autonomy, and the faculty of justice." As the unilateral self-disclosure of the Wholly Other, grace is a new state, "an opening into a kind of life that has nothing to do with your petty pretensions, but that truly does not come from you. You are not the owner. Yet you try to transform it into your property."[20] In the end, from our own self-sufficient viewpoint, grace is unacceptable and intolerable.

The work of Ellul highlights the basic struggle to cultivate a vibrant spiritualty in our Western cultural ethos. Our difficulty lies in how the images of Babel, sabbath, the kingdom, the soil, and the seed direct us toward a position of receiving rather than producing. These offend us at heart because of their inefficiency, being—like grace—independent of our demonstrated ability to construct a reality. Occupying the center of my argument is the need to find a different context in which our accomplishments do not predominate. We must discover a setting that allows us to become intimate with the reality of grace and its nature as something bestowed. This forces, once again, a consideration of what landscape dominates our horizon: What

19. Ellul, *Subversion of Christianity*, 158–59.
20. Ellul, *Subversion of Christianity*, 160, 163.

is the specific environment that is determinative for how we engage our spirituality, our Creator, our world? How do we develop a posture of receptivity which is at the center of the Christian experience?

What has become especially important for my own life in developing this posture is increasing exposure to an environment that I don't control or build; a setting which minimizes my self-sufficient capabilities to affect change and which at the end of the day does not serve as a demonstration of my own mastery. This is how the wild—the wastelands—of our world serve a pivotal role as the physical environment becomes a setting of a deeper and more basic reality than any constructed landscape. William Dyrness connects the natural world with a receptive posture when he writes,

> . . . the first movement in human relationships toward the earth is not active but passive. . . In the Western tradition the earth is encountered as an object that must be managed, without any larger context in which it can simply be received. . . Creation, as the work of God, is first of all received as a gift that speaks to us of purposes and interests that transcend our own, and thus should be received with humility."[21]

In light of the nature of grace and the idea that the created-by-God world is itself a gift that can reformulate our purposes, I want to suggest that exposure to an unpeopled, undeveloped, untrammeled wilderness serves a sacramental role. This idea will undoubtedly require close attention, as the idea of sacrament has been a contentious issue throughout church history, and to associate wild spaces with the idea can potentially lead to further confusion. The practice and relevance of the sacraments of baptism and communion were initially given their theological underpinnings early in the fifth century by Augustine, who indicated that these practices were outward signs of an inward grace. By the thirteenth century, and particularly due to the systematizing work of Thomas Aquinas, the Christian church had solidified seven sacraments which were believed to *confer* grace simply by being performed. Specifically, the sacraments of baptism, confirmation, and ordination were said to immediately effect a seal on the soul.

As theologian Stanley Grenz indicates, the sacraments developed through the medieval church period into sacred rites which were able to *infuse* divine grace. The rites had actually come to be understood as God's chosen means of dispensing grace.[22] The Reformation of the sixteenth century rejected the perceived corralling and institutionalization of God and his grace and reduced the sacraments to two ordinances: baptism and the

---

21. Dyrness, *Earth is God's*, 116.
22. Grenz, *Theology for the Community of God*, 513.

Lord's Supper. Even amongst Protestant churches today, it is still not agreed upon if the sacraments—ordinances—are merely symbolic, effective rites that confer anything, or whether or not there is a magical presence inherent in the exercises.

Regardless, the idea of sacrament has always been closely associated with and dependent on a human need for the grace of God. In pursuing the idea that an experience in an undeveloped environment entails sacramental qualities, I do so firstly by considering some cautions voiced by theologian Donald Bloesch regarding the ideas we can too often associate with sacrament. Bloesch emphasizes that whatever other function they serve, the sacraments always direct attention away from us to Christ. This is central because nothing—and Bloesch emphasizes *both* the rite of sacrament *and* nature—has the capacity to effect faith or our ought apart from the activity of God. To pretend that nature itself is a sacred reservoir of redemption is to err on the side of closing the distance between God and his creation, which is as presumptuous as it is to bind God to ceremonial acts performed by clerics. God is free to reveal or hide himself and we are never in a position to presume God will act when the church acts.[23] With these cautions in mind, Bloesch emphasizes that the sacraments announce the presence of God, faith receives that presence, and faith then working through love demonstrates and manifests that presence to the world.[24] I would contend, then, that if a natural landscape can announce the reality of a God fundamentally different from us and our efforts, then we are closer to fulfilling our responsibility to the world.

In his *Theology for the Community of God*, Grenz indicates that the ordinances are rites to act out our faith. They are "enactments of our appropriation of God's action in Christ."[25] Their role is to affirm faith in a symbolic manner. If combined with faith, these rites facilitate our participation in the reality God is enacting in his world. Sacraments graphically depict the truth verbally declared in the gospel message: the good news of the kingdom.

As much as I may like to, I am not attempting to create a backpacking trip as a new church sacrament. My intent is to draw on the imagery of a graphic acting out of a spirituality vitally connected with all that has been said thus far about righteousness, *shalom*, the kingdom, and grace. These are the acts of God beyond any human construct and therefore beyond our over-confidently established tendencies toward the sufficiency of the

---

23. Bloesch, *Church*, 175.
24. Bloesch, *Church*, 175.
25. Grenz, *Theology for the Community of God*, 516.

built-by-us. Wilderness is thus *sacramental* (though not itself a sacrament) in its function of allowing us to physically rub up against the idea of grace in a context where God does what we could not.

The natural environment serves to remind us of—and furthermore, connect us with—the heart of the good news: God is the creator, he initiates re-creation in the kingdom announced by Jesus, and he invites us to participate in *shalom* in our very marginality: our inability and the weakness of the cup and the basin. Wilderness is itself marginal space for Western culture because it is essentially nonproductive and noninstrumental. But in its foreignness of space, wilderness maintains the unique capacity to resource a spirituality that is of grace and dismantle a faith built from our own self-referent construction.

Wild nature as a connective point to the power and intervening sufficiency of God has been the vital experience of countless people throughout human history. This is certainly how John Muir experienced his environment. One of this country's earliest and most eloquent spokesmen for the value of undeveloped wild spaces, John Muir was born into a highly religiously conservative Scotch-Presbyterian family in Dunbar, Scotland. The family immigrated to the United States in 1849, eventually settling in Wisconsin. At the age of twenty-nine, Muir would begin his wanderings and eventually settle in the San Francisco area. While certainly far removed later in life from the harsh and austere religion of his upbringing, Muir appears to have never lost his spiritual underpinnings. The writing of Muir is littered with references to the reality of God, but an approach formed through years of wandering expansive western wildernesses which served to develop an understanding of the Creator sometimes at odds with the tightly controlled and narrowly formed religion of his youth.

John Muir "was intensely religious. The forests and the mountains formed his temple. His approach to all nature was worshipful. He saw everything evolving yet everything the direct handiwork of God. There was a spiritual and religious exaltation in his experiences with nature."[26] In his reflections on his multiple trips to Alaska, gathered as *Travels in Alaska*, Muir writes of the grinding and crushing of the "huge ice tool" of a glacier in which "every feature glowed with intention, reflecting the plans of God," while "the careladen commercial lives we lead close our eyes to the operations of God as a workman, though openly carried on that all who will look may see."[27] It would be unfair to characterize my point as advocating for the dismantling of any and every value of the corporately gathered people

---

26. Teale, *Wilderness World of John Muir*, xiii.
27. Muir, *Travels in Alaska*, 53, 177.

of God to worship and hear the word preached. At the same time, there is a sense in too much of our faith exercise that reflects more of our own constructs and self-reinforcing categories rather than space which would lead us to a meeting with the absolute otherness of God.

The recognition of the capacity of the natural world to clearly reflect a Creator beyond our own secondarily creative abilities is part of what Muir is emphasizing. If grace is indicative of something only God is capable of, then it often appears that the created-by-God environment is a more readily accessible contact point with such grace than a tightly controlled space and theology which appears to have God figured out. This is not about going fishing every Sunday instead of gathering as a church. It is rather about a different kind of space which would increase our posture as recipients of revelation and grace, a posture which should then inform how we would pursue our own spiritual health and our corporate practices toward the re-pair of the world.

To a similar end, Muir writes in *My First Summer in the Sierra*, "No wonder the hills and groves were God's first temples, and the more they are cut down and hewn into cathedrals and churches the farther off and dimmer seems the Lord."[28] As he sat atop a boulder located midstream in a cataract, Muir exclaimed that "the place seemed holy, where one might hope to see God,"[29] which is in contrast to too much of our casually engineered religious space. Something needs to counter our tendency to be self-sufficient, and natural space is especially adept in this regard: "All the wilderness seems to be full of tricks and plans to drive and draw us up into God's Light."[30] The unique otherness of the not-built-by-us world is a powerful, I would argue even sacramental, reality which resists our fabricated reality and restores us to a position wherein we have a renewed capacity to receive.

This is another way to emphasize that we will inevitably take our cues of reality from what we surround ourselves with. Our environment shapes our understanding of and approach to God because we are not capable of formulating a conception of existence out of a vacuum. In his reflections on the desert environment, Joseph Wood Krutch points out that the character of land and the very look of the landscape powerfully influences what we feel and what we think about. "And nothing, not even the sea, has seemed to affect men more powerfully than the desert, or seemed to incline them so powerfully toward great thoughts, perhaps because the desert itself seems to

28. Highland, *Meditations of John Muir*, 3.
29. Highland, *Meditations of John Muir*, 15.
30. Highland, *Meditations of John Muir*, 125.

brood and to encourage brooding. To the Hebrews the desert spoke of God, and one of the most powerful of all religions was born."[31]

Krutch points out that the emphasis of the desert is starkly different from any other environment because the shore, the mountains, the valleys, and the plains, especially in their conditions as early locations of settlement, invite action and suggest limitless opportunity, while the implications and mood of the desert are something different. "It is more likely to provoke awe than to invite conquest. . . The heroism which it encourages is the heroism of endurance, not that of conquest."[32] My own formulative experiences with the desert of the Colorado Plateau are steeped in such endurance, which is to say: the desert invokes *need*.

The receptive posture emphasized in the seed is paramount because grace must be predicated on need. We do not experience what only God can do in the midst of anything we can accomplish on our own. So long as we are immersed in a comfortable atmosphere indicative of our capabilities to formulate the right conditions for our understanding of progress, God's activity remains conspicuously absent. That is an unsettling and disturbing notion. But if we can define and establish our own ought—in any realm of human activity—then why would God need to intervene and distribute grace? There must be a basic *in*capability on our part; an incapability that is acknowledged and even embraced. We too often fail to turn fully in dependence on God except on the basis of need. Solitary trips into the empty corner of hundreds of miles of deeply incised desert space accentuate inability.

A few years ago, I descended into a deep maze of canyons in nearly the center of the immense region of the plateau country, an expanse on the map specifically chosen for its absence of roads and trails and the almost obscene number of nameless canyons. It took me most of a day to wind the several hundred feet down steeply walled smaller canyons into the larger canyon, which served as a gathering point for a labyrinth of twisting gashes which could provide months of lost wandering. I camped by a narrow, meandering, perennial stream and proceeded the next day to walk and twist and scramble and climb up deep but narrow canyons which themselves branched off into countless hidden destinations. Late in the day, on a high rim at the head of a cliff-rimmed plunge back to the only source of water I had encountered, I decided to make my way back to my spot of the previous night.

It was the worst possible time for a migraine. I have experienced debilitating migraines throughout my life, but never in such an inhospitable location, running short on water, and in no place to assume my normally

31. Krutch, *Voice of the Desert*, 220.

32. Krutch, *Voice of the Desert*, 220–21.

comatose position: prone on the cold tile of the quietest and darkest and most convenient location of the bathroom floor. To get into the bottom of the tributary canyon I was above, I would traverse several hundred yards to a small break in an otherwise cliffed slope, descend a few feet, and traverse back along the bench, paralleling below my route of a few minutes earlier until I found another short drop I could navigate, only to turn back in the other direction. I was in excruciating, nauseating pain and making only small gains by way of enormous effort. It seemed torturous hours when I eventually found myself above the final thirty-foot drop of wall guarding the inner sanctum of the canyon. Out of water and with a head screaming and throbbing with the boulders of all the flash floods that had carved this narrow gash in the earth, I was forced to rig a rappel to negotiate the final step.

Perhaps it sounds overly dramatic, but I can assure you this narrative is nowhere close to being as dramatic as the experience itself. But the point is—and the reason the trauma has not yet been blotted from my memory— is because nearly a decade later I still experience that day as one of my most profound encounters with grace. I was reduced to a hunched, shuffling, blubbering shell who could only beg for God to somehow see me back to a collapse by the stream bank. When all is comfortable and controlled and easy, even thrilling, we rarely give thought to the way in which we stand in need of the intervention of God. And if we have everything covered, why would he intervene anyway? If grace is indicative of God doing what does not get done any other way, then grace naturally requires the end of our efforts and the suspension of self-sufficiency.

More recently, my wanderings landed me deep in Utah's Grand Gulch over a few frigid January days. I walked far down the gulch to a point near where it drains into the San Juan River and broke off into a side canyon, hoping to ascend to the sagebrush flat of Cedar Mesa where I would walk cross-country back to my vehicle. I had no idea if this particular canyon would provide an exit, but if it did not, the two and a half days of walking already behind me would entail an enormous effort to repeat. Hours of twisting and curving canyon with no more than a hundred-yard view of what lie ahead finally brought me to the final caprock cliff guarding the mesa, the cliff band I had been dreading since the beginning of the ascent. High above the canyon floor, at a low break in the cliff I hoped would provide a short enough step to climb, I encountered a stout trunk of pinyon leaning against the wall. It was just thick enough to support my weight and reached just high enough to allow me to scramble to the bench above. I climbed the log, hoisted my pack behind me, and sat down in desperate reflection.

I am willing to allow that my delivering log may have simply been a convenient coincidence. But that's not really the point. The point is that I *experienced* the occurrence as grace. That is always the value of exposure to an environment we don't have control over. The wilderness, still in the possession of the Creator, contains the tricks and plans that drive and draw our attention to God by accentuating our own incapacity to be self-sufficient.

Bruce Chatwin pointed out that Charles Darwin found the *negative* qualities of the Patagonian Desert irresistible. Darwin could not, however, successfully explain why those arid wastes had taken such firm possession of his mind, especially in light of all the other magnificent wonders he had seen throughout his wide travels. W. H. Hudson visited the same desert in 1860 and he devotes an entire chapter of *Idle Days in Patagonia* to addressing the dilemma. As Chatwin observes, ". . . he concludes that the desert wanderers discover in themselves a primaeval calmness (known even to the simplest savages) which is perhaps the same thing as the Peace of God."[33]

The peace of God—*shalom*—is what we are ultimately created for. The seed as something received from Another is the point at which we counter all the cultural realities of part I, mitigate the cost, and embrace the lessons of Job, Babel, the temple, our ought, *shalom*, and the kingdom; lessons that what we long for must be given, not produced. There is much to be said for the peculiar value of the landscape of an arid waste: the space which will form the figure of the final chapter.

33. Chatwin, *In Patagonia*, 15.

Chapter 8

Space

Soon after our youngest daughter graduated from high school, my wife and I accompanied her on a backpacking loop through two canyons in Utah's Cedar Mesa area. Our trailhead started on top of the mesa and dropped into a red rock canyon bursting in vibrant color in the warmup of spring in the desert. We walked under a high arch along potholes of water to a point at which our entry canyon met another canyon flowing in from the north which we would follow back up to the top of the mesa. For most of two days we thought this a rather ideal walk in a beautiful setting.

Rarely do the canyons of Cedar Mesa gradually descend from the plateau top at about 6,400 feet to their sandy floor of more than 1,000 feet below. What is most typical is a series of steep drops over various geologic strata which are often encountered as 100 feet or more of a pouroff over a cliff. Neither my wife nor I are particularly comfortable with heights, especially those consisting of open exposure to an immense vertical drop. Many of my travels in desert canyons and on alpine peaks have provided me with the ability to mitigate my fear and I continue to climb despite the discomfort, but only due to long years of practice. We were fortunate on this first day to discover that our route utilized a steep, broken gully to the canyon bottom, hemmed in by vertical walls and filled with a mass of boulders and other detritus. While steep, it was closed in and crowded just enough to hide any open exposure to the possibility of a devastating fall. The descent was a rather enjoyable, challenging scramble.

The exit from the connecting canyon back to the plateau was an entirely different matter. As we ascended the second canyon the following day, it eventually worked its way to the foot of an impassable, vertical pouroff. The route turned south to climb nearly straight up a hillside crossed by cliff bands, but broken at places just enough to allow passage without needing technical climbing gear. The primary issue for my wife on this day was not the physical nature of the climb, she had rather enjoyed the scrambling drop of the entry canyon. The problem was the exposure. While no more techni- cally demanding than our entrance, we were no longer squeezed in between walls and surrounded by house-sized boulders. We were on an enormous empty slope, often forced to climb above and traverse across vertical cliff bands which accentuated the cost of a potential slip. Nearly in tears with me guarding a fall by climbing closely behind, Colleen quickly worked her way up the slope with never a view into the open air pulling at her heels.

Fortunately, everyone looks back at the trip with (mostly) fond memo- ries and my wife still allows me to lead her into remote backpacking des- tinations, albeit with a little more care in route selection. I sense that the experience in Utah over that long spring weekend illustrates a profound reality about our place in the world: we are generally uncomfortable with— perhaps more likely fearful of—*space*. This is certainly not just about a physical fear of exposed heights, which not everyone experiences like my wife and I do; it's more about our experiencing any exposed, open spaces in our world and life as somehow disagreeable, perhaps even troublesome, often wearying. This is a function of the physical environment we surround ourselves with which serves to form a certain kind of interior life.

Individuals might occasionally talk about the need to find some open space for life, but our entire experience with cultural formation and practice betrays a basic devaluing of any space that is not used productively; and that is a specific productivity, culturally defined, based on the categories of value we have inherited as members of Western society. As was emphasized in exploring the cost of our cultural paradigm in chapter 3, we have little tolerance for a free-flowing river which could be made productive by build- ing enormous dams. Our roads and mines push into our spaces because the empty and uninhabited is useless until we can extract or access it on an ever-increasing scale. Open space that exists on the margins of habitation is generally confronted on the basis of how it can best serve as a context to further the advance of Western aims.

Enormously tragic human and natural consequences accompany these views of space as useless unless put to some productive use, even if that use is as a space to contain the deadly waste of an aggressive society. A cultural ethos obsessed with progress and profit marginalizes not only arid—and what is therefore assumed to be unproductive—land, but by default any people who might occupy such unprofitable space. It is thought acceptable to ignore the legacy of uranium mining on the Navajo Reservation because the land—and by extension, its people—are not useful for much else in a society bent on production. The wastelands of deserts in Nevada and New Mexico are suitable for decades of on-the-ground nuclear testing and waste disposal because they are too marginal for any other use.[1] Space exists to be filled up as a demonstration of how it can become valuable. This is true of *any* space: physical or social or emotional.

On some level I have been exploring this theme of space and its value/nonvalue throughout this work, which makes this an appropriate figure to come to in the final chapter. We demonstrate little tolerance for the empty or the marginal because these don't accord with the values of productivity, profitability, and, therefore, progress. This is unfortunately true with regard to not only the physical environment, but our understanding of people and our own pursuit of meaningful existence. There is an intimate connection, even if too often unacknowledged, between our cultural approach to the landscape as space and how we receive other people from a perspective of marginality. This additionally informs our particular approach to the edges of our soul that would otherwise serve as the location for the reception of grace and the kingdom.

I want to briefly explore some of our understanding of space, especially from the perspective of my own western context, because this is a stark illustration of the ways in which we pursue meaning as an experience of the whole of life. Empty, nonindustrialized space is, as it stands undeveloped and unoccupied, unprofitable. Land not somehow used properly demonstrates a waste of potential and therefore represents lost productivity and a blight on progress. This is a belief that pervades Western thought as a whole to the degree that even people who don't pursue or give unwavering support to the means of profit and progress are viewed as outsiders to the cultural mainstream and are therefore somehow missing out on their potential. We tend to approach life with the belief that nonproductive space—even the empty space of an interior life—needs to be occupied and put to beneficial use. The examples abound in controversial western land use.

At just over 97,000 square miles, Wyoming is the tenth-largest state, but the least populated. Its unique landmass with relatively few people means it is home to some of the most intact, large ecosystems in North America. Wyoming is also home to thousands of indigenous Western Mule Deer. Along the western portions of the state, the Sublette Herd of up to 5,000 deer travel 150 miles every fall from the Hoback Basin just south of the Tetons to the lower elevations of the Red Desert, repeating the route

---

1. See Kuletz, *Tainted Desert*; Solnit, *Savage Dreams*; Ward, *Canaries on the Rim*.

north every spring. The deer follow a set corridor of migration which is the longest for any other mule deer and the second-longest migration of *any* kind recorded in North America.[2]

In 2018, 1.5 million acres of public lands in Wyoming were offered for lease to oil and gas companies by the Bureau of Land Management (BLM). Some of these leases were located in the center of the migration route used by the Sublette Herd and at times selling for as little as two dollars per acre.[3] The problem is, unlike other big game species, mule deer "can't adapt their migratory strategy or route as the landscape changes around them. They learn their migration route—scientists hypothesize that they are taught by their mothers—and keep to it for the rest of their lives. These unique traits are compelling but maladaptive in the context of an increasingly disturbed landscape." Mule deer do not ever get used to oil and gas activities.[4]

Conflicts with development are similarly experienced by the iconic western predator: the grizzly bear. Grizzlies once roamed western forests, mountains, and plains from Texas to California to Montana. There are currently only two large populations left in the lower forty-eight: about 1,000 bears in and around Glacier National Park and a little more than 700 in the area of Yellowstone National Park.[5] Development around both of these parks is growing at enormous rates: Flathead County, near Glacier, experienced a 12 percent increase between 2000 and 2018, while Gallatin County northwest of Yellowstone saw a 25 percent increase over the same period.[6]

Near Glacier National Park, the Northern Continental Divide Ecosystem grizzlies are facing the effects of the possible expansion of the Whitefish Mountain Resort ski area. If approved, helicopters and heavy equipment will be used over the span of three years to enlarge the resort terrain. Machines and hand felling would remove trees from over 800 acres for additional ski runs and chair lifts.[7] A 2018 conservation strategy requires the Forest Service to "maintain the habitat conditions that existed [in 2011]." As Laura Lundquist reports in the *Missoula Current*, "Grizzly bears don't do well in regions that have higher road and trail densities, which is why limits were mandated for grizzly habitat."[8]

2. Gunther, "Should Energy Interests Outweigh Wildlife?," para. 6.
3. Gunther, "Should Energy Interests Outweigh Wildlife?," paras. 7, 10.
4. Gunther, "Should Energy Interests Outweigh Wildlife?," para. 8.
5. Mott, "Who Owns the Wild," paras. 6, 7.
6. Mott, "Who Owns the Wild," para. 8.
7. Lundquist, "Swan Valley Groups," para. 8.
8. Lundquist, "Swan Valley Groups," paras. 11, 18.

To briefly revisit a controversial issue referenced in chapter 6, Christopher Ketchum notes in a recent *LA Times* editorial that 7.4 million acres of pinyon and juniper forest land administered by the BLM in Nevada, Utah, and southern Idaho are targeted for destruction. Junipers can live up to 1,600 years and these forests host more than 700 bird species.[9] Ketchum asks, "Why wipe out millions of acres of thriving pinyon-juniper trees, trees that are superbly adapted to the heat and drought that climate change will throw at the West? To satisfy the demands of the cattle industry for grazing forage on public lands."[10]

The loss of a migration route, an iconic species, a few acres of squat pines, or in the most egregious case, the health of an indigenous desert-dwelling people, is generally justified in our culture as a necessary tradeoff in order to maximize prosperity and progress. What is defined as "empty" space from the perspective of the center of the mainstream and dominating Western worldview is generally disposable. We think little of sacrificing unoccupied space if our own definition of growth and advance can be perpetuated.

We too often fail to understand the impact our environment makes on the ways we organize our personal lives and the meaning we derive from the space we inhabit and our uses of that space. A basic intolerance and undervaluing of any empty space inevitably produces a people who will strive to fill up space in the interest of progress. We get used to being hemmed in and surrounded by all of the trappings of our engineered environment. For most of us there is a certain security from the crowded and the built. Not only as an experience of the cities we inhabit, but we fill up our time and crowd our minds with continual thoughts, plans, and worries. We expose ourselves to the ubiquitous noise of music, media, and image. Because we are uncomfortable with the exposure of space, our various spaces always have to be filled and something always has to be happening. And as long as *something* is happening to insulate us against space, we comfort ourselves by the thought that we are making progress.

In *The Solace of Open Spaces*, Greta Ehrlich writes, "We have only to look at the houses we build to see how we build *against* space, the way we drink against pain and loneliness. We fill up space as if it were a pie shell, with things whose opacity further obstructs our ability to see what is already there."[11] The space we physically inhabit and our uses of that space are pivotal realities because being in and making use of space forms our spirituality.

9. Ketchum, "Pinyon and Juniper Woodlands," paras. 7, 8.

10. Ketchum, "Pinyon and Juniper Woodlands," para. 2.

11. Ehrlich, *Solace of Open Spaces*, 15; emphasis original.

This is what lies behind our human cultural formation and meaning-making. In an additional sense we ourselves *are* space. This is the lesson of the soil and the seed. We can be a space for the rich and world-remaking reality of the gospel. This is potentially true, however, only if the spaces that constitute our soul haven't already become too crowded by cultural conceptions of the real and meaningful. The gospel as *shalom*, kingdom, grace, has been demonstrated as too often antithetical to the world we have constructed.

This brings us to Jesus' parable of the growth of the seed in Mark 4:26–29. Mark is the only gospel writer to share this parable, and he rightly places it within the context of what Jesus already told his audience about soil and seed. It is again a very natural setting, bringing to mind a lesson embedded in the organic environment. Both the figures of the soil and the seed naturally prompted a reflection on the unknowability of God within the categories of our Western scientific and triumphalist thought. This brief story of how good seed in good soil comes to produce fruit increases the sense of mystery. The seed sprouts and grows, but the planter doesn't know how. The earth produces by itself. There is a remarkable lack of human instrumentality and interference in this parable as the farmer merely sleeps and rises day after day. Paul makes a similar point, also speaking about the kingdom, when he says "God gave the growth. So neither he who plants nor he who waters is anything, but only God who gives the growth" (1 Cor 3:6–7).

In his comments on this parable, New Testament scholar Craig Blomberg sees the emphasis in Jesus' point being that God's kingdom will grow into all he intends for it, despite the many signs of uncertainty present in human culture. The kingdom grows in the mystery of God's own action, often apart from (and too often in contradistinction to) human instrumentality. As Blomberg points out, referencing Albert Schweizer, "The surprising omission of any reference to ploughing, harrowing, or cultivating may point to the message that God's people must wait with a 'carefree attitude' for God to act, 'without any spiritual maneuvering or misguided efforts.' At the very least, Jesus is teaching that human beings cannot control or predict the growth of the kingdom."[12] I anticipate the idea of a "carefree attitude" may be most difficult for many of us to accept who were raised in the confines of a heroic, active church.

This is why I frame the parable as a figure of *space*. Our efforts to fill everything up and render everything—even the spaces of the interior life—productive, can at times have devastating and unforeseen consequences. Space serves as a counternarrative to our all-too-crowded and actively

---

12. Blomberg, *Interpreting the Parables*, 264.

prone existence. We tend to artificially thrive on being always hemmed in and crowded and noisy because it provides us with a sense of not only safety but control. Space, without a road or a building or the reinforcement of societal messages that affirm we are contributing as we ought, strips us of destination and therefore our own constructs of value. It is unnerving to look into open air with the earth falling off steeply beneath one's feet. That is not simply a function of an external environment, but equally the internal landscape. We build our spiritual selves against space and mystery through study and activity and a litany of assured answers and perspectives, all the while seeking the security of power, productivity, wealth, and a well-ordered, culturally acceptable way of life.

A number of years ago a close friend of mine had the opportunity to take a work associate from the eastern United States on a driving tour across some of the vast expanses of the west. My friend related that his passenger was perpetually gripped with fear, even within the safe confines of the vehicle, because of the unusual exposure to empty space. Where this individual came from in the east, everything was shrouded by a dense growth of forest, limiting one's view to a few yards at a time. Highways quickly emerged into huge population centers where traffic and buildings engulfed the horizon and perspective. The wide-open expanses of many western states with any kind of town often hours away meant that, perhaps for the first time in his life, this individual could glimpse how vast his surroundings were and was not provided a comfortable, close boundary of people or forest. The exposure to immense space was unsettling.

The brief story from Mark 4:26–29 emphasizes that what good seed in good soil needs is primarily space, not first and foremost our interference. This is what apophatic spirituality and a receptive posture reinforce. Space is about exposure. It is exposure to a condition where one is not hidden or hemmed in or otherwise constrained by a self-created and self-referent world, but rather laid bare to the elements. For the sake of *shalom* it is vital that we experience the exposure of our dependency and inability; the exposure of our broken and damaging ways of operating; the exposure of what we have constructed life around; the exposure of our own agenda that keeps the kingdom from happening. We require the reminder of our own limitations for the sake of our own landscape and the sake of world repair.

Space as a category has a central role in biblical thought. The defining event for the Hebrew experience was the act of Yahweh to intervene in their situation as slaves in Egypt and effect their deliverance, thereby forming them as a whole and free people. It was an intervention acted out physically on a world political stage that the Hebrew prophets and later writers of the New Testament would refer back to as the defining feature of Yahweh's activity in the world: the effecting of salvation. Immediately following the escape from Egypt through the Red Sea, Moses sang "The Lord has become my salvation" (Exod 15:2). The prophet Isaiah would later repeatedly refer to the experience of salvation as an overarching and normative experience for what God's intervention in the world looks like.[13] In Luke 2, Simeon celebrates the appearance of Jesus as the one who would enact the salvation of God.[14]

As is too often the case with biblical categories of such enormity, akin to what we have already experienced relative to the closely related ideas of peace, righteousness, grace, and the kingdom, there is a tendency to constrain these ideas to a narrowly interior experience which allows one to feel at ease with the condition of their soul while leaving the main of life conducted under a received cultural narrative untouched. This is not how the Hebrew people experienced their salvation as the experience was intended to shape an entirely new way of being in the world.

The Hebrew word is *yasha*, serving as the root of both Joshua and the Greek form Jesus, and originally referred to a wide-open space. This was space that was roomy or broad, specifically as opposed to a space of oppression which was characterized by its narrowness. The opposite of *yasha* is to be hemmed in, constricted, without options. This was a spatial concept which counters the oppression of imprisonment, so to be rescued—to experience salvation—is to move out into the open. It is "to make spacious" or that space is given to the one constricted.[15] While *yasha* has the sense of escape, for Hebrew thought, in every case, it refers to having been intentionally rescued. It always takes place by the saving intervention of a third party without the self-help or cooperation with the oppressed. *Yasha* is help of the kind that the oppressed would be lost without.[16] This is why Isaiah emphasizes that salvation is found not in striving, ceaseless activity, but in quietness, rest, and trust (Isa 30:15).

The deliverance from a condition of slavery in which they were constrained as marginal members of society into a spacious experience of freedom and option was, for the Hebrews, meant to be an experience that would inform their own interaction with other marginal populations in their midst. Israel emerged as aliens and strangers from a condition of marginality into a wide-open space which formed a certain kind of identity as those steeped in the formulative experience of salvation. Their interactions

13. See Isa 12:2; 33:2, 6; 45:8; 56:1.
14. Luke 2:30; see also John the Baptist's declaration in Luke 3:6.
15. Kittel, *TDNT* VII:973.
16. Kittel, *TDNT* VII:973.

with the world around them were directly correlated with their own identity as strangers, aliens, and sojourners: "When a stranger sojourns with you in your land, you should do him no wrong. You shall treat the stranger who sojourns with you as the native among you, and you shall love him as yourself, for you were strangers in the land of Egypt: I am the Lord your God" (Lev 19:33–34).

Not only did Israel "know the heart of a sojourner" from their Egypt experience (Exod 23:9), but they were now attached to a God who "executes justice for the fatherless and the widow, and loves the sojourner, giving them food and clothing," with the natural expectation for the people to "love the sojourner, therefore, for you were sojourners in the land of Egypt" (Deut 10:18–19).[17] Foreigners and "strangers" to Israel were expected to share in the same benefits and allowed access to the rights afforded to Israel in their salvation experience.[18] Their space was to be experienced and ordered in such a way that space would be provided for others around them. In her work entitled *Making Room*, Christian ethics professor Christine Pohl points out that, "Embedded within the covenant between God and Israel was Israel's identity as an alien and its related responsibility to sojourners and strangers."[19] The condition of oppression from which Israel had experienced their move into a wide-open space was expected to inform the core of the people's identity. As Pohl writes,

> The Bible makes the experience of marginality normative for the people of God. For the Israelites and the early Christians, understanding themselves as aliens and sojourners was a reminder of their dependence on God. It provided a basis for gratitude and obedience. For the Israelites, especially, it was also connected to recognizing the feelings and vulnerabilities of the literal aliens who lived among them.[20]

Yasha as space for outsiders informed the early Christians' formulative practice of hospitality. The idea of hospitality, which appears in the New Testament as literally "love of strangers,"[21] is a much-diminished concept in our engineered and all-too-self-centered world. As a figure of our general way of being, hospitality has become an industry specializing in food, lodging, and entertainment now relied upon by millions of people to meet these needs

---

17. This is a frequently repeated theme. See Exod 22:21; Lev 19:10; 25:23; Deut 23:7; 24:14–20; 26:12; Jer 7:5–7; 22:13; Ezek 22:7, 29; Zech 7:9–10.

18. See Exod 23:12; Lev 16:29; 24:22; Num 15:15; Deut 1:16.

19. Pohl, *Making Room*, 27.

20. Pohl, *Making Room*, 105.

21. See Rom 12:13; 1 Tim 3:2; Titus 1:8; Heb 13:2: 1 Pet 4:9.

when away from home. While not denying how much the world depends on these services, the industrialization of the practice takes us far from the concept as a vital Christian practice. And while there remains great value in hosting friends and family, embedded in the biblical idea is service rendered to those who are in one way or another strangers to us as a function of their habitation on the margins of our world of experience.

New Testament hospitality is predicated on our treatment of those outside of the cultural mainstream. In the midst of an entire chapter that could fit under the theme of hospitality, Jesus instructs his host in an apparently large gathering in Luke 4, "When you give a dinner or a banquet, do not invite your friends or your brothers or your relatives or rich neighbors, . . . invite the poor, the crippled, the lame, the blind" (Luke 4:12–13). Hospitality is not merely envisioned as entertainment or as a means to an end, but is the embodiment of the gracious outflow of the kingdom of God. In what is likely regarded as the seminal New Testament passage on hospitality, Jesus associates the expression of the kingdom specifically with giving food and drink to the hungry and thirsty, welcoming the stranger, clothing the naked, and visiting the prisoner (Matt 25:31–46).

In the Matthew 25 story of the sheep and the goats, Jesus indicates a further mystery of himself being embedded in the experience of the marginal peoples of the world. This undoubtedly stems from the model of the exodus in which the very identity of the people of God was formed as they remembered and acted on their condition as outsiders. As Jean Vanier remarks in his work on community and hospitality,

> There is a mystery in the heart of the poor. Jesus says that everything we do for the hungry, the thirsty, the naked, the sick, the prisoner, or the stranger, we do for him. . . . The poor, in their total insecurity, their anguish and their destitution, identify with Jesus. Hidden in their radical poverty, in their obvious wounds, is the mystery of the presence of God.[22]

The apostle Paul, in his letter to the Philippians, further connects the acts of hospitality—looking to the interests of others—with the experience of the entire lifestyle of Jesus. Jesus set aside what we would construe as the wealth, power, and privilege of God to empty himself and take on the form of a servant in order to associate with the outsiders: humanity as outsider to God. The humility of Jesus, even to the experience of the cross, was the act of connection with a foreignness that Paul encourages us to emulate (Phil 2:1–11). An important piece of the Philippians 2 model of love to strangers is the realization that it is not dependent on an act stemming from the

---

22. Vanier, *Community and Growth*, 33.

maintenance or distribution of wealth and status, but is a powerful enact-
ment of grace in its very poverty and humility.

In this light, I believe we can correlate hospitality with the image of
the wide-open space of *yasha* and understand hospitality as the creation of
space where people can experience the reality of God. In this way, Jesus *is*
the hospitality of God. He embodies *yasha* and creates the space—the kingdom—whereby *shalom* can be experienced. As the body of Christ (1 Cor
12:27), the church should be creating this space. Henri Nouwen emphasizes,
"Hospitality, therefore, means primarily the creation of a free space where
the stranger can enter and become a friend instead of an enemy. Hospitality is not to change people, but to offer them space where change can take
place."[23] For Nouwen, this space is about options and the opening of oppor-
tunities not available in a culture otherwise occupied and busy with bodies,
minds, and words filling our experience with noise and constant motion.
Creating space is both difficult and fear-inducing. But, "the paradox of hospitality is that it wants to create emptiness, not a fearful emptiness, but a
friendly emptiness where strangers can enter and discover themselves as
created free. . ."[24]

Sometimes hospitality has to do with physical space. It is possible to
frame an environment that reflects a harmony and rightness; a place or
home which embodies peace and grace and the generosity of God. But it
is too often the case that the creation of physical space can become more a
reflection of our own penchant for designing and building, being a preoccupation with what we control through effort.[25] As Nouwen again emphasizes, "The first thing we need is an open receptive place where something
can happen to us. Hospitality, therefore, is such an important *attitude*. We
cannot change the world by a new plan, project or idea."[26] Hospitality as
space, as an attitude, then, has more to do with the very space of our lives:
what we bring with us into our spaces. Of course, this depends on how
crowded our own sense of self is. The condition of our internal, spiritual
selves becomes apparent to our world in often hard-to-describe ways and
often regardless of physical location.

In Luke 7 we find Jesus as the guest of a Pharisee. It was common
practice in first-century Palestine to host lavish banquets which not only
demonstrated the position of the host but additionally provided a setting

23. Nouwen, *Reaching Out*, 71.

24. Nouwen, *Reaching Out*, 72.

25. See the story of Mary and Martha in Luke 10:38–42; additionally, Pohl, *Making
Room*, 144.

26. Nouwen, *Reaching Out*, 76; emphasis added.

for the learned to discuss important topics. The setting would have been relaxed, if not somewhat opulent, according to the standards of hospitality of the day. As Craig Blomberg sets the scene: "Since Simon is a Pharisee and Pharisees frequently invited guests of honor to large lunchtime meals after Sabbath morning worship services, perhaps we are meant to envision that kind of banquet here."[27] As Jesus reclines with the prominent of his day in a well-stocked environment, "a woman of the city, who was a sinner," (Luke 7:37) makes her way to the feet of Jesus where she weeps copiously enough to wash the feet of Jesus and uses her own hair to wipe them clean. This naturally creates a scandal and prompts Jesus to explain this woman's action as stemming from a profound love and gratitude in response to what she understands is Jesus' welcome to an outsider, somehow embedded in his very presence.

While some may fret over the nature of this woman's particular life-style (which is not entirely settled) or the effusion of her physical act, the emphasis lies in the contrast between the lavish hospitality of the host and the way this woman was specifically drawn to something inherent in the presence of Jesus. While Simon's exercise of hospitality was not such that an outsider could come and sit at the table and experience the loving forgiveness of God, Jesus brings another expression of space into this physical space which this ostracized woman was drawn to as an experience of a God who intervenes for the oppressed. Hospitality as space can be carried with a person, and it is space which is capable of countering an established cultural paradigm too often at odds with the gospel.

This scene is not an isolated incident. Luke 14 again opens with Jesus attending a meal hosted by prominent religious authorities. Jesus again acts on behalf of someone marginalized by society, an act of hospitality in contrast to the attitude of the host culture. The differing responses to this outsider are highlighted by the noted silence of the ruling elite to Jesus' question about doing good. Later in the meal, Jesus illustrates very different types of responses to his own life as a space to experience God when he tells a story about a man hosting a banquet—again, an act of first-century hospitality—who is snubbed by those involved in activities of the cultural mainstream while the "poor and crippled and blind and lame" as well as any inhabiting the margins of commercial society (those on the highways and hedges) are welcomed in to enjoy the banquet (Luke 14:16–24). There is frequently a notable difference in response to the space that constitutes the life of Jesus between those crowded with conventional societal expectations and those who occupy the margins of the given culture.

27. Blomberg, *Contagious Holiness*, 131.

Christine Pohl indicates that biblical hospitality serves as a definitive form of resistance to the Western narrative of progress: "Although we often think of hospitality as a tame and pleasant practice, Christian hospitality has a subversive, countercultural dimension."[28] Jesus created a different kind of space in his very being which is often directly in opposition to lavish and comfortable settings—a space which demonstrates the kingdom of God. Jesus was himself safe space that embodied *shalom* and drew the marginalized who did not fit cultural patterns of value. He was wide-open space for women, children, the poor, the sick, and the otherwise ostracized.[29] This in part stems from the way Jesus often withdrew into unoccupied space to cultivate a different sense of reality.[30] The kingdom of God has its own inner qualities for growth and prompts its own responses that our constant activity and tweaking can only frustrate.

It is apparent that the space for encountering the reality of God is not merely a function of a physical setting. The kingdom and the experience of *shalom* is about people as space. We do not become the space for our world to contact its Creator primarily by efforts to order our physical world in just the right way, but through a promise. A man, woman, or child of God takes something with them into their space by virtue of having experienced *yasha*. In what some theologians see as the foremost promise giving shape to the entire flow of the Bible, God appears to Abraham in Genesis 12 where he indicates that Abraham and his descendants are primarily meant to serve as a blessing: ". . . in you all the families of the earth shall be blessed" (Gen 12:1–3).

"Blessing in the Bible refers to God's characteristically generous and abundant giving of all good to his creatures and his continual renewal of the abundance of created life. Blessing is God's provision for human flourishing."[31] When Jesus sends out his original twelve disciples in Matthew 10, he instructs them to enter a house and "greet it" which is a way of saying "give it your blessing" (Matt 10:12). Jesus indicates that if the home is inclined toward *shalom* then the blessing will indeed effect peace (Matt 10:13). It is important to keep in mind that this is relatively early in the ministry of Jesus, which indicates he cannot be referring simply to the homes in these remote locations of those who are already followers of Jesus. The point to be recognized is that Jesus is telling his disciples that they have

---

28. Pohl, *Making Room*, 61.

29. See especially the woman of Samaria in John 4:1–20; the woman caught in adultery in John 8:1–11; and the outcast among the tombs in Luke 8:26–39.

30. See Matt 4:1; 28:36–39; Mark 1:35; 6:31–32.

31. Bauckham, *Bible and Mission*, 34.

something granted by God which they take into their spaces with them. *Shalom* accompanies the disciples, not by virtue of an ability or anything they specifically have—the disciples ventured forth in weakness and poverty (Matt 10:9-10)—but by virtue of the fact that God wants to distribute the blessing of *shalom* and does so through otherwise empty space. It is still the way of the basin and the cup.

It is expected that having been led into the wide-open space of *shalom*, a person will themselves become a space for the embodiment of the kingdom which contains its own qualities necessary for flourishing growth. Again, it depends on how crowded and hemmed in by human achievement and noise we allow our lives to be. This is why in the New Testament the kingdom of God is so often experienced by and from the margins of society. At the margins exist the settings which are the most free from the constraining preoccupation with grasping, accumulating, and building. It is difficult in the center of our built environment, which screams of human ability and achievement and wealth, to find the necessary space to experience the *shalom* of God steeped in the grace that counters human posturing.

Our use of the physical landscape demonstrates that we have little tolerance for the empty; for the unoccupied. Over the past 500 years, our ruling paradigm has formed a people with a too-low tolerance for mystery, unproductivity, or space without an agenda or program. It follows that we have an equal intolerance for the exposure these empty spaces entail. We will countenance nothing that may possibly expose limit, weakness, or anything short of complete mastery. Our environment, our churches, our very spirituality are built against the open spaces so central to the experience of the people of God. It is one of life's profound paradoxes that what we fear and will not tolerate is precisely what we most need.

I want to offer the perspective that the category of space—unoccupied, unindustrialized, wild space—both as an external and internal reality, is more vital to true humanness that we imagine. Empty, exposing space provides the necessary connection to the experiences of beauty, freedom, and life itself which are a few of the fundamental realities standing at the center of what it means to be finally and fully human.

While beauty may be in the eye of the beholder, it is nevertheless a category of response to existence that surpasses momentary appreciation and envelopes the entirety of the human experience. Beauty is an idea, inherited as a quality specific to being human, thousands of years in the making. If someone were to marvel at a city skyline or a modern work of art or a piece performed by a symphony, they still do so on the basis of a response to an immensity, a quality of beauty, which is inherited from historical human experiences of the world which are not dependent on or associated with our modern ways of ordering and internalizing the world. Beauty as a concept, therefore, surpasses the things we build and is formulated as a category of human response from a context much older than our own. The idea of beauty has its roots in a world that extends back far beyond our current constructs. The appreciation of something beautiful is an expression of internalizing the external and thereby an expression of our capacity for spirituality. Apart from the ancient experience of and response to a natural environment, the category of human conceptions of beauty are robbed of meaning.

We are diminished apart from an exposure to a beauty not of our own making. The externality that affects the full vitality of the internal person is by necessity one we did not create. We require exposure to the grand vistas of a canyon or mountain range millennia in the making. The utter apart-from-us wildness of bears and wolves and lions is a conduit to the far-older-than-us context in which the concept of beauty is formed. An 800-year-old pinyon pine in Escalante National Monument or the 3,200-year-old President Tree in Sequoia National Park reach into the distant past where the interactions of color, form, and light produced a human response to their world which they conceptualized as "beauty." Apart from this connection, we are squeezed into the narrow confines of a secondary world of our own making without the necessary immensity of time and scale to match the breath of life in the soul. Our very humanness is thereby diminished.

Conceptions of freedom as a quality of being fully human stretch back to the oldest stories we have. Where freedom is lacking, something precludes a society from viewing all of its members as being truly human. Wars and strife are more often than not predicated on the basic desire for the condition of freedom wired into the human experience. Freedom requires space on more than just a physical level, as our physical and spiritual spaces are so vitally connected. The Old Testament people of God, more carefully than most, associated their very existence as a people with the wide-open space of freedom.

My own experience of empty space has been a necessary setting to understand how basic to my own being freedom is. As a product of my culture, I participate in the grand endeavor to define and achieve my ought in the universe. Because we cannot create out of nothing, our definitions of our own fitness tend to be derived from a cultural narrative which results in being caught in an unsatisfying condition that requires ceaseless effort to demonstrate our competency. We have to prove to ourselves that we belong in a world defined by unending economic and technological growth. Wild spaces are spaces of negation: in stripping us of oppressing and constraining definitions of reality imposed on us by a contingently created culture in a setting where such things cease to matter, we are exposed to an environment which is not nor ever could be built by our own efforts. The scale of such uninhabited space surpasses our smallness of life while the solitude and silence silences our restlessness in the face of created reality. Space is terrifying precisely because it exposes the basic *un*reality of our own definitions of what life and our world ought to look like. It is no wonder that the Hebrew people viewed their very salvation as a wide-open space.

My assertion that life itself is dependent on an experience of exposing space can be best illustrated by a personal story. Fifteen years ago, I was climbing a high peak in the Colorado Rockies in March when I was swept 2,000 vertical feet off the face of the mountain in an enormous avalanche. Avalanche experts point out that many victims who die in avalanches are crushed to death; entombed under a crushing weight of consolidated blocks reminiscent of concrete. As loads of unstable snow are swept at incredible speeds down a steep incline, the speed and friction create a melting effect which is quickly overcome by the freezing of ice and snow, forming a tightly bonded mass, likely more tightly packed than the original snowfield. As the chaos ensued around me, I was pulled under the surface of the cascading snow and began to feel the avalanche squeezing the life from me.

My particular route of the day had begun with a bypass around a cliff band located at the foot of the couloir I was ascending. Undoubtedly, this line of cliffs awaiting tons of snow blowing off the mountain saved my life that day. The avalanche was grinding down the gully, pulling everything it could with it into a quickly freezing mixture, until it was forced into the open space created by the cliffs. I remember being conscious of the enormous, crushing weight being lifted off my body as the boulders of snow now had empty space into which they could fly. Of course, I was flying in open air as well, but ironically the landing was somewhat cushioned by the very elements that moments before had been trying to kill me.

The incident serves as a picture of the need for the lifting of the crushing and consolidating blocks and debris of an ethos that means to determine all of our intentions and actions but which will eventually bury us. We are not merely economic animals and the depth of human being cannot be reduced to a factor of external technologies. Our economic and technological narrowness has been robbing us and constraining us, walling us off from the source of a fully experienced and integrated humanity. Life requires a greater spaciousness if it is to reflect the full horizon intended by its Creator. Wilderness advocate Howard Zahniser asks, "Are we not truly and in reality *human*, essentially, as spiritual creatures nurtured and sustained—directly or indirectly—by a wildness that always must be renewed from a living wilderness?"[32] To refer back to Wallace Stegner, who was quoted in the introduction, "We were born of wilderness and we respond to it more increasingly for relief from the termite life we have created."[33]

Empty, exposing space is the final word in response to the Western faith delineated in part I. Space is necessary for the growth of the seed. It serves as the definitive experience of the people of God as their salvation and follows our own experience of the Creator in the hospitality that is the person of Jesus. Space is what we carry as blessing into our world as our own humanity fills out in beauty, freedom, and life.

Our landscape becomes the landscape of the soul, and *space* is what makes the landscape what it is. ". . . [I]n the desert, weathering evokes beauty. The absence of rock mystifies and captures the imagination more than the actual sandstone. It's the holes, the ellipses, the arches, and the pillars—possible only through emptiness—which give this place such character. And so it is with the landscape of the psyche."[34] In the general absence of an appreciation for space, it is little wonder that we have lost our way as a faith. There is no space left for the seed to grow. We have taken over the prerogatives of the Creator, left to wonder why our soil is unproductive toward *shalom* and where any flourishing growth has gone. We've no space left in the landscape of the soul.

32. Harvey, *Wilderness Writings of Howard Zahniser*, 131; emphasis original.

33. Stegner, *Wilderness at the Edge*, 8.

34. Gordon, *Landscape of Desire*, 186.

Conclusion

The Scandalous Parable of the Good Samaritan

JUST BEFORE COMPLETING MY work on this manuscript, I disappeared for four days into the Maze District of Canyonlands National Park. By now I would expect the reader to anticipate another tale of self-exposure and things gone wrong. Not one to disappoint, my recent January solo backpack was spent mostly lost under a shroud of low clouds and at times heavy, obscuring snowfall. I use the term "lost" rather loosely as I generally knew how to exit the region; I simply could not locate myself on a map for most of three days I was far off-trail.

The Maze is aptly named. In the northern reaches of the region, where I had conducted all of my previous visits, the earth falls away from a large basin below the Orange Cliffs into a puzzling array of interlaced canyons that twist and turn in a massive, natural labyrinth. These deeply set vertical gashes are separated by sharp sandstone ridges, usually only a few yards wide, resulting in a more densely packed concentration of narrow canyons than anywhere else on the Colorado Plateau. If one does not pay close attention to landmarks it would be an easy place to get permanently lost.

A few miles south of the depths of The Maze proper is the region known as The Fins—my destination for this particular trip. While the entrance to Horse Canyon from The Maze Overlook entails a steep drop utilizing steps carved into sandstone and squeezes through narrow crevices, in The Fins the confusing chaos is generally positioned above the primary entrance point from the Dollhouse Road. The appropriately named region evokes an image of sharp ridges of abruptly rising sandstone, ridges themselves further eroded by sharp cuts that separate rock towers of hundreds of vertical feet, lined up like long rows of towering sails. Endless meanders and openings converge in a few canyons that drop precipitously into Cataract Canyon of the Colorado River.

If I am so often misplaced, as I was on this recent hike, it is partially because I gravitate toward mysterious regions like The Fins where trails are nonexistent and maps are not entirely useful; but it is also certainly at times due to my own mistakes. I was already unsure as to my exact location when I woke up on the second day and loaded my pack as snow began to fall. As I followed a narrow cleft upward to a low saddle and began a descent through another tight passageway, the snow began to fall in earnest. By midmorning I was in a vast open wash rimmed by fins and cliffs of rocks with snow accumulating from a low ceiling of clouds. Hard as I tried with my dad's old surveying compass in hand, I could not intelligibly place myself anywhere on my 7.5-minute USGS quad. I was confident I could reverse my course, so I proceeded to wander for miles up and down the wash throughout the day hoping to somehow fit my location on the map.

When I returned home a few days later, I reflected back on three circumstances that had contributed to my disorientation. The first problem was I had underestimated my progress of the first day. I thought it unlikely I would have progressed so far into the region and kept attempting to place myself further back on the map in a region I had already passed through. The second issue was the fact that I had somehow missed an important landmark that would have definitively determined my location. I spent a day looking for something in a region ahead that was actually behind me which I had unknowingly walked by early on the second morning. The third problem was a function of the low ceiling I was under, where major formations were obscured by clouds and left me wandering in the low light of a gray day with poor visibility. Of course, after wandering so far over my four days I know the region well enough now that on a return trip I would be able to place myself with a certain degree of confidence.

Landscape of the Soul has been an effort to frame our location in both time and place as participants in the human experiment that is Western culture. My attempt has been to locate us on the map, to establish the parameters and boundaries in which our travels through life are being conducted. Whether we can identify a road or path we are on, or alternately feel we are wandering aimlessly until we accurately position ourselves on the map, it is impossible to know where we are and what a way forward would entail. I am convinced that a significant bulk of our current societal polarization stems from people having no idea where they are, how they got there, and how to walk forward in a meaningful way.

I have endeavored to place us on the map of our particular society by framing two competing, and I think at many levels incompatible, myths. These mythologies are not fairy tales or fantastic stories of unlikely titans occupying a distant peak. Our mythologies are the all-too-real and believable conditions of our everyday experiences that firmly establish our place in this world. Whether or not they are ever acknowledged or defined or understood, our myths get us out of bed in the morning and compel our acting. These stories form a bond for a society which builds our world—both for good and evil—into the neighborhood we now occupy. Myths are the storage reservoirs that collect our assumptions, motivations, values, and priorities that, when released, become the moving, acting flow expressive of our central, distinguishing sense of the meaningful. Cultural mythologies answer the questions of how we endeavor to order and act on the world as conscious, creative beings. They are our maps of reality that *place* us.

These reservoirs are constructed from our personal narratives and until we adequately recognize our own narrative, we have little capacity to determine whether our specific location is where we want to be or not. It is one thing to claim to occupy a position on the cultural map indicative of meaningful value, but another thing entirely to actually be where one thinks they are. It is possible to be on a different map altogether and to convince oneself that what they see is what the map—the narrative structure—says they should be seeing. This has been an effort to clear the clouds so we can recognize the crucial landmarks of our forming context.

Placing ourselves in our world, whether where we currently are is where we think we ought to be or not, is the product of recognizing personal and cultural shaping narratives. I rely so heavily on my own formulative context because it is so firmly reflective of the competing visions of reality that this work has been exploring. I was born and raised and have spent the overwhelming majority of my nearly five decades on this earth in the West of the United States. I see the West as a region uniquely expressive of the culturally determinative values of labor and productivity. The West fueled dreams of expansion and wealth extraction—both of which are a part of my personal journey—and solidified the derivation of meaning for the whole burgeoning Western cultural experiment. The explicitly religious conception of value and redemption played out in the conquest and engineering control of Western lands in ways that have rarely been so vivid. Here was a unique opportunity to build order into an empty region which provided meaning to human existence while it compelled the continuation of the paradigm of progress well into our own time.

At the same time, these western environs are uniquely contentious as visions of what is most worthwhile confront one another more forcefully in this region. Differing views about land use, personal rights, and the role of the other abound in stark display in the Western states. My experience of Western land is not unusual, as natives of the region often talk about their identity being steeped in the landscape which envelopes the Western experience while a growing number of in-migrants express an interest in slowing down, appreciating the viewsheds, and all-too-often naively invoking the idea of getting back to the land. The West is still largely unpeopled apart from a few large urban settings, a region characterized by wide expanses and large swaths of public lands that contain many of the nation's forest reserves and the iconic natural wonders of our national parks. The Grand Canyon, Yellowstone, Glacier, Zion—these and other national parks invoke the idea of "Americanness" as clearly as the cowboy, logger, or hard-rock miner. Both the natural setting and the inhabitants' zeal for transforming that setting bear equal weight in forming our national identity and value system.

The other—what I identify as competing—formulative paradigm is the narrative of Christianity. While immersed more deeply than many in both the industrial and natural settings of the Western experience, my narrative is equally formed by a unique intimacy of involvement with American Evangelical Christianity. My theological degrees led to twelve years of vocational ministry. As a denominational executive, I traveled widely and visited a large number of local faith communities. But studying and teaching theology for nearly two decades does not preclude struggling to locate oneself on this map. Simply invoking the Christian title is no guarantee that a church body is not more thoroughly a reflection of the Western cultural paradigm than it would be of a biblical worldview. I experienced too much of the same lifeless irrelevance that a growing contingent of our culture is ascribing to the Christian church. And still my own narrative is shaped by the alternatively compelling vision of being a created being who must rely on an uncreated externality to form my existence as it was always meant to be.

This narrative places me in a particular location on the cultural topography. These two aspects of my experience serve to inform the two sides of our shaping myth which are at best competing for adherence and at worst utterly incompatible. Are our best interests as human beings served by our unquestioning adherence to the ideas of Western cultural progress? How does a biblical vision of existence differ and where does the modern American church find itself relative to our cultural ethos? Are we actually lost in the enveloping cloud of cultural formation, thinking we are one place (*shalom*) when we are in all reality somewhere far away and moving in the other direction?

The Western cultural mythology I have here expounded is steeped in the confidence that as humans we can affect our most meaningful existence through our intellect and effort to achieve an always-expanding and fulfilling sense of progress. In these terms, humankind is self-referent as value and meaning must emerge from and be an expression of our own capable efforts. Nature stands in need of an act of redemption, which is an idea no longer aimed at human failure but at the inefficiencies and lack of value inherent in a natural world not yet mined, paved, or otherwise controlled. "The greatest of these" is no longer love, no longer an other-oriented care and concern, but the premier value of labor, growth, productivity, and progress.

Part of my emphasis in the opening chapters is that the conflict between worldviews is not primarily a struggle between religious and irreligious outlooks. Progress is an idea that has been ascribed a sacredness. Our very nature is to be religious beings, always granting a significance beyond the mundane. When all we have left is the mundane, it must fulfill the role of the meaningful. Our effort and accumulation are our connective lines or tethers to meaning; our sacraments exposing us to something beyond the acts themselves. This is the faith exchange Western culture has affected. The faith or religious dynamic alive in our conception of progress partially exposes why Christianity in America can be so easily co-opted by this particular cultural myth.

Religion is determinative for being, and always has been for a humanity designed with the additional capacity to consciously internalize the external. When something takes on a sacred significance, whether granted explicit religious verbiage or not, it derives a certain power of devotion from the human mind. The sacred is referent to something beyond, something that always surpasses the merely physical and temporal. The meaning of a transcendent quality ascribed to Western ways of acting on our world commands a devotion demonstrated in the use of time and energy every bit as enveloping as the most demanding monastic vow. It is little wonder that this belief system proves to be more compelling than much of our Christian confession which minimizes the otherness and mystery of God out of a concern for self-sufficiency and personal validation.

As deeply immersed as we are within the Western ethos, the modern church is not exempt from the constraining qualities inherent in the myth of progress. This condition lies behind my intent in the arguments of the preceding chapters. We as Christians are too often subject to the failures of the Western project experienced under the heroic labor to build our own best world. We can too often reflect being constrained under a morally senseless paradigm which perpetuates a restlessness and lack of confidence. We ignore the reality of human limit and misplace the source of meaning, beauty, and freedom. The church is generally as disengaged and displaced as the culture in which she lives. The cost is borne in the formation of the church as a kind of society which justifies and ignores and delays the repair of the damage we perpetuate on both people and land which lie at the margins of a culture of progress. The cycle of culture has reached a vicious loop in which we are locked into ever-greater expenditures and ever-increasing ingenuity simply to maintain where we are, let alone achieve progress.

I have endeavored to cast an alternative cultural paradigm drawn from what I hope is an accurate and fair reading of the biblical conception of full and flourishing humanity. In light of the ways our efforts to build and extract value and meaning have issued in irreparable damage to environments and people, it is crucial to realize that we did not make our own life or world but are dependent on Another. We are not constrained to perpetuate unintended consequences as a means to construct a useful existence. Humankind also requires the sobering realization that our knowledge is the very source of dissolution—our death and decay—and so would do well to exhibit greater humility in any exercise of creative ability. The biblical understanding of humanity anticipates all of our efforts to build significance by our own effort and communicates the incapacity of the works of our own hands through the stories of Job, Babel, and the struggles with the temple.

The alternative possibility is figured prominently in the encompassing ideas of *shalom*, sabbath, and the kingdom of God. The stark difference in the two competing paradigms is on full display in these images as the conditions for human flourishing are not found in endless production and accumulation but in cessation. It is counterintuitive and countercultural, residing as a tension and paradox those of us steeped in Western culture undoubtedly have difficultly receiving. The repair of the world is not the product of a perfectly engineered environment, but the distribution of the kingdom of God that we facilitate in our *in*capability. The image of the cup precludes us from insulating and isolating ourselves from the suffering of the world within the comfort of our own consumptive society, as if we had already built something worthwhile enough to meet the depth of a created soul. The basin requires the kneeling posture of a servant which is paradoxically where the fullness of true being is found.

In this opposing vision of reality, we are never given any indication that what we most need and are created to experience will be the result of something we accomplish or build. The very idea grates against our cultural ethos. I sought to formulate a different conception of being through the earthly parables of Jesus, a way of being which would counter any conceptions of capable strength and knowledge and independence which are always referred to as *in*capable when placed alongside the ground of being.

This position relative to the Creator is what is emphasized by soil, seed, and space. To move beyond our current location on the cultural landscape requires firstly the commitment to stop moving and to act through nonacting. This places us in a position to receive the grace of God's self-disclosure and experience the open space wherein the repair of the world occurs.

The world we surround ourselves with, the specific landscape we are immersed in, serves to create and subsequently reinforce the inclinations of our inner spirituality toward meaning, naturally followed by our impetus toward acting. Because humans have the capacity to act beyond instinct, we have to be especially aware of what externality we internalize. Until our formulative context consists primarily of a natural environment not made by us, we will continue to be constrained in a narrowly mechanistic and materialistic worldview. I am aware that completely untouched and utterly pristine environments have not occurred on our earth for millennia. Human beings have undoubtedly been manipulating the hidden corners of the natural world for their own ends throughout human history. Nevertheless, there are still spaces that speak *primarily* to the act of Another as opposed to those spaces dominated by our own constructs. The perspective I am promoting depends on what *dominates* the horizon: the world created-by-another or the self-reinforcing, constructed environments of our cities, roads, industrialization—any space that directs the attention first and foremost to an order we impose on the world.

This is about changing our narrative. Human narratives of being and acting are changed primarily through loss and exposure. This goes far in explaining why we so seldom change our constitutive stories. Loss and exposure are what we build life *against*, protecting personal and communal existence from any perceived regression or disclosure that what we have expended so many resources and so much energy constructing may actually be a chimera. We much prefer to continue hidden in the enveloping cloud than be exposed to the wide perspective which may reveal to us that we are nowhere near the location we had hoped we were moving toward. Because of the overwhelming strength of the Western ethos, this has become the unfortunate condition of too much of American Christian spirituality.

Loss is an experience we all confront to one degree or another, but all-too-frequently steel ourselves against actually facing or learning from. The myths that form us resist the acknowledgment that they may be insufficient for the depth of human meaning they were constructed to provide. The experience of loss becomes minimized at best, utterly ignored at worst. My own views on the all-too-typical American approach to Christian spirituality have grown out of more than a decade of losses of differing kinds and degrees which left me scrambling to fill a space created by the absence of a critical tether point.

Prior to becoming a land surveyor, my dad worked for years in one of the world's largest open-pit uranium mines in central Wyoming. He died in 2003 at the age of fifty-four, having been consumed by cancer, likely the result of years of exposure to uranium ore. Two years after his death, the avalanche I referred to in chapter 8 took the life of a twenty-three-year-old, recently married young man I was climbing with. Later that same year is when I resigned from my work in the church and shortly thereafter began work in the Colorado oil and gas industry. That shift in vocation and the accompanying change in lifestyle was experienced by me as a loss due to the dramatic upheaval in the source of my forming identity, which up to that time had been centered in vocational ministry. My experience of loss extends to many of my tethers of life and meaning that became severed in the years that followed, some of which have been mercifully repaired by God's intervention. As an unfortunate reflection of a western climate in which suicide among middle-aged men is growing to nearly epidemic proportions, I have lost too many close friends of my own age in the past few years to an act of their own hands. The litany of losses any of us have been exposed to can either be shuffled to the recesses of our mind or confronted as a pathway to a more significant story of where life and beauty and meaning are found.

Loss properly met and received then issues in an exposure to a different landscape. Space becomes opened in the soul where the elements we crowd ourselves with have to be viewed in light of a greater immensity. This is the exposure we are uncomfortable with and build against because exposed space threatens the perceived safety of our hemmed-in, controlled environments. Our narrative of sufficient and heroic ability cannot be challenged apart from an exposure of where we are in light of a wider landscape into which we might wander. The move from the life of a pastor to the life of a roughneck exposed me to too many of the failures of the church to be self-aware enough to actually be the gospel for a population marginalized from North American faith expressions. My weeks away from the rig served to expose me to the limitations of the job and our ever-increasing industrial environments which were compromising not only the land but the communities that had inhabited that land for generations. The stories of my trips to mountains and deserts which litter this book are intended as stories of encounter, of *exposure*, to both myself and to another way of being in the world. I have been indelibly changed through my exposure to dependency on a Creator who is other, rather than relying on my own capacity to construct a fulfilling environment. The church in America will not have the capability to embody the ought, *shalom*, the kingdom, or the blessing until it is willing to be forthright about loss and be exposed to a nonconstructed reality which refuses to reinforce our own abilities.

I have pursued two central contentions in this work. The first is that American Christianity has relinquished its ability to be an expression of *shalom* and the kingdom of God because these foundational realities are not received as a gift of God but sought as the product of our perceived capability to cooperate with a Western paradigm bent on progress, power, and profit. The ethos of progress robs the gospel of its power and reality. The second contention has been that when our ruling ethos becomes one dominated by the value of production—at any cost and in alliance with any power perceived to advance our own aims—then the landscape which is the soul will be little more than an anemic reflection of a contingent creation of our own making which becomes a poisoned, choked soil with no space to receive the seed of the gospel, let alone cooperate in the repair of the world.

I want to draw this to a close by looking at what I believe is the scandalous message of the parable of the good Samaritan. This is perhaps the most recognizable parable of Jesus, yet one that too often fails to challenge the church appropriately. At heart, this parable confronts our ideas of who gets to define the center of reality. What context or universe do we *really* inhabit? Who and what determines what is central to life and what occupies the margins? The unique power of this parable is its ability to pinpoint a center of meaning and authority on the map of our landscape and thereby challenge the source from which we think we derive life and being.

The parable of the good Samaritan from Luke 10:25–37 is fundamentally a story about life at its deepest and most basic level. It transcends the typically narrow—albeit critical—consideration of hospitality and actually serves to address meaning, our ought, *shalom*. The meeting between Jesus and the lawyer that sets up the story is laced with the language of something larger than the specific acts of care of the stranger would indicate. Jesus is questioned in verse 25 by an expert in the details of the Jewish religious system who wants Jesus' interpretation about the way to "eternal life." A similar question posed by a rich ruler in Luke 18:18 and Jesus' association of the question with the kingdom of God (Luke 18:24–25) means that we are to understand this as a question about life in the kingdom, which we recognize is at least in part about a present reality.

Jesus further associates life in the kingdom with God's act of covenant indicated in the Old Testament Law. The law was initially an expression of the lovingkindness of God who endeavored to form a people with an alternative culture steeped in the rhythms of sabbath and justice for the marginalized. The lawyer in this scene appears to understand that the heart of the law—the life of *shalom* in the kingdom—is about an orientation of love to the Creator which also issues in love for the neighbor. The quotations in Luke 10:27–28 from Deuteronomy 6:5 and Leviticus 19:18 indicate the summation of the law and prophets. Additionally, Luke 10:29 invokes the idea of the rightness or ought embedded in creation when he editorializes that the lawyer is basically seeking to "*justify* himself." The word "justify" in this context is drawn directly from the Greek form of the word "righteous-ness," which indicates that the lawyer approached Jesus with some sense of seeking this condition of "oughtness." Everything leading into the parable indicates that what is at stake is the *shalom* of the kingdom where life is as it was designed to be as a function of an orientation of love to God and neighbor.

But we also know the expert in the law was seeking the right means of existence in self-referent ways, which begins to implicate us in the story. While knowing the right answer—Jesus does affirm this man has a proper perspective on life in the kingdom—the lawyer was actually seeking the confirmation that he was already living as he ought. To this end he asks what I believe he thought to be a relatively harmless question: "And who is my neighbor" (10:29)? This has become a self-referent universe with a self-serving feedback loop. This man knows the right answers and presum-ably the proper actions and the right kinds of people. Being a scholarly and well-heeled Jew in Palestine, he could likely look around his context and identify crowds of people similar to himself. He would inevitably be among his own people—not as learned or as obedient or as blessed, perhaps—but still occupying a received and assumed culture which accorded with his own perspective. He might have to put up with some minor discomfort, but any action to a neighbor in his world would not likely be too much of a stretch for someone already so firmly in-the-know.

The scandal, and something too often missed, is the fact that Jesus never answers the question, "Who is my neighbor?" Into this loop feeding back on itself, referring to itself, reinforcing itself, Jesus introduces some dissonance. Because this is a scene about life, about the *shalom* of the king-dom, Jesus wants his listeners to consider who really occupies the *shalom* universe. Who is at the center, defining reality, and in so doing establish-ing what then constitutes the margins? We presume from Jesus' story that the traveler making his way from Jerusalem to Jericho, a 3,200-foot drop in elevation over the span of seventeen miles, also occupies the cultural mainstream: a Jew traveling in his own country. Fellow occupants of the central societal faith pass by the damaged man without further consider-ation, actually making the effort to "pass by on the other side" (vv. 31–32). It falls to the despised Samaritan—the definitive designation of an outsider, a margin-dweller—to perform the acts of neighborliness that establish a new center wherein *shalom* is seen to dwell.

Jesus does not just recenter the map, pointing out a missed landmark or meander to reorient the lawyer's location. Jesus pulls out a different map altogether to demonstrate the lawyer is not even on the same page. The question is not really, "Who is my neighbor?," but instead, "Who gets *life*? Who is as they ought to be? Who occupies the world of *shalom*?" The injured traveler finds himself in the compromising position of having to *receive* the expression of blessing from a despised outsider. Is it possible that Jesus is communicating that the world, the context of kingdom *shalom* and righteousness, is not primarily about specific acts furthering a particular cultural paradigm but instead about receiving the condition of *shalom* from an outsider? If life, covenant, love for God is about the neighbor, then this despised outsider somehow gets it right and simply demonstrates what setting of meaning he occupies. The perspective apparently offends the lawyer, who cannot even bring himself to say, "It was the Samarian."

Love of God and love of the other—an orientation of value and action—occupies the center of the *shalom* universe. And while modern American Evangelicalism will undoubtedly assume a posture of receptivity to grace relative to God, the posture to the other is an entirely different matter. Despite the close connection established between God and the neighbor through the commonality of love, we tend to think we *receive* from God while we *do* for others. What I am emphatically *not* saying is that love does not issue in action. A proper orientation to God and the other cannot help but express a formative value through certain exercises of care and concern. What I *am* proposing is that in this parable Jesus changes the very notion of where *shalom* resides and emphasizes how life flows from the margins because he does not even address "Who is my neighbor?" He casts an occupant of the center of received culture as a recipient of the kingdom from an unexpected source. Jesus defines a new center from which life emanates.

I think we sanitize this parable as an impetus to further activity on our part, which simply reinforces our inclination to take charge of the kingdom of God and build it into being through all the wealth and power we can put at our disposal. If some compromises have to be made in people and environment in order to position ourselves to build what we think the kingdom looks like, that is a small price to pay for the perceived and predetermined end. The problem is, I wonder if we are even on the map any longer. We do not get to define the center of reality and it appears that Jesus has shifted the reality of life from the center to the margins. The people and the landscape who do not fit our definition of productivity are ushered to the edge of our map, which is the very place this parable emphasizes *shalom* is received.

Our perspectives and treatment of people and landscape are far more intimately intertwined than we imagine. Marginal people occupy and come from marginal space: space and people defined as that which does not measure up to the standards defined by Western notions of progress. Land and people then both become marginalized, disposable, utterly inconceivable as a context from which to receive anything of value. The further a person or place is from the center of our culturally determined paradigm, the more disposable they become. The center gets the privilege of defining what occupies the edges. As a product of the Western ethos, the American church too often cooperates in advancing the perspective of the center, ignoring the values of the outliers, the space that actually occupies the center of the *shalom* universe.

I will leave it to the reader to consider the political implications of such a perspective in such a highly charged and contentious climate. In the end, the point of *Landscape of the Soul* is that the landscapes—as well as the people—of nonutility that occupy space against a Western ethos of progress and growth are the very spaces from which we learn dependency, receptivity, and the nature and quality of the gospel of *shalom*. These are the very contexts that work on us in a profound way that our own work can only devalue and destroy. We will lose the center if we are not careful enough to recognize that our manipulated landscape too often becomes the landscape of the soul.

Bibliography

Abbey, Edward. *Confessions of a Barbarian: Selections from the Journals of Edward Abbey*. Boulder, CO: Johnson, 1994.

———. *Down the River*. New York: Plume, 1991.

Achs, Jordan. "Andrew Hamilton Shatters Colorado 14ers Speed Record." *Cimbing* (July 9, 2015). https://www.climbing.com/news/andrew-hamilton-shatters-colorado-14ers-speed-record/.

Anderson, Bryan. "Taxpayer Dollars Fund Most Oversight and Cleanup Costs at Superfund Sites." *Washington Post* (September 20, 2017). https://www.washingtonpost.com/national/taxpayer-dollars-fund-most-oversight-and-cleanup-costs-at-superfund-sites/2017/09/20/aedcd426–8209-11e7–902a-2a9f2d808496_story.html.

Baillie, John. *The Belief in Progress*. New York: Scribner, 1951.

Bair, Julene. "She Poured Out Her Own." In *Homeland: Ranching and a West That Works*, edited by Laura Pritchett et al., 85–98. Boulder, CO: Johnson, 2007.

Barth, Karl. *The Epistle to the Romans*. Oxford: Oxford University Press, 1968.

Bauckham, Richard. *Bible and Mission: Christian Witness in a Postmodern World*. Grand Rapids Baker Academic, 2005.

Bauman, Zygmunt. *Does Ethics Have a Chance in a World of Consumers?* Cambridge: Harvard University Press, 2009.

Bell, Daniel. *The Cultural Contradictions of Capitalism, 20th Anniversary Ed.* New York: Basic, 1996.

Berry, Thomas. *The Dream of the Earth*. San Francisco: Sierra Club, 1990.

Berry, Wendell. *Another Turn of the Crank*. Berkeley: Counterpoint, 1995.

———. *Home Economics*. Berkeley: Counterpoint, 1987.

———. *Sex, Economy, Freedom, and Community*. New York: Pantheon, 1993.

———. *The Unsettling of America: Culture and Agriculture*. San Francisco: Sierra Club, 1996.

———. *What are People for?* Berkeley: Counterpoint, 2010.

Bloesch, Donald. *The Church: Sacraments, Worship, Ministry, Mission*. Downers Grove, IL: Intervarsity, 2002.

Blomberg, Craig. *Contagious Holiness: Jesus' Meals with Sinners*. Downers Grove, IL: Intervarsity, 2005.

———. *Interpreting the Parables*. Downers Grove, IL: IVP Academic, 1990.

Boster, Seth. "Colorado 14ers Keep Getting Busier, Report Shows." *The Gazette* (Oct 13, 2019). https://gazette.com/news/colorado-s-ers-keep-getting-busier-report-shows/article_fa627818-ec35-11e9-8273-73869de51511.html.

Bouma-Prediger, Stephen C. *For the Beauty of the Earth: A Christian Vision for Creation-Care,* 2nd ed. Grand Rapids: Baker Academic, 2010.

Bromiley, Geoffrey. *Introduction to the Theology of Karl Barth.* Grand Rapids: Eerdmans, 1979.

Brown, Colin, ed. *New International Dictionary of New Testament Theology.* 3 vols. Grand Rapids: Zondervan, 1979.

Brueggemann, Walter. *Living Toward a Vision: Biblical Reflections on Shalom,* 2nd ed. New York: United Church, 1982.

———. *The Prophetic Imagination.* 2nd ed. Minneapolis: Fortress, 2001.

Burton, Lloyd. *Worship and Wilderness: Culture, Religion, and Law in Public Lands Management.* Madison: University of Wisconsin Press, 2002.

Butler, Tom. "Lives Not Our Own." In *Keeping the Wild: Against the Domestication of Earth,* edited by George Wuerthner, et al., ix–xv. Washington, DC: Island, 2014.

Cannon, Brian. "There are Millions of Acres in Our State: Mormon Agrarianism and the Environmental Limits of Expansion." In *The Earth Will Appear as the Garden of Eden: Essays on Mormon Environmental History,* edited by Jedediah Rogers and Matthew Godfrey, 195–214. Salt Lake City: University of Utah Press, 2019.

Carson, D. A., et al. *The Expositor's Biblical Commentary: Matthew, Mark, Luke, Vol. 8.* Grand Rapids: Zondervan, 1984.

Cather, Willa. *Death Comes for the Archbishop.* New York: Vintage, 1971.

Chambers, Clarke A. "The Belief in Progress in Twentieth-Century America." *Journal of the History of Ideas* 19 (April 1958) 197–224.

Chatwin, Bruce. *In Patagonia.* New York: Penguin, 2003.

Cronon, William, et al., eds. *Under an Open Sky: Rethinking America's Western Past.* New York: Norton, 1992.

Dawson, Christopher. *Progress and Religion: An Historical Inquiry.* New York: Sheed and Ward, 1929.

Decker, Peter. *Old Fences, New Neighbors.* Golden, CO: Fulcrum, 2006.

DeVoto, Bernard. *Across the Wide Missouri.* Boston: Houghton Mifflin Co., 1975.

———. *The Western Paradox: A Conservation Reader.* New Haven: Yale University Press, 2001.

Dyrness, William A. *The Earth is God's: A Theology of American Culture.* Eugene, OR: Wipf & Stock, 2004.

———. *How Does America Hear the Gospel?* Grand Rapids: Eerdmans, 1989.

Egan, Timothy. *The Worst Hard Time: The Untold Story of Those Who Survived the Great American Dust Bowl.* Boston: Mariner, 2006.

Ehrenfeld, David W. *The Arrogance of Humanism.* Oxford: Oxford University Press, 1981.

Ehrlich, Greta. *The Solace of Open Spaces.* New York: Penguin, 1986.

Ellingson, Stephen. *The Care for Creation: The Emergence of the Religious Environmental Movement.* Chicago: University of Chicago Press, 2016.

Ellul, Jacques. *The Presence of the Kingdom.* New York: Seabury, 1967.

———. *The Subversion of Christianity.* Grand Rapids: Eerdmans, 1986.

———. *The Technological Society.* Toronto: Knopf, 1964.

Farella, John. *The Main Stalk: A Synthesis of Navajo Philosophy*. Tuscon: University of Arizona Press, 1990.

Finley, Bruce. "Development Devours U.S. Natural Landscapes to Rate of 2 Football Fields Per Minute, Study Finds," *Denver Post* (August 6, 2019). https://www.denverpost.com/2019/08/06/how-much-nature-should-america-keep/.

Flores, Dan. *The Natural West: Environmental History in the Great Plains and Rocky Mountains*. Norman: University of Oklahoma Press, 2003.

Franke, John R. *Barth for Armchair Theologians*. Louisville: Westminster John Knox, 2006.

Frehner, Brian. "The People Cannot Conquer the River: Mormons and Water in the Arid Southwest, 1865–1938." In *The Earth Will Appear as the Garden of Eden: Essays on Mormon Environmental History*, edited by Jedediah Rogers and Matthew Godfrey, 173–94. Salt Lake City: University of Utah Press, 2019.

Fuellenbach, John. *The Kingdom of God: The Message of Jesus Today*. Maryknoll, NY: Orbis, 1997.

Galbraith, John Kenneth. *The Affluent Society, 4th Ed*. New York: Mentor, 1985.

Goetzmann, William H. *Exploration and Empire: The Explorer and the Scientist in the Winning of the American West*. New York: History Book Club, 2006.

Gordon, Greg. *Landscape of Desire: Identity and Nature in Utah's Canyon Country*. Logan: Utah State University Press, 2003.

Gouzwaard, Bob. *Capitalism and Progress: A Diagnosis of Western Society*. Toronto: Association for the Advancement of Christian Scholarship, 1979.

Grenz, Stanley. *Theology for the Community of God*. Grand Rapids: Eerdmans, 2000.

Gunther, Kristen. "Should Energy Interests Outweigh Wildlife? In Wyoming, Trump's Energy Dominance Mandate Could IrreparablyDevastate Mule Deer Populations." *High Country News* (January 17, 2019). https://www.hcn.org/articles/wildlife-oil-and-gas-threaten-wyomings-ungulates.

Gunton, Colin. *The One, the Three, and the Many: God, Creation, and the Culture of Modernity*. Cambridge: Cambridge University Press, 1993.

Hall, Douglas John. *Imaging God: Dominion as Stewardship*. Grand Rapids: Eerdmans, 1986.

Harvey, Mark W. T., ed. *The Wilderness Writings of Howard Zahniser*. Seattle: University of Washington Press, 2014.

Hausdoeffer, John. "Wild Partnership: A Conversation with Roderick Frasier Nash." In *Wildness: Relations of People and Place*, edited by Gavin Van Horn and John Hausdoeffer, 243–53. Chicago: University of Chicago Press, 2017.

Havel, Vaclav. *Open Letters: Selected Writings, 1965–1990*. Reprint ed. New York: Vintage, 1992.

Highland, Chris. *The Meditations of John Muir: Nature's Temple*. Berkeley: Wilderness, 2011.

Jackson, Richard H. "Mormon Wests: The Creation and Evolution of an American Religion." In *Western Places, American Myths: How We Think about the West*, edited by Gary Hausladen, 135–65. Reno: University of Nevada Press, 2003.

Jardine, Murray. *The Making and Unmaking of Technological Society: How Christianity Can Save Modernity from Itself*. Grand Rapids: Brazos, 2004.

Johns, David. "With Friends Like These, Wilderness and Biodiversity Do Not Need Enemies." In *Keeping the Wild: Against the Domestication of Earth*, edited by George Wuerthner et al., 31–44. Washington, DC: Island, 2014.

Jones, Robert P. *The End of White Christian America*. New York: Simon and Schuster, 2016.

Jones, Robert P., et al. "Exodus: Why Americans are Leaving Religion—And Why They're Unlikely to Come Back." *PRRI*. 2016. http://www.prri.org/research/prri-rns-poll-nones-atheist-leaving-religion/.

Jung, C. G. *The Earth Has a Soul: C. G. Jung on Nature, Technology, and Modern Life*. Berkeley: North Atlantic, 2002.

Kelly, Tyler J. "The Fight to Tame a Swelling River with Dams That May Be Outmatched By Climate Change." *New York Times* (March 21, 2019). https://www.nytimes.com/2019/03/21/climate/missouri-river-flooding-dams-climate.html.

Ketchum, Christopher. "Pinyon and Juniper Woodlands Define the West. Why is the BLM Turning Them to Mulch?" *LA Times* (January 30, 2020). https://www.latimes.com/opinion/story/2020–01-30/bureau-of-land-management-deforestation-pinyon-juniper-great-basin?fbclid=IwAR36mqtYhTRYHLD3ocUUpOPIX D73OQ6hYpBxLzBEBDxla8UPArftJlJFHdo&utm_campaign=Rockies%20 Today&utm_medium=email&utm_source=Revue%20newsletter

King, Martin Luther, Jr. "Letter from a Birmingham Jail" https://fee.org/articles/letter-from-a-birmingham-jail/?gclid=Cj0KCQiAtrnuBRDXARIsABiN-7DY9nyYn5OI 12Z5TVasVjpeW7GLtmew7moUeuCwk_WD3JKvkGu9P4oaAtWOEALw_wcB.

Kittel, Gerhard, et al., eds. *Theological Dictionary of the New Testament*. 10 vols. Grand Rapids: Eerdmans, 1977.

Kittredge, William. *Owning it All*. St Paul, MN: Graywolf, 1987.

Krutch, Joseph Wood. *The Desert Year*. Tucson: University of Arizona Press, 1985.

———. *The Voice of the Desert: A Naturalist's Interpretation*. New York: Morrow Quill, 1955.

Kuletz, Valerie. *The Tainted Desert: Environmental and Social Ruin in the American West*. New York: Routledge, 1998.

Ladd, George Eldon. *The Presence of the Future: The Eschatology of Biblical Realism*. Grand Rapids: Eerdmans, 1996.

Lane, Belden. *Desert Spirituality and Cultural Resistance: From Ancient Monks to Mountain Refugees*. Eugene, OR: Wipf & Stock, 2018.

———. *The Solace of Fierce Landscapes: Exploring Desert and Mountain Spirituality*. Oxford: Oxford University Press, 1998.

Leech, Brian James. *The City That Ate Itself: Butte, Montana and its Expanding Berkely Pit*. Reno: University of Nevada Press, 2018.

Limerick, Patricia Nelson. *The Legacy of Conquest: The Unbroken Past of the American West*. New York: Norton, 1987.

Lopez, Barry. *Crossing Open Ground*. New York: Vintage, 1989.

Lundquist, Laura. "Swan Valley Groups Oppose Ski Area Expansion in Grizzly Habitat." *Missoula Current* (January 13, 2020). https://www.missoulacurrent.com/outdoors/2020/01/swan-valley-grizzly/.

McIntosh, Emma, and Mike De Souza. "Alberta Warned it Could Take 2,800 Years to Clean Up Oil Patch." *Canada's National Observer* (June 3, 2019). https://www.nationalobserver.com/2019/06/03/investigations/exclusive-alberta-warned-it-could-take-2800-years-clean-oilpatch.

McKibben, Bill. "The Christian Paradox—How a Faithful Nation Gets Jesus Wrong." *Harpers*, August 2005. https://harpers.org/archive/2005/08/the-christian-paradox/

————. *The Comforting Whirlwind: God, Job, and the Scale of Creation*. Cambridge, MA: Cowley, 2005.

————. *Enough. Staying Human in an Engineered Age*. New York: Holt, 2003.

Meier, Carl A. *Testament to the Wilderness*. Santa Monica, CA: Lapis, 1985.

Merton, Thomas. *The Asian Journal of Thomas Merton*. New York: New Directions, 1975.

————. *Thoughts in Solitude*. New York: Farrar, Straus and Giroux, 1999.

Mott, Nick. "Who Owns the Wild: Grizzlies or Humans?" *Outside Magazine* (October 3, 2019). https://www.outsideonline.com/2402436/grizzly-bears-habitat-humans?utm_campaign=Rockies%20Today&utm_medium=email&utm_source=Revue%20newsletter#close.

Muir, John. *Travels in Alaska*. New York: Modern Library, 2002.

Murray, Emma. 'Andrew Hamilton Becomes First to Summit All Colorado 14ers in One Winter." *Climbing* (March 27, 2018). https://www.climbing.com/news/andrew-hamilton-becomes-first-to-summit-all-colorado-14ers-in-one-winter/.

Nash, James A. *Loving Nature: Ecological Integrity and Christian Responsibility*. Nashville: Abingdon, 1991.

Nelson, Paul T. *Wrecks of Human Ambition: A History of Utah's Canyon Country to 1936*. Salt Lake City: University of Utah Press, 2014.

Nichols, Jeff. "Before the Boom: Mormons, Livestock, and Stewardship, 1847–1870." In *The Earth Will Appear as the Garden of Eden: Essays on Mormon Environmental History*, edited by Jedediah Rogers and Matthew Godfrey, 155–72. Salt Lake City: University of Utah Press, 2019.

Nichols, John. *On the Mesa*. Salt Lake City: Smith, 1986.

Nouwen, Henri. *Reaching Out: The Three Movements of the Spiritual Life*. New York: Doubleday, 1975.

Olalde, Mark. "Forever Mines." *High Country News* 51.20 (November 25, 2019) 24–31.

Oldham, Jennifer. "Forests on Utah's Public Lands May Soon Be Torn Out. Here's Why." *National Geographic* (September 3, 2019). https://www.nationalgeographic.com/environment/2019/09/pinyon-pine-juniper-forests-utah-torn-out-why/?fbclid=IwAR0RyANTgAwuuCg2wjL5YMLO1FENdY4Z3Ef1l-QfF6ONL4Z2t8TZUnbTRzg.

Pasternak, Judy. *Yellow Dirt: A Poisoned Land and the Betrayal of the Navajos*. New York: Free Press, 2011.

Pieper, Josef. *Leisure: The Basis of Culture*. San Francisco: Ignatius, 2009.

Plantinga, Cornelius, Jr. *Not the Way it's Supposed to Be: A Breviary of Sin*. Grand Rapids: Eerdmans, 1995.

Pohl, Christine D. *Making Room: Recovering Hospitality as a Christian Tradition*. Grand Rapids: Eerdmans, 1999.

Quinn, D. Michael *The Mormon Hierarchy: Wealth and Corporate Power, Vol. 3*. Salt Lake City: Signature, 2017.

Reisner, Marc *Cadillac Desert: The American West and its Disappearing Water*. New York: Penguin, 1987.

Rogers, Jedediah S. *Roads in the Wilderness: Conflict in Canyon Country*. Salt Lake City: University of Utah Press, 2013.

Rohr, Richard. *Falling Upward: A Spirituality for the Two Halves of Life*. San Francisco: Jossey-Bass, 2011.

Roszak, Theodore. *The Making of a Counterculture: Reflections on the Technocratic Society and its Youthful Opposition*. Garden City, NY: Anchor, 1969.

Samuelson, Robert J. *The Good Life and its Discontents: The American Dream in the Age of Entitlement, 1945–1995*. New York: Times, 1995.

Saner, Reg. *The Four-Cornered Falcon: Essays on the Interior West and the Natural Scene*. Baltimore: Johns Hopkins University Press, 1993.

Santmire, H. Paul. *Nature Reborn: The Ecological and Cosmic Practice of Christian Theology*. Minneapolis: Fortress, 2000.

Shephard, Paul. *Man in the Landscape: A Historic View of the Esthetics of Nature*. Athens: University of Georgia Press, 2002.

Smith, Henry Nash. *Virgin Land: The American West as Symbol and Myth*. Cambridge: Harvard University Press, 1970.

Solnit, Rebecca. *Savage Dreams: A Journey into the Hidden Wars of the American West*. San Francisco: Sierra Club, 1994.

Stegner, Wallace. *Beyond the Hundredth Meridian: John Wesley Powell and the Second Opening of the West*. New York: Penguin, 1992.

———. *Mormon Country*. Lincoln: University of Nebraska Press, 1970.

———. *The Sound of Mountain Water*. Lincoln: University of Nebraska Press, 1985.

———. *Wilderness at the Edge: A Citizen Proposal to Protect Utah's Canyons and Deserts*. Salt Lake City: Utah Wilderness Coalition, 1990.

Stegner, Wallace, and Page Stegner. *American Places*. New York: Penguin, 2006.

Stoll, Mark R. *Inherit the Holy Mountain: Religion and the Rise of American Environmentalism*. Oxford: Oxford University Press, 2015.

Tarnas, Richard. *The Passion of the Western Mind: Understanding the Ideas That Have Shaped Our World*. New York: Ballantine, 1993.

Teale, Edwin Way, ed. *The Wilderness World of John Muir*. Boston: Mariner, 2001.

Thayer, Joseph H. *Greek-English Lexicon of the New Testament*. New York: American Books, 1889. https://www.christianresearcher.com/uploads/1/6/2/9/16298120/01greekenglishlexicongrimmthayer.pdf.

Thompson, Derek. "Three Decades Ago, America Lost its Religion. Why?" *Atlantic* (September 16, 2019). https://www.theatlantic.com/ideas/archive/2019/09/atheism-fastest-growing-religion-us/598843/.

Thompson, Jonathon P. *The River of Lost Souls: The Science, Politics, and Greed Behind the Gold King Mine Disaster*. Salt Lake City: Torrey House, 2018.

Tomlinson, Dave. *The Post-Evangelical*. Grand Rapids: Zondervan, 2003.

Turner, Frederick. *Beyond Geography: The Western Spirit against the Wilderness*. New York: Viking, 1994.

———. *Of Chiles, Cacti, and Fighting Cocks: Notes on the American West*. Golden, CO: Fulcrum, 2004.

Turner, Jack. *The Abstract Wild*. Tuscon: University of Arizona Press, 1996.

Van Dyke, Charles. *The Desert: Further Studies in Natural Appearances*. New York: Scribner's Sons, 1901.

Van Dyke, Fred H., et al. *Redeeming Creation: The Biblical Basis for Environmental Stewardship*. Downers Grove, IL: IVP Academic, 1996.

Vanier, Jean. *Community and Growth*. Toronto: Griffin House, 1979.

Virtanen, Michael. "WV Officials: Billions Needed to Clean Up Old Mines." *The Herald-Dispatch* (January 29, 2017). https://www.herald-dispatch.com/news/wv-officials-billions-needed-to-clean-up-old-mines/article_3410b71a-328d-5699-905e-a3b3300f80a7.html.

Volf, Miroslav. *Exclusion and Embrace: A Theological Exploration of Identity, Otherness, and Reconciliation*. Nashville: Abingdon, 1996.

Voyles, Traci Brynne. *Wastelanding: Legacies of Uranium Mining in Navajo Country*. Minneapolis: University of Minnesota Press, 2015.

Ward, Chip. *Canaries on the Rim: Living Downwind in the West*. New York: Verso, 1999.

Webb, Walter Prescott. *The Great Frontier*. Austin: University of Texas Press, 1964.

Welch, James. *Winter in the Blood*. New York: Penguin, 1986.

Wenham, Gordon J. *Genesis 1–15, Volume 1*. 2 vols. Word Biblical Commentary. Grand Rapids: Zondervan, 1987.

West, Elliot. *The Contested Plains: Indians, Goldseekers, and the Rush to Colorado*. Lawrence: University of Kansas Press, 1998.

White, Lynn, Jr. "The Historical Roots of Our Ecological Crisis." *Science* 155 (1967) 1203–7.

White, Richard. *It's Your Misfortune and None of My Own: A New History of the American West*. Norman: University of Oklahoma Press, 1991.

Whybrow, Peter C. *American Mania: When More is Not Enough*. New York: Norton, 2006.

Williams, Terry Tempest. *Red: Passion and Patience in the Desert*. New York: Vintage, 2002.

Wilshire, Howard, et al. *The American West at Risk: Science, Myths, and Politics of Land Abuse and Recovery*. Oxford: Oxford University Press, 2008.

Woodley, Randy. *Shalom and the Community of Creation: An Indigenous Vision*. Grand Rapids: Eerdmans, 2012.

Worster, Donald. *The Wealth of Nature: Environmental History and the Ecological Imagination*. Oxford: Oxford University Press, 1993.

Subject Index

Scripture Index